Trained To Be An OSS Spy

Author at OSS-Bari Station (1945)

Trained To Be An OSS Spy

Helias Doundoulakis

With Gabriella Gafni

To order additional copies of this book, contact:
Xlibris
1-888-795-4274
www.Xlibris.com
Orders@Xlibris.com
663876

Contents

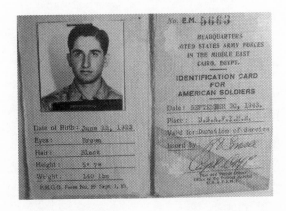

Previous Accolades

"A superb memoir that any fan of a well-told tale will savor."

— BlueInk Review

". . . Doundoulakis is able to evoke the suspense and thrilling detail of his many narrow escapes and also convey his youthful sense of excitement and adventure. His intimate rendering of the adversity Greek civilians faced during the war is particularly moving . . ."

— Kirkus Reviews

"Not every hero of World War II was forcing their way forward on the front lines. This is the true life story of Helias Doundoulakis, who served as a spy during the thick of World War II. Witnessing the early days as a citizen . . . he was trained as a spy, then found himself blending among the Greek people, whom he lived with during much of his life. Telling his full story from his early life to his life after . . . [Helias doundoulakis presents] the exciting story of a real spy."

— The Midwest Book Review

"'The Greatest Generation' is fading away, and there are very few among those left who had as adventurous an experience as Helias Doundoulakis . . . . The narrative is almost wholly exposition. That said, the understatement of the stark drama and danger make the straightforward storytelling all the more powerful . . ."

— *Foreword/Clarion Reviews*

Acknowledgments

My life has exceeded many expectations. The success that I have enjoyed as an American citizen is a direct result of my experiences during World War II. Therefore, it is only fitting that I pay tribute and dedicate this book to the three most influential people in my life: my brother and exemplary role model, George Doundoulakis, whose courage never faltered, my incomparable friend, Patrick Leigh Fermor, whose display of bravery I tried to emulate and, most significantly, my beloved wife, Rita, to whom my heart owes a perpetual debt of gratitude.

Author's Foreword

More than seventy years have elapsed since the events recounted in this book. Nevertheless, I have tried to be precise as to facts, dates, and names of individuals. I regret any errors that may have occurred as a result of time's passage. In narrating my experiences (every word of which is true), my goal is to remain objective, while authentically conveying the emotions that surrounded each circumstance and event.

My love of recording history is tied to my enthusiasm for photography. The images featured in these pages provide a backdrop for my life story, and give the reader a glimpse into nearly a century gone by.

Here and there, the narrative contains Greek expressions, slang words or phrases, and their corresponding English translations. The reader should be aware that Greek surnames identify given individuals' origins or hometowns, each connoting "son of." For example, *-akis* is the typical suffix for

Cretans, *-oglou* indicates origins in Asia Minor, and *-opoulos* identifies Athenians.

My surname, however, is an exception to the rule. The name "Doundoulakis" does not mean "son of Doundou;" rather, it signifies a sound that was given to my great-great-grandfather by the Cretan workers to whom he sold wine in the villages. Apparently, my great-great-grandfather was a wine aficionado, who traveled by mule, carrying wine in tin containers to thirsty village workers. As soon as he left our hometown of Archanes, he would indulge in the pleasure, himself. The more wine he drank, the emptier the containers became. The sound of the remaining wine created a *doun, doun* tympanic melody that echoed through the fields, letting the workers know how much wine was left in the barrels. The diminishing wine's distinctive tone made the workers pause, look at one another, and say, "Here comes our friend, Mr. Doun-dou-las, who seems to have little wine left." Eventually, my great-great-grandfather's actual surname, Vrondakis, was permanently changed to Doundoulakis.

It is especially poignant, at this time in my life, to set my thoughts on paper and to create a legacy, memorialized in words, for my family, friends, and anyone willing to acquire that knowledge. I thank my readers for coming along with me on my road of memories.

Preface

We were told that time would heal the wounds of war—not the physical scars, but the horrific sights and sounds of war. To this day, at age ninety-one, I still remember the bombing of Salonica's railroad station, the cries of innocent civilians, and the American airmen who were shot down. The sights, the sounds, the memories still loom before me as if they occurred yesterday. Thoughts of the German occupation of Greece call to mind starving people, burned homes, the loud, deafening whistle of German Stukas, the random searches at Gestapo checkpoints, and the fear on the faces of everyone around me. Names may elude me, but never the sights and the sounds—not ever. For many, it was a time of suffering, for others, a time of death; but, for me, it was a time of adventure—in many ways, the time of my life, with lots of spending money, friendly attention from the female persuasion, and wondering—always wondering what tomorrow had in store. No doubt, I was scared by the prospect. With all of those feelings and emotions churning within me, by good fortune or God's will, I was never caught. Although constantly under German scrutiny, I was never suspected of being an American spy. My all-too-frequent escapes from the enemy became like a cat-and-mouse game, in which I miraculously survived.

Even if I tried, I could not erase these memories, which are coupled with other unforgettable sensations and feelings that are—and always will remain—seared in my conscious and subconscious thoughts: the smell of bombs and, most horribly, the rotting of flesh. Only those of us who have shared these experiences truly understand their impact—such as the members of the Veterans of Foreign Wars ("the VFW") and the Disabled American Veterans ("the DAV") who meet here on Long Island. Recollecting and imparting stories, memories, and impressions have helped us to cope with our past and find inner peace—our shared objective.

Yes, time may have served to soften the indescribable blow of memories, but the events remain as vivid today as when they occurred. Yet, upon reflection, I realize that from the ashes and ruins of Greece, I emerged alive, and my trials and tribulations informed my entire life, molding me into the man I have become. I didn't know it then, but out of tragedy, triumph often flourishes. The Office of Strategic Services ('the OSS") was as much a form of rescue as it was a danger, as much a comfort as a venue of isolation. I owe a great deal to those who trained me. The men and women, soldiers and civilians whom I met along the way heroically and courageously faced horrific circumstances. Their influence on my life has been profound, and I hope that this work will pay due homage to their sacrifice.

As I once told my friend, Spyros, you will see why the art of escaping with one's life was, through it all . . . just a game.

Helias Doundoulakis

Chapter 1

Initiation Into OSS Spy School
Cairo, Egypt, 1943

That memorable fall day in October, 1943 was mostly warm. I remember the weather because of the unusual circumstances that attended it—at least in my world—and that of fifteen fellow patriots. I was being introduced to a peculiar form of war called "spy training" in the Secret Intelligence ("SI") and Special Operations ("SO") section of the OSS (the Office of Strategic Services) outside Cairo, Egypt. A white-haired man, with strong piercing eyes, entered and, although we were sitting, he commanded our attention.

"Good morning, gentlemen. I am Major Vassos, head of the training school for the Secret Intelligence section of the OSS. The fifteen of you are the chosen group to prepare for beginner's spy training. Now, let me ask each one of you. Ah . . . Let me ask this gentleman in front . . . What is your name?" Turning to me, Major Vassos looked at me with a fixed gaze. As our eyes met, I paused and, in a stern monotone, he continued, "And, remember, while you are here, you have no last name, and will not use it."

"I am Corporal Helias D., Sir," I said, rather unsure of my use of the abbreviation. By his wide stare, I knew that I had erred.

"Tell me, Corporal Helias," he went on. "Is it day or night outside?"

Hoping to rectify my error, I quickly responded. "It must be day, Sir, six o'clock in the afternoon, and it will be dark soon."

Once more, Major Vassos looked at me disapprovingly. "Gentlemen, as you can see, the corporal is not really sure whether it is day or night! Well, after you're done training, I can assure you that you will be able to convince anyone—even *me*—that it is nighttime, even though the sun is still shining! Your minds will be able to fabricate imaginary scenarios or concepts that will convince anyone you speak to—friend or foe—that whatever you are saying is true. Your training will last for five months, and will mostly consist of absorbing instructions, and your ability to demonstrate your readiness to undertake important, dangerous missions. Not everyone can be a spy, but your presence here proves that you will be capable of doing so. The instructions will be given by either the OSS teaching staff or by members of the English Intelligence Service. They've been around longer; so much the better for us. Their organizations possess more experience in certain matters, which I'm not at liberty to discuss with you right now, men."

The training was to be divided into eight classifications, as follows:

- Parachute training from various heights
- Morse code and wireless operation
- Defense-type commando training
- Environment assimilation
- Techniques for opening locks and safes, photographing or stealing documents
- Story fabrication and lying

- Methods of escape during capture
- Annihilation (how to kill in order to escape)

Clearly, the tasks ahead were not for the faint of heart. Consequently, Major Vassos (who, I later discovered, was named "John") had a tough veneer, but I liked him from the start. His impressive appearance made me believe that he had been a spy himself at some point in the past. After introducing himself, he presented his group of instructors (all of whom were officers), and described each one's specialty.

Along with the officers and instructors, there were many other soldiers in the compound, all with at least a sergeant's rank, assigned to a variety of tasks. In addition, there were over twenty helpers, cooks, cleaning personnel, and others.

I was awe-struck, and just took it all in. When the major spoke, I stood there as if I were hypnotized, and I asked myself, *Did they really call me? Had I actually been chosen to be part of this—a young man from a humble background who, not long before, just came from a small village in Crete?* To think that I was really there, a corporal in the U.S. Army and an OSS member, preparing for spy training and would become an OSS agent—an integral part of the American spy network in Greece!

In truth, my presence there had nothing to do with happenstance. On the contrary, I had been carefully chosen by the OSS, which took several factors into account: my prior two years as a member of the Cretan resistance under the English Intelligence Service, the fact that I spoke English, Greek, and a little German, and my American birth and citizenship.

As the major dismissed us, I sat quietly, slowly grasping the reality. I had come a long way from Heraklion, Crete and the high school boy that I had been just two years before, in 1941. Step back with me now through the time tunnel of my youth, and then forward again, toward a future that I never could have envisioned.

Chapter 2

Invasion, Destruction, and Vengeance

At an early age, my brother, George and I immigrated to Crete from Canton, Ohio. Though we journeyed far, we never forgot our American roots. The family had settled in Canton, where my father had a successful restaurant business. Life proceeded on an even keel, until my maternal grandmother was injured and rendered blind after a devastating fall from a fig tree while harvesting fruit. Eager to fulfill our familial responsibilities, we returned to Crete to care for her. Upon our return, we became known as "the little Americans," and everyone called me "Louis." Since my brother and I spoke English, we became popular among those who shared that language. Prior to the invasion of Crete, we especially enjoyed speaking to the English soldiers billeted in the vicinity.

By the end of April, 1941, German troops had occupied most of Greece. Some of the Greek islands, however, were not under Nazi control. Crete, the largest Greek island, situated between mainland Europe and North Africa—close to Libya and Egypt—was of great strategic importance. The large British force on the island consisted of those who had been driven out of mainland Greece by Hitler's advancing army. Later, the Germans bombed the island, targeting various areas of infrastructure (mostly airports and harbors), and rumors of a German invasion spread. The issue was not *if*, but *when* and, most significantly, *how* and *where*.

Canton, Ohio, 1924

George and Helias, 1927

Then, it happened. On the memorable afternoon of May 20, 1941, my father and I were spraying the fields in our vineyard. Not too far away was the ancient palace at Knossos, seat of the Minoan civilization, where the famous British archaeologist, Sir Arthur Evans, had recently been excavating. It seemed inconceivable that our little village, filled with a history and beauty of its own, would ever be the site of an enemy invasion.

Unsuspecting and intent upon our tasks, we walked up and down, harnessing our spraying equipment to our backs. Two miles away, across from us, behind a hill, was Heraklion's airport. Looking up, we observed two German planes flying very low—almost touching the tops of the trees— coming toward us. Most likely, we appeared to be soldiers with backpacks. As the planes flew closer, the pilots began firing at us with shots so loud, they sounded like a thousand simultaneously bursting balloons. Bullets struck the leaves and the ground; but fortunately for us, the first strafing was not accurate and missed my father and me as we ran for cover.

Shaken but thankful to have emerged unscathed, we were surprised to see that the planes had turned around and headed straight in our direction again, in an attempt to make another attack. I quickly yelled to my father to remove the spraying equipment and take cover in a nearby ditch. By the time the second strafing began, I had barely taken cover in the ditch, as I felt the bullets striking the ground near my shoes. The loud machine gun fire came perilously close . . . and ever closer . . . to us. It was strange to be so young and, yet, so keenly aware of mortality—particularly of my own; but such was the nature of the times. By the grace of fortune, God, or destiny, we survived.

Anticipating yet another momentous occurrence, we gathered our equipment and prepared to walk back to Archanes, our village. Our plans were thwarted, however, by the sight and sound of airplanes coming from the north, dropping hundreds of multicolored parachutes in the vicinity of Heraklion's airport. Given these dire circumstances, we ran south in the opposite direction, to our village. All of our hometown's villagers had been listening to radio reports of the invasion—the ominous news of German paratroopers descending all over the island.

At the time, my brother, George, worked as an interpreter for the joint Greek and British military headquarters at the post office in Archanes. The British forces were our only hope, since most of the Greek forces in northern Greece had surrendered, and the forces in Crete were scanty by comparison. To assist the British, small Greek forces joined Cretan civilians to form bands of fighters.

Fierce resistance to the German invasion escalated, and by the time their initial attack ended, the Germans had suffered the loss of fifteen hundred men. The paratroopers were easy targets, susceptible to annihilation before they reached the ground. Still, they continued to arrive, and by the third day, the Fallschirmjäger (Hitler's elite paratroopers) had sustained a loss of more than half their manpower.

Incredibly, the tiny island resisted with noble defiance, never yielding or backing down. Not to be outdone, the German high command responded by increasing the number of troops flown into Maleme Airport, outside of the city of Chania, where the Germans had a foothold; and in preparation for a continued invasion, they also bombed the major cities.

**The German Forces Occupying Chania, Crete.
British Forces Retreated to Crete's South Shore
and Began Evacuating on May 28, 1941.**

Along with the Cretan Resistance, the British, Australian, and New Zealand troops nearly won the battle. Eventually, however, the Germans were able to secure Maleme's airport on the island's western side, allowing them to fly in continuous reinforcements.

Meanwhile, the English maintained their reserve troops on the northern shores of Crete, awaiting a large invasion by sea. A German and an Italian flotilla were repulsed, but were only feints. The British were incredulous that the Germans attacked via their paratroopers instead of on the beaches. When British Commander Freyberg finally employed the main attack plan, it was too late.

In contrast to the western part of the island, the British and Cretan troops in Heraklion valiantly faced and fought back the German onslaught. Cretan men, women, and even children held out for ten days, bravely weathering the attacks with the British and Greek forces. A British destroyer rescued King George of Greece on the northern coast. The king had narrowly escaped, while most of the Greek, British, Australian, and New Zealand forces were evacuated from Sphakia on the southern coast. Tragically, about five thousand troops were left behind and captured.

Devastated by their losses, the Germans were bent on revenge against the participants in the uprising, who fought with only simple weapons, such as knives, *drepania* (i.e., sickles), and even rocks. In response, they carried out barbaric atrocities against the Cretan civilians whom they suspected to be complicit in the revolt. For every German soldier killed, ten Cretans would be executed at random. To compound these heinous attacks, the Germans burned entire villages, and gathered men and older boys into forced labor camps to perform work on various projects.

One of the Germans in charge of the roundup, named "Hans," was a tall, blonde, imposing man—particularly formidable to the locals who were chosen for forced labor. "Hans is coming! Hans is coming!", everyone would shout at the sight of him, as they ran to hide. One day, as I left my home near the market, I saw Hans choosing people for the day's work. Before I had a chance to hide, he grabbed me. There I was, in his clutches, along with three others whom he had previously caught. As we proceeded to the market's center, Hans spotted another man sitting in a tavern, and decided to also use him for the work detail. When he turned his back, I seized the chance to escape and ran toward my house. With the pounding sound of Hans' boots behind me, I ran up to the second floor terrace of my house, hoping that Hans would give up his pursuit; but he barged right in. "No *piculo* here!", my mother said, using the slang for "little boy;" but the menacing man was relentless— true to the reputation that "no one escapes Hans." He ran past my mother, trapping me on the second floor. Hearing his heavy footsteps on the stairs, I climbed out over an eight-foot wall onto the roof, and hid inside the chimney. Standing on the terrace, Hans never imagined that I could climb over such a huge wall; so, he descended the stairs and left.

Covered in soot, I appeared before my mother, who could not help but laugh out loud at the sight of me. She was worried, however, that Hans would eventually catch me—and she was right. Two days later, when he was out in search of workers again, he spotted me, grabbed me, and began to hit me with a heavy wooden stick. Along with three other civilians, I was taken to a house where we had to build a shower for the Germans in the landlady's yard.

The aroma of freshly baked bread from the landlady's outdoor oven smelled so inviting to us hard-working, hungry laborers, that we nearly salivated. Noticing our desire to partake of the bread, Hans went over to the oven, pulled out a big loaf, and cut it into pieces for all of us—a display of momentary kindness.

Another unforgettable encounter occurred during the destruction of my father's vineyards, purportedly carried out for the purpose of building a military hospital. I vividly recall the day and the moment when that happened. A group of villagers were driven out to our property in Archanes, where the Germans staked out a large area. As I looked on in disbelief, workers were rounded up, and began to destroy our vineyards. Nearby, a German sergeant called out and demanded my participation. Observing my dismay at the prospect of destroying our vineyards and my resultant disobedience, the sergeant began to hit me on my upper back with a hard stick. Before I could turn around, a worker from my hometown who observed the sergeant's conduct, approached and said to him in German, "Do you see all of these vineyards? They belong to this boy. You took them from him, you want him to destroy them and, now, as if that were not enough, you hit him. Nice German, nice German!" The sergeant stopped, pointing around the entire vineyard and then at me. By all appearances, he was surprised to learn that these were my family's vineyards, and regretted beating me. He took his leave, and I never saw him again.

In his path, the sergeant and his compatriots left behind an excavated area filled with dirt and covered with concrete. On that foundation stood a large wooden military hospital, a façade for contempt and destruction. Upon their retreat, the Germans torched the structure. Such was the enemy's vengeful disregard of life—the end of my world as I had known it.

Chapter 3

Master Plans and Impending Adventures

After the surrender of Crete, George and I sought refuge in the mountains with some English officers and soldiers awaiting transport to Egypt by ship. My brother and I considered leaving with them; but after communicating with the SOE captain, Christopher Montague Woodhouse (or "Monty," as we called him), our plans changed, and we embarked on a major turning point in our lives.

Deeply impressed by George's initiative and intellect, Monty encouraged him to form a Cretan resistance organization. "Why leave for Egypt? As an SOE official, that is my duty," he reasoned. "Take your brother, Helias, go to Heraklion, and form an organization with people you trust. I won't leave either but, instead, remain in Crete, taking cover in mountains, caves, or private homes, while you gather information regarding the German operations and report back to me."

George readily accepted the proposal, and I left for Heraklion, intent upon recruiting my high school friends and former classmates to join our underground resistance movement. Many eagerly obliged. Our headquarters were located at the home of our trusted friend, John Androulakis, whose name and unparalleled acts of courage will be referenced often in these pages. At the outset, we recruits barely fathomed the nature, extent, and repercussions of our responsibilities.

**High School Friends, John Androulakis and
Helias Doundoulakis (1942)**

As time passed, our resistance group encountered more and more risky ventures and operations. Monty left his post as head of the SOE on April 14, 1942, and was replaced by Thomas Dunbabin on that very day; and as an increasing number of informants scoured Heraklion to gather reports for Dunbabin, the organization began to grow. We were all links in the SOE chain, and our organizations' recruits (along with other Cretan men) had to perform mandatory labor for the Germans. When it was my turn, I was taken along with many others to Heraklion's airport, where I repaired holes in the runways left by the strafing of British aircraft. On the first day that I was there, I mentioned to George that I had seen huge transport maneuvers from the airport to El Alamein, Egypt, where fighting was taking place. George asked me to take mental note of how many airplanes were being loaded and the times of day when they left Heraklion's airport. A master strategist, George outlined his plan for our secret transmission of reports.

"I'll pretend to sell fruits outside the airport's entrance," he said, "and I'll have someone there who'll pretend to sell peanuts *at* the entrance. It will be your responsibility to communicate with that person by acting as though you want to buy peanuts."

Never could I have imagined that such a simple transaction (or, I should say, the *appearance* of it) could carry such import; but so it did! The next day, I was escorted to the airport again for the purpose of repairing the runway holes. My fellow workers and I began at 9 a.m., at which time (and in the ensuing hour), a long line of German soldiers were preparing for takeoff. There were nineteen planes, fifteen of which pulled gliders.

My mind was racing. How was I going to get out of there and notify George?

Suddenly, a light went on in my head, and I approached a German sergeant who was supervising us. "Excuse me, sir," I began. "I haven't eaten anything since yesterday. Could I possibly go outside the airport gate and buy some peanuts?"

"First, fill these five holes in front of you. Then, you can go," the sergeant replied decisively.

I set to work quickly, and observing my diligence, the supervisor allowed me to leave, beckoning a guard to watch me. Under the guard's vigilant scrutiny, I approached the man masquerading as a peanut vendor. Of course, the ruse had been planned, and the man expected me. Still, the adrenaline rush was tremendous. *Can I really pull this off?* I silently asked myself. Mentally calming my nerves, I leaned over and spoke in Greek.

"Nineteen planes filled with soldiers, fifteen of which were pulling gliders, just left at 10 a.m."

The would-be vendor summarily poured the peanuts into a bag, took my money, and handed me the snack. Eating voraciously, I re-entered the gate, inwardly breathing a sigh of relief. The impostor vendor then gave the information to George who, in turn, communicated it to Dunbabin, who passed it on to Cairo.

The day went by, and at 4:30 p.m., only eight planes and eight gliders returned. I wondered whether the others had remained in Egypt; but there would be no reason for that to have occurred. More soldiers required transport out of Crete, and the others, therefore, had to return. I pondered for only a moment and, then, realized that if such was the extent of the returning group, eleven airplanes and seven gliders filled with soldiers and equipment must have been shot down. Reports from English pilots sent to meet the German planes confirmed my suspicion. I was profoundly impacted by the news—particularly by the fact that I had been a conduit for the fulfillment of George's master plan.

George's sabotage of the Kastelli Airfield was also highly noteworthy. Along with his high school friend, Kimon Zografakis and two English commandos, George was able to penetrate the heavily guarded perimeter, place explosives on seven German planes and hundreds of barrels of aviation fuel, and set fire to the airfield. As Dunbabin once noted, the sabotages on airfields and oil depots had to be timed to occur close to one another. Only after the war did I learn that these sabotages were clever ploys, designed to deceive the Germans into believing that the invasion of southern Europe would be through Crete (instead of through Sicily, the true invasion route).

In yet another instance, George received information from a girlfriend, Eleni, who had become a female "acquaintance" of a German colonel. The latter informed her that he would soon depart for North Africa on a large convoy of ships and submarines. George's timely receipt and conveyance of this report to Dunbabin led to the destruction of the German convoy. As it turned out, the convoy was heading to resupply Field Marshal Erwin Rommel's Afrika Korps. As a result of his astuteness and courage, George was awarded the King's Medal in the Cause of Freedom, and Dunbabin received the Distinguished Service Order.

In July, 1942, an unexpected event took place. Captain Patrick Leigh Fermor (who went by the pseudonym "Mihalis")

joined the SOE team, replacing Thomas Dunbabin as head of
that organization a couple of months later. George befriended
the new charismatic SOE member, becoming his trusted
associate and chief representative on the civilian side. From
Dunbabin's description of him, we learned that our prospective
leader was a rather strange figure who, since his youth, had
accomplished some extraordinary feats. In fact, in his late
teens, he walked from Holland to Constantinople and, by all
accounts, that adventurous, intrepid spirit and penchant for
dangerous missions never ceased.

When he decided to come to Heraklion, Mihalis called
George to request that someone meet him at the bus station
and escort him to John Androulakis' home, our headquarters.
When George assigned me to that duty, I wondered how I
would recognize the newcomer.

"Just go over to the loudspeaker and say, 'Patrick Leigh
Fermor, the new SOE captain, please come to the desk,'" George
quipped. Then, smiling, he added, "Don't worry. You can't
miss him. He is tall and handsome, with a dark moustache.
He will be dressed in traditional Cretan garb—a black mandili
[kerchief] with tassels covering his brownish-blonde hair,
an ornately decorated black vest, olive-colored trousers, and
knee-high black boots."

Eager to greet the intriguing newcomer, I arrived half
an hour early at one of the four exits out of the Venetian-
wall-barricaded city of Heraklion. The place was famously
known as "Chania Porte," the last bus stop, where Mihalis
was scheduled to meet me. In order to enter the city, one
had to pass the German checkpoint by displaying proper
identification.

Patrick Leigh Fermor (1940)

**George Doundoulakis and Captain Leigh Fermor
in the Psiloritis Mountains (1942)**

The Psiloritis Mountain Hideout (1942)
George Doundoulakis, John Androulakis, and Patrick Leigh
Fermor, with Manolis Bandouvas and His Bodyguards

I had barely arrived when I saw Mihalis' bus approaching, and my heart quickened. There was something about this meeting that ignited extreme curiosity and anticipation. Then, I spotted him. George was right. There was no mistaking the new SOE captain. "Patrick Leigh Fermor!" I blurted out, momentarily forgetting to guard our new leader's anonymity.

"No!" he declared. "I'm 'Mihalis'!"

"Oh, excuse me! I'm sorry!" I quickly replied, regretting my impulsiveness.

Mihalis' kind expression immediately put me at ease. "Don't worry," he said. "George told me about his brother—a very important member of his organization—and I hope to have a good working relationship with you."

Suddenly, the air changed around me. The man carried an aura of importance about him, coupled with a tinge of impishness—a "devil-may-care" approach. I instantly liked him and knew that he would ultimately become a very significant part of my SOE experience—and, perhaps, my future.

"By the way, have your identification ready," I instructed Mihalis, acknowledging the seriousness of the moment. "The Germans perform very strict inspections, you know."

Mihalis assured me that he had his identification card, and we proceeded toward the inspection post. There, not one, but two German officers stood guard. Observing Mihalis' tasseled kerchief, they laughed and joked. Instead of dismissing their comments, Mihalis approached, pretended to take off his kerchief, and placed it on one of the officer's head. In a broken Greek-English dialect, he exclaimed, "Put it on! It looks good on you!"

"*Nein, Nein!*" the officer responded, still laughing uproariously.

38

There I stood, shocked that the new SOE captain would deign to risk imperiling himself and our organization with his gesture and heavy British accent. *If they discover that he's a foreigner, we're done for*! I told myself. Luckily, however, we passed inspection and, at that moment, I felt compelled to speak my mind.

"We were just lucky that the Germans didn't know better and didn't recognize your foreign accent. They could have called the police!"

"Don't worry, Helias!" Mihalis replied jocularly. My accent sounds good to them. They're all wet behind the ears."

"Yes," I said, collecting myself. "But next time, they might not be!"

Mihalis' proclivity for adventure and risk-taking would not be denied. Certainly, a youth such as I could not even try to restrain him. This fact immediately became apparent when, on our way to our headquarters, we sat down for coffee at an outdoor café. German soldiers paced back and forth, and one of them paused and repeatedly tried to light a cigarette. Gesturing to light the German's cigarette, Mihalis reached into his pocket, picked up a pack of matches, and rose from his chair. Stunned like a deer in the headlights, I pulled at his arm.

"Please, not again!" I begged the gallant Mihalis.

"OK, Helias." Mihalis smiled at me, and returned to sit down and enjoy some leisure time.

Idleness, however, did not have a place in the newcomer's heart. Sitting in the café located in Lions Square, the site of the Venetian Morosini Fountain (constructed in 1628 A.D.), Mihalis glanced into the distance toward Heraklion's harbor. After a long pause, he asked me whether we could go there before proceeding to John Androulakis' house. Since the harbor was just a short distance away, I had no objection to the detour. When we reached our destination, Mihalis looked at me pointedly. "There are many ships in this harbor, Helias. We should sink some of them."

I proceeded to tell the adventurous new captain about the underground sewer tunnels beneath Heraklion's harbor, which would allow us to approach the ships undetected (that is, if the Germans had not already barricaded them). The only obstacle to accessing the tunnels were the huge, rusty steel bars, semi-coated with seawater, obstructing the entrance. I explained that I had discovered the secret tunnels in my early high school days, when I used to go swimming in the harbor. Intrigued by my idea, Mihalis requested that John and I explore the harbor area, in order to determine the possible existence of blockades.

Yet again, Mihalis' plans and pronouncements left me wondering how the charismatic stranger would impact my future and that of our organization. We had not even reached headquarters, and our new leader was already setting us on a dangerous course.

Now, as I think back, I recall that time as being one of intense excitement—a vast panorama of dreams for the open, wandering mind of a young boy such as I; and even though I didn't know it then, I was growing up all too quickly.

Chapter 4

Survival Tactics

B y the time I entered my last year of high school in 1943, I had already witnessed life from a very unique perspective, far surpassing my years. Still, an entire lifetime had yet to unfold and, under very trying conditions, my parents had to accommodate the needs of growing boys. In order to facilitate George's and my easy commute to school, my mother rented a small room in Heraklion near the old Venetian castle. Life was far from simple. The extreme shortage of food in the area made eating almost a luxury and, according to a doctor's account, I was suffering from malnutrition—and, as I quickly learned, I was not the only one. Many Cretans endured such deprivation, and some even died. Finally, the Greek authorities managed to convince the Germans to rectify the scarce food supply, since the occupiers prioritized their own soldiers' nourishment. In response to that request, the Germans ordered that all of the schools terminate their spring semester in February rather than June (as per the custom), so that the students could return to their villages. However, there was an ulterior motive underlying the instruction: the Germans could then recruit able-bodied male graduates to join their labor camps. Those who rejected that option (as I did), chose, instead, to study German under the tutelage of instructors brought in from Germany for that purpose (I studied the language for about nine months).

While working in my brother's organization, I met the demands of schoolwork with focus and resignation. My real learning venue, however, was the classroom of life, and one of my most influential teachers was Captain Leigh Fermor. At Mihalis' command, John and I thoroughly investigated the harbor's underground tunnels and found, to our excitement, that the steel plates could be sawed and removed from the inside out. Therefore, with his plan for the sabotage in tow, Mihalis requested that time bombs be sent to him from Cairo. John and his friend, Katsias, then prepared to deliver the mines from Crete's south shore to Rethymno—not an easy feat to accomplish under the Germans' watchful scrutiny. They hid the magnetic time bombs (called "limpet mines") in two burlap bags, which John carried onto one of the buses traveling to Rethymno. On his way to Heraklion, the bus broke down, and was replaced by an open-bed truck. As John transferred from one conduit to another, the ticket collector who helped him to load the bags inquired about their content. "These are much too heavy," he remarked. Instinctively, John responded with a bribe, which the ticket collector accepted. Then, John boarded, placing the bomb-filled bags at his feet.

On the way to Heraklion, two German soldiers entered the truck and sat down right next to John. Since there were no seats, one of the soldiers, intent on making himself comfortable, began to rest his feet on the bomb bags, and even palpated them with his hands. Miraculously, no words were spoken. However, at Heraklion's western gate (Chania Porte), the last stop, John encountered the ticket collector again. Apparently bent upon exacting another bribe from John, he paced back and forth, eyeing him suspiciously. "What is in the bags?" he queried again. At first, John feigned indifference, pretending not to hear him. Determined to elicit a response, the ticket collector began to look around for German soldiers. Silently unnerved, John turned and replied, "They're canned goods." Before the ticket collector could say another word, John placed his hand on the ubiquitous gun in his pocket, and pointed it at the meddlesome ticket collector.

"Remember!" John intoned menacingly. "We're Cretans first; so, mind your own business, and keep quiet. If you don't, I will kill you outright, and detonate the bombs, too. They are powerful enough to destroy this entire bus depot and all of western Heraklion, as well!"

John's decisive words rendered his adversary silent. Nearby, our friend, Mihalis Kokkinos, looked on. Without flinching, he hastily carted the bags through Chania Porte, right past the German guards on patrol, and loaded them onto a mule. As John and Mihalis Kokkinos departed for our headquarters, the ticket collector gaped after them, without recourse to do or say anything further.

Back at our headquarters, John proceeded to unload the bombs. *Where are we going to hide them?* we wondered. Suddenly, a thought flashed through my mind. "In the fireplace!" I declared. Everyone agreed. We drew back the cloth curtain covering the fireplace ashes, and placed the time bombs safely behind it. Never did we imagine that a commonplace, almost nondescript area of the house would serve as a hiding place for limpet mines, potentially capable of mass destruction.

Once we had the bombs in our possession, George notified Captain Leigh Fermor (also known as "Mihalis"—not to be mistaken for Mihalis Kokkinos), who was in the mountains, conferring with partisans at the time. Mihalis stated that he would come to inspect the bombs that Sunday, and George asked that I arrive at our headquarters at 10 a.m. on the appointed day. Dutifully, I kept my promise, and, on that Sunday morning, I left my home in Archanes. My heart quickened at the thought of seeing the new SOE captain again, wondering what he had in store for us. Just as I stepped up to the house, I was surprised to find him ringing the doorbell.

Once inside, after greeting John's mother, Kyria Maria and his sister, Iro, George directed Mihalis' attention to our hiding place. Smiling, he said, "It was Helias' idea to place them here."

"Bravo, Louis!" Mihalis replied, addressing me by my American name, adding, "I never would have guessed that the bombs would be behind this little curtain."

With due haste, I untied one of the two bags containing the time bombs, removed two, and handed them to Mihalis. As the SOE captain inspected it, George became slightly agitated. "It's not safe to do this in front of the downstairs entrance. We had better go upstairs," he advised.

The four of us concurred. Before following the others, I carefully tied up the open bag and restored it to its camouflaged spot behind the curtain covering the fireplace. When I went upstairs, I found the other three men immersed in conversation. Mihalis was seated in a chair, George sat on the bed, and John propped himself up on an unstable stool. In the minds of my fellow SOE members, our mission was their sole consideration; comfort was not an issue.

Kyria Maria Androulakis (1941)

Mihalis railed about the atrocities committed by General Müller, commander of the Axis forces in Crete, who systematically executed Cretan civilians in retaliation for attacks against his soldiers. Enraged by such ruthlessness, Mihalis was determined to "fix that son-of-a-bitch, Müller" and destroy German ships in Heraklion's harbor. As mentioned, such was the impetus behind the limpet-mine transport which John and Kokkinos so bravely undertook. All along, I surmised that Mihalis was also contemplating Müller's abduction; and, as it turned out, the notorious kidnapping of Müller's successor, General Kreipe, about eleven months later bore out my assumption.

As the four of us—Mihalis, George, John and I—were talking, we heard the doorbell ring. John looked out of the upstairs window and, seeing a German officer, called downstairs to his sister in a whisper.

"Is he carrying a weapon?"

"No, he's just holding the book that I lent him on the Greek classics. He probably wants to return it." Iro tried to sound casual.

Undoubtedly captivated by Iro's charm and beauty, the officer had befriended her. It was obvious, however, that the book was a mere excuse to accomplish his purpose: to enter the house, observe and, possibly, conduct a search.

As Iro opened the front door, stone silence descended upon the house. Abruptly pushing past her, the officer entered. Protective of the property and its use as our headquarters, Kyria Maria, John and Iro's mother, became irate at the officer's brashness. While the two ladies conversed with him and diverted his attention, Mihalis pressed his finger to his lips and admonished us to remain silent. As the officer took a seat in the living room downstairs, we listened intently to the conversation. Suddenly, without warning, the stool on which John was sitting gave way beneath him, crashing to the ground with a loud thud. Startled, the officer became suspicious, and we could hear Kyria Maria and Iro desperately trying to calm him down.

"Oh, its only a broken window shade that keeps falling off the hinges," they said, strategizing their every word.

"Let me take a look. I wouldn't mind repairing it," the cunning officer replied, his ominous footsteps resonating on the stairs.

John reached for his pistol, but Mihalis shook his head, demanding that he refrain from taking action. Unbeknownst to us at the time, Iro instinctively devised a plan and pretended to faint. Kyria Maria recognized the ruse, and began to scream at the top of her lungs. As the German officer rushed over and knelt down beside Iro and tried to help her, Kyria Maria persuaded him to take her outside for some fresh air. When Iro regained composure, the officer took his leave. What a narrow escape—for all of us! In those critical moments, the ladies hardly suspected that Mihalis was preparing to kill the officer with his dagger; but, fortunately, his forcible intervention was not necessary. Later, he commended Kyria Maria and Iro for their courage and quick-wittedness. He remarked that because of them, lives were saved—including that of the German officer.

There were many unsung heroes in those tension-filled, life-altering days; and although their deeds were not always acknowledged, when faced with praise, they would, most likely, have replied, "We were only doing what we had to do."

Chapter 5

The End of the Beginning

Two years had passed since the Germans invaded Crete, and we expected the other ominous shoe to drop—the discovery of my brother's association with the British and his connection to the SOE. Sadly, before we knew it, the worst did, in fact, occur. After a traitor's failed attempt to buy George's silence for one million drachmas, he informed the Gestapo. George then ordered John and Sifis Migadis (who was also a member of our resistance movement) to kill him; but the malevolent deed had already been done. Aware that his life was in danger, the traitor rushed to Gestapo headquarters with a letter in hand, revealing our organization's activities.

To his anguish, George learned of the betrayal from his friend (a young girl) who worked with our organization as an informant and, simultaneously, as a translator at Gestapo headquarters. Just before closing time, the traitor rushed there and surreptitiously slipped a letter under the door. George's friend was still there, and quickly retrieved the traitorous missive from the floor. Instinctively wanting to destroy it, she refrained when she observed her Gestapo co-workers around her who potentially could have reported her. Therefore, she decided to put the letter in a bin to delay its delivery until the following morning. After she left the office, she immediately notified George.

Sifis Migadis (1941)

Later that evening, Captain Leigh Fermor was informed of the events that had taken place, and sent a wireless message to Cairo, requesting the immediate evacuation of our organization from Crete. The dangers ensuing from the betrayal were all too obvious. George and all of the SOE resistance fighters, along with their families, were at risk of being tortured and killed. Fearing that we would be caught first, George told his close associates to leave Heraklion immediately.

That night, I received word of the evacuation at my home in Archanes, and prepared my parents for our imminent departure from Crete. I told them to be brave but, understandably, they were devastated that the Gestapo wanted their sons captured, dead or alive. They wept at the thought of being apart from us for a very long time—or, worse, that they might never see us again. Sleep eluded all of us that night. As I lay in my bed, I heard the sobs of my mother, Eva, as she spoke with my father, Demetrios, in the next room. The nightmare was very real—and I live it still, in my memory.

The next day, I had an early lunch with my parents in our kitchen—our last repast together. Emotions ran high, surpassed only by the love that would sustain us throughout every trial we had yet to face. While wiping her tears, my mother sewed George's and my birth certificates inside the lining of our jackets. "These may be useful when you travel to Egypt, as proof of your American citizenship," she said. My mother was very wise and resourceful. If, for any reason, the Germans stopped and searched us, our birth certificates would be well hidden, and our lives would be spared; yet, that documentation would be on hand when needed. In that moment, we never envisioned just how useful it eventually would prove to be.

When the time came to leave, I said a tearful "goodbye" to my mother and father, and loaded my clothes and our jackets onto my bicycle. Then, as I looked up, I saw Retired Colonel Antonios Betinakis walking through our front gate, carrying a letter for George. Since Colonel Betinakis worked with our resistance movement, he was very familiar to me. At least twice a week, he would hand me information to take to my brother in Heraklion, who then passed on the intelligence to the British. Each time Colonel Betinakis saw me, he was glad . . . but on this occasion, he was peculiarly glad to have caught me in time, and said, "Please, Helias, take this letter to your brother immediately. It contains very important plans which reveal the names of new associates; so, please be extremely careful!"

I took the letter, and put it inside the hollow end of my bicycle's right-side handlebar, leaving about half an inch outside for easy access, and covered the end with the rubber grip. As he watched, the colonel must have approved of my mode of transportation and the means by which I secreted the letter. "Bravo, Helias! Very smart idea! Nobody would ever suspect that you are carrying top-secret information. You are a first-rate messenger. That is why you are entrusted with such important missions." Colonel Betinakis's approval meant a lot to me, and when I saw him on the all-important day of our departure from Crete, I felt pride in the fact that I had participated in something deeply meaningful.

Because we didn't want to reveal our plans or the fact that my brother had appointed Mikis Akoumianakis to be in charge in his absence, Colonel Betinakis was oblivious to the events about to take place. Therefore, concealing my inner anxiety, I dutifully took his letter and placed it in its customary hiding place, inside the right handlebar of my bicycle.

Of a kind, reverent disposition, the colonel turned to my silently bereaved parents. "You should be very proud of your two sons, who have fought so valiantly for the cause of freedom," he said with an expression of compassion and gratitude.

My mother, who moments earlier tried to swallow her tears, let forth a wellspring. "Colonel Betinakis, she began haltingly, "I hope that God is looking out for my sons because the freedom you speak of may come at a high price."[1]

Pretending that nothing out-of-the-ordinary was happening, my father, with a wave of his hand, said to me, "Now, go on your way!" For the last time, I turned and waved back to my parents, summoning every ounce of strength within me.

As I pedaled along, I heard a German soldier (with whom I had often conversed in the past), call out, "Helias, halt!" Not intending to stop, I began to pedal faster. The soldier got up from his place on the stoop near the local high school, where he had been sitting with some other German officers, and ran after me at full speed. When he caught up with me, he reached out and pulled at my right handlebar, dislodging the rubber grip. Suddenly, I noticed the colonel's letter protruding from within the handlebar. By the grace of good fortune, the soldier didn't notice the letter, and was very apologetic.

"I'm sorry! Let me put it back," he insisted.

---

[1] Tragically, my mother's words were prophetic. Five months later, Colonel Betinakis, along with Heraklion's mayor and ten prominent citizens, was shot by a firing squad as retribution for sabotages committed in and around the city.

Undaunted, I calmly took the rubber grip from his hands, and replaced it myself. "I'm in a big hurry!" I called, briefly looking over my shoulder as I sped toward SOE headquarters, leaving the flustered soldier behind me.

What had just happened? Maybe, the soldier simply wanted me to slow down and prevent any falls or self-injuries; but that brief exchange could have cost many lives. One turn in the road could have led to . . . who knows where or what? To be alive in those times was often sheer luck.

Such were my thoughts as I reached John's house, entered through the back door, walked over to the fireplace, and stared at the time bombs. "Make sure that there's nothing left in here, Helias!" my brother George said. "Did anyone follow you?"

I shook my head and tried to catch my breath, wondering where we would hide the bags of limpet mines. Everyone agreed (including Kyria Maria and George) that it was too late to bury the bombs outside—all except the ever-fearless John Androulakis, who suggested that he load them onto a mule and bury them somewhere far away; but that wouldn't have been practical. Something had to be done with them immediately. As usual, the wheels were turning in my brain.

"Why don't we take bricks from the yard outside and cover the fireplace where the bombs are presently hidden behind a small curtain? In that way, the bombs will be safe from the heat—and the Germans will never find them!" I said, feeling relieved and proud to have devised a solution.

Everyone endorsed the idea; and, so, with some bricks, mortar, and stone, we proceeded to conceal the time bombs safely beneath the hearth. We then quickly looked around to see whether or not we had left anything in the house which potentially would point to our organization's existence. Thankfully, not a trace of evidence could be found—at least to our eyes.

Once we cleared the house of evidence, the indomitable Kyria Maria saw us off. In that last stand—the end of our lives as we had known it—she was as valiant and steadfast as any soldier. Her hugs and kisses were salves for the emotional wounds that would take a very long time to heal, and forever served as reminders of where we began.

Chapter 6

Flirting With Danger

We had hardly walked a few blocks when the Gestapo raided and searched John's house, turning everything upside down and trying to uncover information about George's organization and its members. A German police officer put a gun to Kyria Maria's head, demanding to know the whereabouts of her son and my brother. Under immense threats and intimidation, Kyria Maria stood her ground and, miraculously, never broke down or was searched. A woman of quick wits and resourcefulness, she concealed classified documents in her brassiere, thus preserving her precious life—and the integrity of our resistance movement—to the last. In those terrifying moments, Kyria Maria was on the front lines of battle and she will always remain a heroine in my life's story.

Minutes after the Germans' raid on our headquarters, there was a knock at my parents' door. The Gestapo demanded entrance, and asked my parents where George and I were. The officers were particularly interested in my brother's whereabouts, since his reputation as a young resistance movement leader preceded him. Recalling our offer of excuse should such a raid take place, my parents calmly said, "Our sons have gone to study at the university in Athens."

One of the officers pointed a gun to my father's head. "Tell us where your oldest son is!"

Thinking quickly, my father replied, "You are an officer in the Gestapo, and you must know that there are many high-ranking officers on the island of Crete. Do you really believe that a boy of twenty-one could be the leader of such an organization? This must be a false accusation by someone who doesn't like my son!"

After a brief reflective pause, the officer determined that he couldn't argue with my father's reasoning. Lowering the gun, the officer turned and left, and my courageous father breathed a deep sigh of relief. Thereafter, he left home and went to stay in a cave for a week to avert further interrogation. During his time in hiding, my father contracted asthma, a condition which he endured for the rest of his life.

Having heard of the dual raids on our headquarters and home, my brother and I knew that we had to leave Crete as soon as possible. The thought of the limpet mines flashed before us. At it turned out, they remained in their secreted place for a while, undiscovered and unused. Evidently, Mihalis' plan to sink German ships in Heraklion's harbor never materialized. Those who were entrusted with the sabotage refused to use the tunnels that John and I had traversed together, and since they could not pass the German guards, the mission was thwarted. The bombs, I surmised, must have been buried somewhere in a cave outside the city of Heraklion.

And what about us? Looming before us was our safe passage out of the island of Crete. As one might imagine, walking out of Chania Porte, Heraklion's western gate, was more than unsettling. Would the traitor's malevolence ultimately sabotage our purpose? Would we be stopped, detained or . . . worse? Such were our thoughts as we approached the exit; but we kept a steady gate, and only breathed again once the door closed behind us. We traveled for a day and a half before we reached the town of Saint Miron. For about a week, I stayed at the home of Mr. Dramatinos, the mayor of St. Miron, where some overly curious neighbors took me for the son of Captain Petrakogiorgis, the well-known partisan leader. George could not stay there with me because there were many people in the mayor's house at the time; so, he took John with him and went to Anogia to meet Captain Leigh Fermor. During my stay at the mayor's home for a week and a half, I felt secure. Then, one night, I heard the mayor's wife whispering nervously to her husband, "The Germans might come to investigate the boy's presence in our house, or one of the neighbors might report us to the Gestapo." Fearing for his family and his village, the mayor apologetically requested that I leave before the Germans discovered me there. Although I assured him that I was not Petrakogiorgis's son, I understood his concerns for the safety of his family and his home. The German police were, in fact, searching for me, and everyone who came into contact with me at that time was in potential danger.

All it took was one telephone call from the mayor, and within a day and a half, a man came to escort me away. I asked to be taken to the town of Anogia, where I would meet up with George and Mihalis. We left the village on foot, and traveled through the Cretan mountains for about a day. Once we reached Anogia (famous for its brave citizens), we stayed in the mayor's home for a few days. We were told that the mayor of Anogia was the wealthiest man in town, and owned extensive tracts of grazing land and hundreds of sheep. Each day, at least one lamb was slaughtered to feed his guests. SOE members and

Cretan partisans were given shelter at the mayor's house, along with our group. There, I reunited with Captain Leigh Fermor and five others from our resistance movement. To repay the mayor's hospitality, Mihalis offered to take his brother with us to Egypt.[2]

On the nomadic trail from Anogia, we were accompanied by a guide who knew the mountains well. Counting me, there were four of us: John Androulakis, Sifi Migadis, Kostas Kastrinogiannis, and me. First, we crossed the Cretan mountains by night, so as to avoid German airplanes. Then, our guide directed us to a large bat-infested cave on the lower foothills of Mount Ida, aptly named for being the highest mountain in Crete (in Greek, it is called "Psiloritis," meaning "very high"). That place of refuge was very secure and, therefore, used by partisans and SOE members, due to its inaccessibility. The guide instructed us to stay inside at all times, and not wander about during the day. Luckily, I had taken a deck of cards with me, and we played bridge by the fire for hours. However, the guide warned us not to light *any fire* at night (not even a cigarette), so as not to be spotted. Without any other diversion, we told jokes to pass the hours in darkness. The best joke-teller was Kostas, who repeated his jokes until our sides nearly burst, and we fell asleep, exhausted from laughter.

The guide promised to bring us food each day, but our hunger persisted. One day, I noticed three partridges trying to enter the cave but, when they spotted us, they became wary. I thought that, perhaps, they were seeking refuge in the

---

2   To our profound dismay and bereavement, months after our departure from Crete, the mayor of Anogia paid for his hospitality with his life. As retribution for sheltering our group, SOE members and Cretan partisans, the Germans executed him and burned his property to the ground.

cave, too. All of us salivated at the thought of a sumptuous "partridge dinner." So, I decided to take the pin that my mother had fastened to my collar, and create a hook. This, in turn, I attached to a thread that I removed from my sweater. I found a few bread crumb remnants that had come from a piece of *paximadi* (hard bread) that I had eaten a while before. Using my saliva, I stuck the crumbs together on the hook, fashioning a lure for the partridges. All of us gaped in wonderment, as the largest partridge became curious and slowly approached the bait. Alas, my little concoction fell off the hook, and the king partridge had a feast. One of our friends and SOE members, Sifis Migadis, literally flew into a rage, dashed after the partridges, and fell right in the spot where the birds had gathered. Not to be outwitted or outpaced, the partridges quickly flew out of the cave, leaving Sifis more disgruntled than ever, enduring my taunts at his foolish chase.

One morning, the guide didn't show up, but returned the following day, with only a lidded container, used as a small dish (called a *galeti*), containing beans and two spoons. "One spoonful of beans per person!" we said, almost in unison. As we sat around our little fire, Sifis poured out one galeti and handed it to me. As I quickly devoured the beans, John and Kostas looked on, eagerly awaiting their turn. Next, Sifis took his turn but, instead of eating one spoonful, he ate two. He was able to trick me by shouting "Look! Partridges!" and as I turned my head, he voraciously downed the second helping. I was furious, and threatened to hit him. Kostas, however, held my anger in check, all the while cursing Sifis. Then, he calmed down and said with a laugh, "We survived the Germans and, now, we're going to kill each other over some beans?"

As we separated, Kostas accidentally kicked the galeti, and the beans scattered everywhere. Enter the partridges, who took their revenge by gobbling up most of our coveted meal. Meanwhile, John and Kostas once again spewed expletives at Sifis for ruining our meager chance to satiate our hunger.

"You deserved it for making fun of my chasing the partridges!" Sifis exclaimed.

Uproarious laughter ensued. Thus, by the light of the fire, amusing ourselves with antics and jokes, we remained in the cave for nearly ten days, with very little food and water. Finally, we were informed that an English torpedo boat was scheduled to rescue us; however, we still had to wait . . . and survive.

Something told us that the trek would not end there— and our hunch was correct. Not long after we arrived at our second cave hideout, another guide, dressed in a traditional Cretan black head scarf, baggy trousers, and high black boots, approached us. I observed that he carried a knife in his sash. His fierce expression, gleaming black eyes, imposing bushy black eyebrows and prominent moustache accentuated his formidable appearance. In the second cave, there were seventeen of us, including the two civilians who had begged to come along.

"I, alone, am familiar with the area through which we have to pass," the guide said decisively. Later, I heard him whisper to George, "If the torpedo boat refuses passage to the two civilians, they will have to be killed."

Upon hearing this, I literally shook in my boots, but quickly brushed off the feeling. The circumstances in which we found ourselves did not allow for faintness of heart. In those desperate conditions, self-preservation meant steadfastly remaining on autopilot.

Our guide emphasized that traveling on foot would be far from easy, and in order to meet up with the English torpedo boat, we would have to cover forty kilometers in two days before reaching Crete's south shore. Looking at us sternly, the guide warned us of the threat of German scrutiny and the risk of traveling in broad daylight.

"In order to cover the required distance by night, we will have to run," he said in a measured, deliberate tone, adding, "I don't know whether you will be able to keep up with me."

In fact, the guide had a point. A shepherd accustomed to mountain running, he could, no doubt, have outrun all of us. At nineteen, however, I felt more than equal to the task; but I wasn't so sure about the other older members of our organization, like fifty-year-old Mr. Kastrinogiannis. On any ordinary day, the city-dwelling chemical engineer could never manage the mountainous terrain—let alone at night. *Would he keep up with us?* I wondered to myself, sometimes half joking with the others about what could potentially happen.

"This is not a laughing matter!" the guide warned our group. "Anyone unable to keep up with the others or too weak to continue will be killed. If compelled to speak under torture, there is no telling what information one might divulge—including the group's departure time and location."

That speech stopped me in my tracks and, with a measure of humiliation, I stared at the ground. Looking down at my feet, I realized that I was wearing a pair of old English army boots without soles. I recall having to improvise, therefore, by cutting rubber from some old tires into the shape of my boots, tying them in place with a thin metal wire. Suddenly, I realized that my own shoes could lead to a death march. If the wire were to break, how could I run? More significantly, the sound caused by the improvised rubber soles would make far too much noise and, hence, draw attention to our group.

My troublesome thoughts were interrupted by our guide's instructions to line up in a single file and follow him. As he walked past me, the guide remembered my playful mockery of Mr. Kastrinogiannis, glanced at my boots and said, "If they fall apart, you won't be left behind. Either you'll run barefoot, or I'll kill you." If a young boy such as I needed a lesson in self-introspection and humility, by no means would I recommend that kind of training ground. I, however, had no choice but to swallow hard and be on my way. I packed a small bag of clothes, which also contained George's and my jackets, and slung it across my back. As I felt for our birth certificates, I recalled the love and care with which my mother had sewn them into our jacket linings before our departure from Heraklion. I kept my own jacket close, as it would not only serve as my lifeline in Cairo but could, quite possibly, be my last and only reminder of my mother. I didn't know when I would see her again, and I was prepared for the worst.

As we formed a line, one behind the other, dusk descended. We were told that during the next five to six hours, no one was allowed to talk or smoke, as even the tiniest light could be detected in the dark for miles. The shepherd guide crossed himself and, one by one, we did the same. Then, we began to jog on small paths. However, our guide tried to save time by using mountainous shortcut routes, jumping like a wild goat across the rocky terrain and running quickly. The group of younger guys had no problem keeping up with him, but Kastrinogiannis was visibly affected. Panting and breathing heavily, he requested a five-minute rest, to which the guide replied dismissively, "I have no time to spare. We have to make it to the next secure area by daybreak, which is fifteen kilometers away." Remembering our guide's admonition about keeping our appointment with the English torpedo boat, the beleaguered Kastrinogiannis fell silent.

"Very soon, we'll also have to come down from the mountainous terrain and travel on flat roads, leading in the direction of Timbaki airport. German patrols guard that area twenty-four hours a day, carrying powerful searchlights that move over the entire region. Therefore, we will be in the most dangerous territory, and we have to be very careful during the next few hours before daybreak," our guide announced.

Within a brief period of time, we were going downhill and I saw the searchlights continuously moving and illuminating the area in the distance. Our guide instructed us to cross the main road up ahead which, I assumed, was the heavily guarded route toward the airfield. For fear of being separated from the guide, I stayed close to him the entire way, knowing that we would soon be crossing the main road. Like a duckling following its parent, I remained close at the guide's heels, trying desperately to keep from falling to the end of the line and getting lost or left behind. All the while, I continuously checked my boots to make sure that they were still intact.

Prior to crossing the main road, the guide noticed a patrol car approaching and told us to jump into a ditch running parallel to the road. While everyone ran in the direction of the ditch, trying to find the proper spot to jump into, I stood in front of the line, behind the guide. Then, as I tried to follow the others, I made a sudden move and, without warning, the wire holding the right sole of my boot fell apart, and my foot came right through the bottom of the boot! As I attempted to fix the wire, the others raced past me, and just as the patrol car rode by us, I found myself last in line. *Oh, my God! My worst nightmare has come true!* I thought to myself, as I observed the searchlight shining from the passing patrol car. I closed my eyes, trying not to breathe, as fear overtook me. In my bare feet, I tried to run but, as the searchlight passed over me, I had to jump back into the ditch. Not only was I last in line, but I was also falling behind the group, in danger of being caught. *What could possibly be worse?*

Once I climbed into the ditch, I remained motionless, feeling tired, hungry and thirsty. We had been on the run for what seemed like days on end, and I desperately needed sleep. Dozing off, I dreamed of happy moments in my hometown, Archanes, of my parents and the friends that I left behind. In a profound sleep, I didn't notice that the patrol car had left and I didn't hear our guide's signal to cross the main road. Maybe, by God's will, I awoke just as the patrol car passed or, just maybe, in my dreams, I actually heard a car speed by; but in all events, I awakened to find myself alone. I broke out in a cold sweat, in fear of losing the group, falling asleep again, and being caught by the next patrol. *They would execute me for sure,* I thought, *but first they would torture me and demand the reason for my being alone near the airport.* Home seemed like a world away. I reached out and felt my American birth certificate sewn into the lining of my jacket, displaying my birth date as July 12, 1923. I felt so fortunate to be alive—but for how long would I survive? *Surely I, the straggler, will pay the ultimate price,* I thought, enveloped by sheer terror.

Chapter 7

Race to the Torpedo

As I was imagining my capture by the Germans, I fixed my gaze in the direction in which the group had been heading prior to my separation from them. Suddenly, I saw something move in the dark, which looked like a man running or, maybe, it was a German soldier on patrol. I couldn't be sure. Maybe, it was someone who, like me, had become separated from our group. I thought to myself, *why should I have been the only one to fall asleep*? I would have thought that old Kastrinogiannis might also have fallen behind. Perhaps, it was he whom I saw in the darkness, running to catch up with the others. Then, the thought occurred to me that this was, most likely, wishful thinking; or, perhaps, destiny had placed me once again on the right side of the war. With no time to ponder, I sped off again.

Finding no other alternative, I had to go in the direction of the moving object. I had no time to worry about my boots; so, I took off the other boot and put both of them in my pack. Then, I began to run barefoot as quickly as I could. Although I was stepping on thorns and sharp stones, my fear didn't allow me to feel anything. That level of fright had once caused me to fall asleep and ignore what was happening in my surroundings. My sleep-deprived body was being put to the test. Although I was running fast, someone ahead of me sprinted at an even quicker pace. Since he was not coming closer to me, I concluded that he must have been from our group—and, therefore, not a German.

Who else—other than those in our group—would be running like a demon in the dead of night? Because my feet had adapted to the rough terrain, I decided to run even faster, and I was able to get close enough to recognize that the "moving object" was, in fact, a member of our group. Soon, I was running last in line and joined my friends again.

I was so overjoyed at seeing my compatriot lagging behind, that I couldn't help but weep while running; but he and the others didn't turn around to witness my emotional outburst. Everyone was simply focused on keeping up with the guide, oblivious to what the others were doing—including George, who didn't check to see whether his younger brother had rejoined the group. Like the others, he was looking out for himself, which was understandable. The truth was that I could have been lost, and no one would have taken note of my absence until reaching the beach. As for our guide, he ran at lightning speed—faster than any of us—and, like the others, probably didn't care for anyone but himself and his mission. Remembering what he had told us about leaving "no one behind," I decided not to reveal what had happened to me. In all likelihood, neither he nor anyone in the group would have sympathized. If I had not awakened in time and was unable to rejoin them, everyone would have been placed in jeopardy, including my brother. Therefore, I decided to keep my thoughts to myself, without telling anyone (not John Androulakis, Sifis Migadis, or even George) about my plight. I also feared that if I divulged the truth, I would lose their trust. In this case, therefore, silence was, truly, golden.

After two nights of running, my feet were bleeding from cuts, thorns, and scrapes; but there was no rest for the weary. Our pace quickened and we began to run downhill, feeling thoroughly exhausted, hungry and thirsty. At daybreak, I saw the sea behind the trees, inhaled the salty air and the distinctive smell of the ocean. Eventually, the shore came into view, indicating that our goal was in sight, at last! The guide told us that after we neared the shore, we would hide under the trees or behind large rocks, and wait until the following night for the torpedo boat. He also cautioned us to be aware of German patrols and the observation post on top of a nearby hill, which afforded the Germans an excellent vantage point for overlooking the shoreline. Because the unobstructed stretch of sand might be used for amphibious assaults on the island, it was monitored continuously. Hence, in our hiding places, we couldn't talk or smoke. Every trace of our presence had to be concealed.

We arrived at daybreak and waited for the English torpedo boat scheduled to arrive the following morning at 1:00 a.m. The meeting place was about twenty hours away, and we had not eaten anything since the previous day. That meager meal consisted of a piece of bread and a handful of olives, the last morsel of which we savored. We would have to spend the next twenty hours without food or water until the torpedo boat arrived. *How can we possibly sleep with hunger pangs and in fear of a German ambush?* I asked myself, searching aimlessly for a place to rest.

Looking around me, I spotted a small broad-leafed tree standing next to a big grayish-white boulder. With fatigue enveloping my entire body, I ambled over and sat down. *This looks like a nice place to sleep for the next twenty hours*, I thought. So, I piled up some of the fallen leaves and created a mattress, with a smooth stone for my pillow. Not a moment after I lay down and closed my eyes did I sense that I was being watched. From under the rock, a greenish-yellow lizard came out and stared at me, opening and closing its eyes, wondering if I was planning to take up permanent residence beneath that tree. *Perhaps,* I thought, *I had taken its rock.* I moved my hand in a shooing gesture, watching the lizard as it ran and hid under the big rock. With my territory established, I felt that I had won a small battle. With that mildly comforting thought, I closed my eyes again and fell into a deep sleep.

At dawn, I saw most of the others spreading out all around me, each having found his own makeshift bed. Just fifteen hours before, I had silently pleaded with *God* in my mind and heart, *if only for today, you could make this sunrise a sunset!* I observed that the sun seemed to be moving very slowly that morning—so incrementally, in fact, that I whispered to the group, "Even the sun rises slower today, fellows. How can we sleep with hunger pangs and sunshine in our eyes? Most important, who's on watch for German patrols while we're sleeping?" Nobody answered. They must have been too weak to comprehend what I was saying. Obviously, all of us had no choice but to surrender to fate; and if we were destined to be found and captured, such would be our lot in life. It was simply futile to worry, therefore. As per the Spanish phrase, *"Que será, será"* ("whatever will be will be"), I just had to let my life run its own course.

As I observed the sun peering out from behind the trees and dancing across the western sky, I realized that it was already late afternoon, and I had slept through the entire day. Fear gripped me. Was I alone or were the others still around me? With some difficulty, I raised my head, and for the first time in days, I smiled as I spotted my beach mate, the lizard. Judging by his expression, I knew that he was certain that I had become a permanent neighbor. To my joyful surprise, John and I spotted each other and exchanged waves and smiles. However, neither of us dared to approach the other or speak, given the presence of the German outpost on the hilltop. For the next six hours, silence pervaded the atmosphere. It was just my boulder-mate, the lizard and me—and the stillness.

At twilight, our guide informed us that we could make our way quietly over to the large rocks near the water's edge, and duck down until the torpedo boat arrived. The wait was nearly over. *It will be only a few hours now*, I told myself. To pass the time and divert my mind from hunger, I envisioned a huge loaf of fresh bread, Cretan cheese, and a large pitcher of water. My wants were few, and that would have been just enough. A large feast would have been too much to ask for—and not even necessary. As my imagination got away from me, I suddenly realized that my humble dream would not manifest, after all—at least, not yet.

The hours crept away, and the wait seemed interminable. My mind wandered back to my hometown and my parents, to whom we bade farewell almost one month before. What could *they* have been thinking in those crucial moments of our young lives? I hoped that they were also dreaming—imagining that their two sons were alive and well, enjoying the Cairo nightlife. I could only imagine how disheartened they would have been if they knew that we were still on the island of Crete, crouching behind rocks on its southern shore! How worried and frightened they would have felt, knowing that their sons had been exposed to such enormous perils, and that some had given their lives to our escape effort!

Lost in thought, I still remembered to watch the time. Midnight approached, and all of us fixed our sights on the moonless beach, anticipating the vessel's arrival; but to our great disappointment, 1:30 a.m., 2:00 a.m., 3:00 a.m. came and went, and there was still no sign of the boat. We began to worry, and thought about what we would do if the vessel did not come by daybreak. Certainly, there was no turning back. Our guide would not know where to lead us. Perhaps, we would have to return to our cave hideouts in the mountains. I shuddered at the thought. On the run from the Germans, without shelter, we were like helpless lambs in a wilderness filled with beasts of prey. I had no other recourse than to pray, *God, please help us!*

While some in our group sat and gaped at one another blankly, others prayed. As I came out of a daze, I noticed two tall figures heading to the shore. I anxiously glanced at my watch, and saw that it was 3:30 a.m. One of the men was my brother and the other was Captain Patrick Leigh Fermor, signaling to something that each of them had spotted offshore. Anxiously glancing into the distance, I distinguished a moving object in the water heading toward the shoreline, which appeared to be a rubber dinghy. Upon its approach, we clearly discerned that the dinghy was manned by two English sailors, rowing very slowly and purposefully. The dinghy was tethered to a long rope that led out to sea, which was attached to the torpedo boat anchored offshore. The sailors attached the other end of the rope to a large boulder onshore, which they used to pull the dinghy back and forth to the torpedo boat, carefully avoiding any splashes made by the oars. "Four people at a time," the English sailors whispered.

As I awaited my turn to be transported by the dinghy to the torpedo boat, I saw the two civilians in front of me who had begged to be taken along on our journey. I was very glad that limitations had not been placed on the number of passengers and that they could board. Seeing them escorted to safety truly did my heart good, especially knowing the dire consequences of their separation from the group. Of course, I never breathed a word of what the shepherd guide once told my brother about them. What they didn't know couldn't hurt them.

Realizing that I would be next in line to board the dinghy, Captain Leigh Fermor ("Mihalis") and the guide approached me. I turned and said "goodbye," and thanked Mihalis who had sent for our safe passage to Egypt. Mihalis embraced me and said, "I will miss your and George's help, but you will return soon, and we will be able to carry out the plans that we all had in mind."[3] I also thanked our guide who, despite his aloofness, deserved credit for ushering us through the most harrowing time of our young lives and for successfully completing his mission. "We'll meet again when the war is over," I said, shaking the shepherd guide's hand. With his characteristic reticence, he just nodded and turned away.

My farewell was interrupted by the approach of the rubber boat, carrying a tall man whom I did not recognize. When the man came ashore, Captain Leigh Fermor and the shepherd guide warmly embraced him and kissed him on both cheeks (a typical Greek salutation). I soon learned that the man was Captain Petrakogiorgis, whose son I apparently resembled. As I noticed the three men standing together, it became clear to me why our guide had been so adamant about not

---

3   I assumed that Mihalis was referring to the capture of General Müller.

leaving surviving people behind. The Cretan resistance leader and the foremost SOE operative were scheduled to convene simultaneously at the shoreline. Ours was, most certainly, not a venture to be taken lightly, and we could not risk having anyone reveal where we were heading or what we intended to do. Secrecy was of the essence. I briefly contemplated telling Captain Petrakogiorgis that I was mistaken for his son in St. Miron, but I decided to lie low and say nothing. As the rubber dinghy began to move away from the Cretan shores, I stared out, watching the three men disappear together into the night, wondering when—if ever—I would see my home again.

Chapter 8

The Road to Cairo

The torpedo boat was formidable—at least fifty feet in length. As we approached, the English sailors assisted us in climbing aboard, and instructed us to move quietly to the bow. All seventeen of us complied and sat down, one next to the other, dangling our legs out in the front of the boat, at the bow. As we sat there, we suddenly realized that not only would we be continuously sprayed by the sea's waves, but completely covered in water (depending upon how rough the waters were and how quickly the boat would be traveling at any given moment). As the boat took up anchor and headed due south, the force of the sea waves and winds muffled the boat's low-throttled engines. As we exited the restricted area, the captain gradually increased our velocity, such that we were literally flying over the waves.

Having told our English rescuers that we had not eaten in over two days, they generously provided all that they had: canned beef hash. Trying to satiate our hunger, we devoured the food so quickly that we became violently sick, and regurgitated all over our clothes. That setback was nothing, however, compared with the trials that we had so recently withstood.

At daybreak, as a German patrol plane spotted us, I believed that our fortunate escape effort had been short-lived. The German plane dipped low in the sky and made two wide circles around us, as the pilots attempted to discover who we were. Then, as soon as it appeared, the plane turned around and headed back north, toward Crete. After general quarters had been called, the English sailors immediately assumed their deck gun positions and awaited a squadron of attack planes. If an onslaught *had* occurred while we were on deck, we would have run the risk of being killed immediately. After all that we had already endured, we wanted to take every feasible measure to save our lives.

As the crew increased our speed, we struggled even more to hold onto the ropes. As the boat ascended to the top of the waves and descended, we alternately pulled the ropes up and pushed them down again. It felt like we were on a fast-moving rollercoaster, while trying to control our reactions to the boat's tumultuous movement. Fortunately, the waters were not as rough as they potentially could have been that morning; however, a few huge waves did, in fact, manage to cover the entire front of the torpedo boat—and all of us, as we clung to the cable and desperately tried to avert being swept away by waves. The intensity of our struggle continued for about an hour, until the gunners observed that the planes had not returned. At that point, they left their battle positions and took off their helmets. At last, we could breathe a collective sigh of relief!

Early that afternoon, the African shoreline loomed up before us. Upon our approach to the harbor of an English army camp in Marsa Matruh, Egypt, we observed that the landscape was bereft of trees, covered only in sand. When we docked, we were told to shave and wash up. After about a week, this was to be our first glimpse of ourselves in the mirror. With our long hair and beards, we hardly recognized ourselves. We looked as though we had been recluses or shackled prisoners, and being ill compounded the state of our disheveled appearances. Fortunately, the English soldiers provided us with new clothes and instructed us to discard our old tatters in a huge barrel.

When I was just about to throw away my boots with the soles tenuously attached by a thin wire, I turned to one of the British soldiers next to me, and declared, "I have travelled such a long distance in these boots!"

Gaping in disbelief, the soldier replied, "You should keep them as a reminder of your ordeal."

"To tell you the truth, I thought about that," I agreed; but, then, after holding the boots in my hands for a few seconds and reflecting upon the difficult times that those ill-fated objects and I had been through together, I simply tossed them away.

After we refreshed ourselves and put on British uniforms, we realized that our group had undergone an enormous transformation. "Just a short time ago, our tired bodies either could have been left to rot in a ditch, killed by the guide, be tortured by the Gestapo or, even, be eaten by sharks!" someone exclaimed. We had come a long way, quickly morphing into adults—almost overnight.

Most of all, we were hungry. Once we were directed to the mess hall, the attendant in charge informed us that dinner was not ready to be served yet. Acknowledging our voracious hunger, however, he brought us five loaves of bread with butter and jam. No sooner did he hand us the bread, than virtually all of them were devoured, as were the next five loaves that he provided. At a nearby table sat two English soldiers who witnessed our ravenous appetites and gave us some of their bread.

"Where are you from?" the soldiers asked.

"We have escaped from Crete, and have not eaten anything for three days," we explained, further detailing our trials.

"If we had known that you were coming, we would have saved our lunch for you," the soldiers replied with feelings of empathy and compassion that I will never forget.

After our interlude of breaking—and gorging—bread, we were informed that we would leave for Cairo in the morning. The distance between Marsa Matruh and Cairo was six-hundred kilometers, which we would traverse by two open army trucks. Predictably, there was no place to sit, except for wooden boxes, placed on the floor. When our departure time arrived, I foresaw yet another arduous journey; and, so, I tested out the box option—which appeared to be more suitable than sitting on the floor. Our truck took off at one-hundred-fifty kilometers per hour and, with the slightest brake pressure, the boxes slid all over the place, hitting the other boxes (and, hence, the other guys around me). *My God!* We thought to ourselves. *What else will we possibly have to go through before reaching our destination?* Given that the roads were all paved with sand— and nothing else as far as we could see—the driver pushed the truck to the limit of its capacity. There we were, in the middle of a desert, surrounded by nothing but sand, without a single tree as far as the eye could see. The drive seemed interminable and we were rapidly becoming languid and fatigued beyond words. Suddenly, up ahead in the distance, we spotted what appeared to be trees.

"Look! An oasis!" I exclaimed.

"Yes, we are now approaching Alexandria and the river Nile's Delta, the source of almost all fruits and vegetables for the entire country of Egypt," the driver informed us. "Next to that oasis is Alexandria, where we will stop and rest for a while before continuing on to Cairo."

At last! Civilization! we thought. In Alexandria, we took a break, and had some refreshments and a few tasty Egyptian cigarettes. Then, we departed again and feasted our eyes on a variety of vineyards and gardens, lined with eucalyptus and palm trees that paved our way to Cairo. Something told me that the barren landscape would soon give way to nature's opulence.

Finally, when we reached the outskirts of Cairo, trees and vegetation came into view—unlike any that I had ever seen on the island of Crete. Wispy mimosa trees, brimming with pink and white flowers, bloomed everywhere and filled the air with their fragrance. As we looked at the people around us, we noticed Muslim men wearing white robes with tasseled red fezzes. The women were austerely dressed in full-body black robes, with only their eyes visible for others to see. Even the children were clad in long black robes. I couldn't help but wonder whether the people were comfortable in such all-encompassing garb. After all, it was early June, and in our culture, we were used to very different attire. Observing such differences made our journey very enjoyable and interesting—at least, for the moment.

The new sights, sounds, and smells of Cairo's streets filled our senses and beckoned us to look everywhere. Overcrowded railed streetcars teemed with passengers hanging outside the windows, so as to avert paying the fare. *What a strange form of transport!* I thought, never having witnessed anything like it in Crete. The stores and cafés were adorned with beautiful blue and white awnings, and the streets were populated with vendors of all kinds, selling rose bouquets, kebabs, watches, and Turkish coffee. Small Byzantine and Ottoman-styled plazas seemed to spring up out of nowhere, packed with afternoon shoppers, young and old, alike. Large arched windows were common along these streets, and vehicular traffic assumed a life of its own. Cairo was, clearly, a bustling metropolis—quite a contrast to Archanes, my boyhood town. My cherished home seemed almost a lifetime away.

Distracted by the new environs, we hardly took note of our departure from the city. We assumed that the driver had treated us to a brief, much-needed detour to enjoy some of the sights of Cairo's bustling streets before we reentered the sandy desert, a shocking contrast. We drove for a while before entering an English army base where, I thought, we would remain until our next assignment. I did not relish the thought. Surrounded by nothing but desert, one-hundred-degree temperatures, and dust pervading the barracks, we felt very uncomfortable, to say the least. Dreaming of a downpour, I turned to one of the Egyptian servants and inquired, "Has it rained here lately?" "No!" the servant replied emphatically, in his best English. "It hasn't rained in Cairo for ten years!" I quickly ran to tell the others, who shared my disappointment.

On our third day, just as we were beginning to believe that our stay in that heat and dust-laden place might be indeterminate, a British sergeant walked in, followed by an officer. In typical English fashion, the sergeant summarily slammed his foot on the floor, raised an open-handed salute to his forehead, and introduced the officer. Then, he called out, "George Doundoulakis, John Androulakis, Kostas Kastrinogiannis,

Sifis Migadis, Pete Petras,[4] and Helias Doundoulakis, report to headquarters."[5] The sergeant saluted again, reversed order, and left with his officer colleague.

Soon, we were told to pack our belongings, and follow another English sergeant to his car, where we were informed that a "surprise" awaited us. As one can imagine, we were a bit skeptical, given that we already had been subjected to more unexpected occurrences than most people had in a lifetime.

"You are either very lucky or very important," the sergeant said, with a twinkle in his eye. "Wait until you see where you are going! It's not a place for just anyone, you know."

We waited silently, in great anticipation, not daring to speculate.

---

[4] The mayor of Anogia's brother. In deference to the gentleman's privacy, I have changed his actual name.

[5] The remaining eleven men (the partisans and two civilians) were taken to the exiled Greek army, stationed in the Middle East.

Chapter 9

From Famine to Feast

After a while, I was getting used to minute-by-minute changes in my environment; but I never expected that I was about to experience a complete culture shock. Breathing a sigh of relief after exiting the miserably hot desert army camp, we crossed a bridge and entered what appeared to be the suburbs of Cairo. Although our group had an impressive brief glimpse of the city before, it was even prettier and more lavish than we ever could have imagined. The driver announced that the place was called Heliopolis, home to the wealthiest Egyptians. The neighborhoods were populated by opulent villas and estates—hardly a place for a group of young escapees on the run—or so we thought.

As we drove along, the sergeant suddenly stopped in front of one of the structures and announced, "This is your destination—the surprise!" Pointing to a breathtaking villa, he explained, "This is being used by high-ranking members of English Intelligence." We gaped in amazement. *Who could have recommended the SOE villa as our destination*? we wondered. Again, the sergeant marveled, "You or the person who arranged for your stay here must have a lot of influence!"

Not until later on did we discover that Captain Leigh Fermor was the prime mover behind the plan. Something told me that he had once stayed at that SOE villa.

As we exited the car, two Greek-speaking Arab men welcomed us, as two others assisted with our belongings. The entrance to the villa was adorned with marble steps and glass doors. As we soon learned, the corridors were covered with similar slippery white marble tiles, and we had to use caution at every step of the way. As if we had not already witnessed the pinnacle of luxury, we were escorted to three bedrooms, each of which accommodated two people. Then, we visited the dining room, where we would eat our meals on tables covered with white linen.

And what a meal we had that evening—a veritable feast, not the first of its kind! In fact, every one of our meals was served in the same style. We felt as though we were living in a dream world. *Surely, our extraordinary good luck will soon run out*, we thought. That had been the pattern. When we were told, however, that we would remain in our fantasy place of refuge for more than a whole month (until we were sent back to Greece), we couldn't believe our ears. At every turn, we were surrounded in lavishness, and we took it all in, as though we had experienced a kind of rebirth. To be sure, we took nothing for granted.

The day after our arrival, John Androulakis discovered a nearby train station. It was not difficult for him to make the discovery, since the noise of passing commuter trains to Cairo was located only two blocks from the villa. "Let's go to Cairo by train!" John suggested with his usual cheerfulness. Being of an adventurous spirit, I agreed. We walked toward the station, without taking note of its designation, boarded the train and sat down. We stayed on until the last stop, then got off, and walked through the streets of Cairo, undaunted by the fact that we were in a completely new environment, filled with strangers; but wait! The place sounded a lot like home. *Could it be that people were speaking Greek?* Yes, there were people all around us speaking our native tongue—some who fled Crete, as we did, and others from various parts of Greece. Some of them even made their home in Cairo, just like one of my relatives, who emigrated to Egypt before the war. As John and I looked around, we could not believe how many Greek restaurants there were on one street.

After spending two hours touring the city's center, we decided to catch the return train to Heliopolis. Just as the train pulled out, we acknowledged a slight dilemma. Since we had absolutely no information as to the address of the villa, a telephone number, or where the villa was situated within Heliopolis, we did not have a clue as to where to get off. All of the stops looked the same to us. *Hmmm. What are we supposed to do now?* I thought to myself. Mihalis had gone to such lengths to find us a safe, luxurious haven, and now, we had no idea as to where we were going! Well, after the trek to Crete's south shore, our thirst and famine, and not knowing whether we would be ushered to safety alive, the setback was merely a minor dent in our plans.

At one of the stops, my intrepid friend, John, said that we should jump off. I refused but, without hesitation, he leaped from the train, leaving me behind. At the next stop, I got out and tried to recognize the buildings; but when I saw one, I saw them all. Observing my bewilderment, a Cairo police officer approached me. I was dressed as a British soldier, without identification or any cognizance of my surroundings. Fortunately, I was able to communicate in limited Arabic that

I needed help, and the officer quickly called a colleague to assist. When the other officer appeared, both indicated that they wanted to take me to their station. In truth, since I was dressed as an English soldier, the two did not have authority to do so; but, under the circumstances, I suppose that they saw no other option.

Of course, I wanted nothing more than to return to the villa, but I was truly at a loss. The only definitive fact that I could recall about the villa's location was that it was across the street from a church. Desperately latching onto this bit of information, I repeated the word "church" several times. The two officers just stared at one another with bewildered expressions, not knowing precisely what to do. Suddenly, out of the blue, a well-dressed English-speaking man approached, drawn by my incantation of "church, church." "There is a church just two blocks from here. I'll take the boy there," the man offered. Looking immensely relieved, the officers were glad to relinquish me to the gentleman's care; and, with a sweeping hand gesture, indicated that I should follow him. I had no idea whether the man would actually help me or whether he had an ulterior motive; but what choice did I have?

After walking about two blocks, just when I thought that the man might be up to no good, he exclaimed, "Here is your church!" To my amazement, I turned to look across the street and, there, in all of its glory, was the villa! In my young experience, I had learned never to give up hope.

Expressing gratitude to the kind stranger, I took my leave, rushed across the street to the villa's entrance, hastily looked at my watch, and realized that it was 1:00 a.m. Fortunately, at that bewitching hour, a brave individual was still in the office, and I waved, beckoning him to open the locked door. With a deep sigh of relief, I climbed the stairs and entered the room that I shared with my friend, John, expecting to find him there; but, to my surprise, he had not returned. *He must have had even more trouble finding the villa than I did! No doubt, he will have some very interesting stories to tell when he returns,* I mused, as I settled into bed.

By the time John finally came back, it was past 4:00 a.m., and although I yearned to hear of his adventures, I thought it best to wait for the following morning. Conforming to my instincts, therefore, I just remained quiet and pretended to be fast asleep. The next day, John told me that his impetuousness had landed him on the wrong side of town, where he got lost and ran through the streets with thieves following his trail. Miraculously, he found his way back to the villa in one piece.

For over two-and-a-half months, from June to mid-September, 1943, we remained in the lap of luxury at the Heliopolis villa, idling and cajoling by night in the local nightclubs and singing on the street corners to the female visions of beauty passing before our eyes. The affluent locals wondered about us, and probably assumed that we were wealthy Greek refugees. Notwithstanding what anyone thought or believed, however, we were simply having the time of our lives, creating memories that would last for a lifetime.

During the day, we often went to downtown Cairo and frequented the Greek restaurants there. While having lunch in a very nice establishment one day, John and I met a Greek pilot who also had escaped from Greece. "Do you hear that voice?" he said, calling our attention to the famous Greek singer, Sofia Vembo, on the radio. Naturally, I recognized her. Her voice was so distinctive, the music so uplifting. "Would you like to meet her in person?" the pilot asked with a serious expression. I could not believe my ears. "Of course! Who would not want to meet her?" I replied, all the while believing that the pilot was joking. "Let's go, then!" the pilot said. He gestured to us. We hailed a cab, took a brief ride and, then, walked for a while. I wondered where we were going and how the gentleman knew the renowned singer, but I dared not ask. I just waited for events to unfold. After all, I was used to surprises by now.

The memory of my recent struggles faded when I encountered Ms. Vembo, a kind lady, sitting under a huge tree, with a crochet needle in her hands. Greeting us with a warm embrace, she was undisturbed by the informal introduction, and behaved as though she had known us for years. "How did you come to be here in Cairo?" Ms. Vembo inquired. I told her our story, after which she sang a patriotic song that brought us to tears. "Don't give up hope, boys!" she said encouragingly. One day, we will be victorious. Greece and the rest of Europe will be free from tyranny!" Her words resonated in my heart and made me hearken back to my home in Greece and the United States. How inspired and uplifted my relatives in Europe and North America would have been! *It's incredible how we met such an extraordinary person in the most unlikely of places!* I said to myself.

Speaking of unlikely circumstances, what were the odds that, in our rooms at the villa, we would fall prey to robbers? Unfortunately, we were unaware of the fact that even our extravagant place of refuge was not immune to intruders.

John and Helias In Cairo (1943)

Sifis Migadis and Helias Near a Pool At the Heliopolis Villa

John Androulakis (1943)

Helias In British Uniform (Cairo, 1943)

On one sweltering summer evening, we left our balcony door open; and, to our surprise, when we awoke, we found that our wallets, shoes, clothing, and watches were gone. The latter accessories apparently had been taken off our wrists as we slept. When the English sergeant discovered what had happened, he chastised us for being careless. "Too bad, they didn't leave their names. They would have made better saboteurs than you!" he quipped. Apparently, the good life had put us in a state of complacency.

Just when we were settling in, it was time for us to say "farewell" and express our thanks to the English for their hospitality and, most of all, for our rescue from Crete. One night, as the SOE officers convened for an unusually late meeting in villa's main office, we had reason to suspect that clandestine plans for each of us were underway. Our hunch was confirmed when our dear friend, John Androulakis, was the first to be called in. Later, he secretively emerged from the office, stating that he had to depart the following day on an important mission, the nature of which was classified for security purposes. We said our goodbyes, wishing John the best. The details of what he had to accomplish and the accounts of his heroism had yet to unfold.

Then came George's and my turn to receive our assignments. We hardly knew what to expect but, in our new incarnation as adults, we braced ourselves and surrendered to fate, never backing down.

Chapter 10

Surprising Transformations

Although we knew that the SOE had planned a mission for both of us, my brother George apparently had ideas of his own (of which he had informed me beforehand). Before we were given our assignment, George declared his objective to be introduced to the Office of Strategic Services ("the OSS"), the newly formed American spy organization. I sat there motionless—without giving away the fact that George and I had already discussed the plan—as did the English Intelligence officers, who just stared at my brother with expressionless faces. Some, however, could not conceal their anger. "It appears that you do not appreciate Captain Leigh Fermor's generosity and good favor," said one. "You're both deserting us!" declared another. George shook his head, and clearly stated that we were, in no way, ungrateful. "On the contrary," George said. "As you know, we have worked closely with the SOE over the previous two years, and have undertaken many successful missions." One of the officers nodded in agreement (evidently, Mihalis had praised our record).

"We are American citizens, and we have our birth certificates to prove it. We would much prefer a formal introduction to the OSS, rather than serving under English Intelligence. Both organizations serve the same cause of defeating the Germans. Therefore, it makes sense to serve our birth country. In no way are we deserters. We will be working with the SOE, hand-in hand. We appreciate your hospitality, particularly during this rest period, and we are your allies, with the same purpose."

The English officers could not find fault with George's reasoning, and promptly notified the OSS office in Cairo of our intentions. Within an hour, James Kellis, an OSS officer, contacted us and invited us to join him. Soon, he arrived at the villa, and we rode with him to the Cairo OSS headquarters by jeep. We were immediately impressed by the organization's triple barbed-wired gates and numerous guards. Judging by the OSS's warm reception and eagerness to have us there, the SOE officers must have strongly endorsed and praised our work as underground members of their organization in Crete.

More warm smiles and handshakes followed when we were taken into a room and met with other officers. The men knew of our American citizenship, and felt that we were trustworthy.

Two significant factors made us prime candidates for OSS membership: we spoke Greek without an accent, and we were willing to return undercover to occupied Greece. The commanding officer specified that although George and I were American citizens, we would have no choice but to enlist as civilians working for the OSS. Immediately, George took issue with our status as civilians. "We are Americans, and we will enlist as American soldiers," he said.

"That is impossible," the commanding officer replied. "To become an American soldier, you will require basic training, and you have no time to be sent back to the United States for that purpose."

"We only need OSS training, not basic training," my brother insisted. "Don't forget, we already had two years in the SOE. Please reconsider. If there is no other alternative for us than to stay on as civilians in the OSS, then we will be better off with the SOE. At least, the British secured our safety, and intended to enlist us as British soldiers, not civilian volunteers," George continued with an urgent tone in his voice.

Listening intently, the commanding officer looked at the others. "I'll be right back," he said decisively. With one call to his superiors at the Pentagon in Washington, the commanding officer secured the permission we needed to enlist in the American Army without basic training. Later, two officers were assigned to assist us in going through the enlistment process (i.e., physical examinations, the swearing in, our uniforms, and other particulars, such as paperwork).

We had achieved our goal of being American soldiers; and, to make matters even more exciting, George had attained the rank of staff sergeant overnight. In truth, he had put in a lot of groundwork in the SOE, and his reputation preceded him. As for me, I became a corporal, and was extremely proud of that promotion. After putting on our American uniforms and stripes, George and I looked in the mirror. A surprising transformation had taken place. "The little Americans" had become respected enlisted men.

As stunned as we were by our metamorphosis, we were content and proud to repay the United States Army with our steadfast commitment and service, and we were prepared to rise to the challenge. Later, the officers in charge told us that we had received an immediate transfer to the OSS, and that we had to attend spy training school.

"Just wait! You're in for something grand!" the lieutenant told us, adding, "By the way, why don't you take anything you'd like from the supply room? After all, you are newly inducted

American soldiers, and you deserve more." He took us to the supply room and said, "Get two more uniforms, more shoes, more underwear, cigarettes, candies, and whatever else you want." After we had filled one large army duffel bag to capacity, the lieutenant announced, "Let's go to school!" All we could do was follow along.

**Induction to the Army for the
Doundoulakis Brothers (1943)**

Chapter 11

A Glimpse of Majesty

George and I followed the lieutenant to his car, carrying our duffel bags.

"Our next stop is the spy school," the lieutenant said. "The place will surprise you, and you will never forget the experience."

As we climbed into the car, we wondered how we could possibly be more surprised than we were by the SOE villa. *What could be better than that?* we thought. We drove out from Cairo, parallel to the Nile river, into a beautiful area. Like Heliopolis, the place was filled with villas and mansions on the opposite side. Suddenly, the lieutenant stopped the car and said, "Well, here we are. This is your school." We looked on in wide-eyed disbelief at a palace, much larger and grander than the Cairo SOE's headquarters.

"Are you sure this is a school? It must be a sultan's palace!" I exclaimed.

"Yes, indeed, it is! It belongs to King Farouk's brother-in-law, who has three palaces. He doesn't need this one, so he's renting it to the OSS, to be used as a training school for their spies. How do you like it?" the lieutenant asked.

George and I continued staring at the splendid structure, feeling as though we were in the middle of a fairy tale—yet again. Tall columns and lush trees surrounded the palace, and across the boulevard, the Nile shone in all of its radiance. As we drove up to the huge entrance, we observed that it led to an enclosed garden. We exited the car and began to walk toward the front steps. Off to the side, I spotted a few men guarding the entrance. After ascending about a dozen marble steps, the lieutenant slid open a large pocket door, made of sculptured glass and wood. Our hearts pounded with excitement as we stepped into the palace. Looking around, we saw a colossal spiral staircase in the style of Hollywood movies.

"Do you see those buttons on the wall?" the lieutenant pointed out. "If you press them, the partitions will slide away and be hidden in the walls, and the first floor can accommodate three hundred people during any type of celebration."

Our eyes darted every which way in amazement. The floor designs were created out of multi-colored marble, apparently displaying works of fine art. They had a shiny, glassy appearance and, as we walked, we had to be very careful, so as not to scratch them. As we ascended to the second floor, we observed that it was separated into four complete individual apartments, each one with distinctly colored marble floors. Each apartment also had two to four bedrooms and dressing rooms, which provided plenty of space for our group of fifteen. Every apartment was a different color marble—either plain white or white with blue, pink, or green lines.

My brother and I stayed in the pink marble apartment with two bedrooms, which was quite acceptable to our taste. After all, coming from a small three-room house in a little Cretan village, without inside electricity, running water, or toilet, how could we possibly complain of such a dreamy environment (even though we did not like the color pink)?

In the back of the structure was an immense garden, with the most exotic trees and birds that we had ever seen—much like those found in a jungle. The basement housed the servants and the kitchen, while on the other floors, there were parlors, billiard and ping-pong rooms, exercise rooms, and lecture halls. The dining room was adorned with tables covered with white linen. At mealtime, Egyptian personnel prepared our food, and we were served by American soldiers who, we later learned, were Congress members' sons or relatives. Apparently, in order to keep them out of harm's way on the front line, their families had secured them positions as servants. Somehow, the fact that they were shielded from harm because of their privileged status seemed unfair to those who had to risk their lives for their country.

Most of our group who were attending spy school were Greeks, along with two Yugoslavians and three Italians. Thirty personnel were assigned to fifteen trainees, including George and me. Major Vassos was the highest-ranking officer, followed by two captains and four lieutenants. The remaining personnel had at least a sergeant's rank.

Our day consisted of seven-hour instructions, and traveling to and from Cairo via the OSS army bus on specified time schedules that, for security reasons, continuously changed. The use of taxi cabs en route to and from Cairo was strictly prohibited, and one student was dismissed for violating the rule. In all events, since the palace had every amenity that we could ever need or want, leaving the grounds was optional. Outside the school area, we had the Nile at our feet, with its beautiful walking spots. Never again would we have to worry about getting lost on a train! Then, there was "the cherry on top of the cake" (as the Greeks say): a one-hundred-fifty-foot yacht (accessible only to OSS personnel), and a smaller forty-foot sailboat at our disposal. Both vessels were moored along the Nile, just a short distance from the palace. That was the life. If only our parents could have shared the experience!

On our second day there, I decided to go for a walk and visit the yacht, instead of going to Cairo. Displaying my OSS identification to the Arab guards, I was permitted to enter. Immediately, two Egyptians wearing white robes approached me.

"What do you wish to do?" they inquired.

"Would you like to go for a sailboat ride?" one suggested. "The weather is perfect today, with only a mild wind."

When I declined, I realized, by the man's disappointed expression, that I must have deprived him of his job—and, possibly, his own desire to go sailing, since he could not so indulge without a guest.

"Would you like to be served dinner in the yacht's dining room?" another asked.

I readily agreed, and was taken on a tour of the whole yacht.

"You can sleep in any cabin that you like," my guide said.

As I passed the rooms, I was mesmerized. One cabin was more lavish than the next. *Such luxuries are fit only for kings*, I said silently to myself. Then, realizing that I should address my tour guide, I responded, "Thank you, supper will be enough for tonight." I concluded that this was my time to fancy myself a king for a day—a fantasy-like prelude to a potentially dangerous mission. *The dream won't last*, I told myself. However, for that moment, I allowed myself to bask in luxury. To be honest, everywhere I went, I was surrounded by opulence. The U.S. forces had rented The Grand Hotel in the center of Cairo, where we could pass the time at any hour.

I would go there with some of my Greek-American soldier comrades, just to play billiards or ping-pong, or simply to pass the time.

One day, the lieutenant who had assisted my brother and me with our army-induction process, saw me in the dining room, and pulled me aside.

"Are you happy with all that you have seen and experienced so far?" he asked.

"Of course, I am," I replied eagerly. "But don't forget, I'm still very confused with all this change. I can't believe that people lived in this extravagant palace, and now I am privileged to do the same. I recently came from a small village in Crete, where I lived in an old three-room house, without plumbing or electricity. Even in winter, I had to go outside to wash or use the bathroom; and, now, I'm living in this palace, in a pink-marbled apartment, like a king!"

"I understand what you mean," the lieutenant replied, with a smile. Then, he added, "Tomorrow, I am going to get some ammunition from the army barracks. Would you like to come with me?"

I agreed and the next day, we drove together into the desert, just outside Cairo, where we found thousands of American soldiers billeted, living in their tents, row after row. It must have been one hundred degrees where we found the army men, disrobed from the waist up, with their bodies drenched in perspiration, glistening in the sun.

"Do you see where your fellow American soldiers are staying?" the lieutenant asked. Instinctively, I knew that a reply was not necessary. Clearly, the lieutenant was giving me a reality check. For the moment, I was privileged, living in the villa; but in no time, I would be alone, without the camaraderie of other soldiers, at risk of being killed or captured behind enemy lines (as opposed to frontline combat).

As fate would have it, the inevitable happened, and paradise quickly gave way to real-world responsibilities. After just a week, the time came for us to begin our training, and some of us gathered in the main lecture hall to receive our assignments.

"For some of you, the first round of instruction will be parachute and commando training, for which you will be sent to Haifa, Palestine tomorrow. There, you will also join the English commandos in training. I know that you love it here, but in a few weeks, you will return to the palace, your permanent base."

So, with more adventures in view, we could do nothing but pack to leave our glimpse of majesty behind, grateful to have had such a wonderful place to plant our feet. Then, in a blink of time, we were beckoned to reach for the sky.

Chapter 12

Mastering the Descent

The next morning, some of us departed for Palestine and I went straight to parachute training camp, where our group was split up into various jumping units. As it turned out, I was the only American in a group of twelve English soldiers assigned to a certain airplane. Each group had a sergeant-in-charge that gave us our pre-jump training and instructions on how to fold our parachutes (roughly, but carefully) and bring them to the pickup point. The sergeant said that the parachute training course would take ten days. During the first few days, we would exercise eight hours a day to make our bodies very "elastic," as he said. So, in the early morning darkness, we ran two or more times around the entire airfield until we collapsed, panting uncontrollably. We then ate breakfast, which consisted of boiled squash and potatoes. These meager sources of nourishment were hardly enough to sustain growing young men. As a result, I lost ten pounds at the camp in my ten-day stay there.

Having exercised to the point of exhaustion, we trained to hit the ground and roll. First, we climbed a thin, vertical ladder to the top of a seventy-five-foot high platform, after which the sergeant tied us with parachute-like ropes and pushed us off. There we were, frighteningly swinging in mid-air. Just before we reached the lowest point, we had to unfasten a buckle, so as to release ourselves from the ropes, turn our bodies, and roll to the ground.

Haifa Palestine Parachute Training (1943)

The so-called "horror swing," similar to falling from a parachute, was not for the faint of heart. Even grown men were terrified of it. I recall a middle-aged English captain who told us, "I will jump from an airplane, but I will not use that swing." The younger group, of course, did not sense the danger. On the contrary, we viewed the area as a huge playground, and even enjoyed the risks associated with hanging perilously in the sky.

Once our bones were "softened" (as the sergeant used to say), we climbed into the airplane, where we were instructed on how to clip our parachute onto a cable, and then slide it toward the exit door. When the red light turned green, we had to jump out as quickly as possible. Each of us was assigned numbers for every jump, the first of which was to be two thousand feet. "Any volunteers to jump first?" the sergeant asked. Since everyone was quiet, I raised my hand.

"For the first jump," the sergeant began, "you will fall out over the airfield, where there are no trees. Then, on the other jumps, you will fall in tree-filled regions." Next, the sergeant demonstrated how to pull the parachute cords sideways and how to fall between the trees. "You don't want to fall on the top of a one-hundred-foot-high tree and get stuck, do you?" he warned.

Being the first to jump made me feel like a leader. I was the number one man in a line of twelve others behind me. Suddenly, a thousand thoughts flashed through my mind. I remembered my friends in Archanes, my small hometown village in Crete. *If only they could see me now . . . leading a group of twelve British paratroopers . . . ready to jump from two thousand feet! What would they think?* I wondered. I hearkened back to the time when I watched German paratroopers fall from the skies of Heraklion. Now, two years later, it was my turn. As pride in being an American soldier welled within me, the light over the exit door turned green.

Without hesitation, I jumped out of the door, feeling the airplane pass over me. As I fell with great speed, I tried to keep my eyes open to enjoy the thrill of falling; but, in no time, the parachute opened. Swaying like a contented leaf in the breeze, I savored each moment. The view was spectacular—as if the world's entire panorama were right before me. I felt as free as a bird. Then, I hit the ground. *I loved it,* I said to myself. To be sure, it was easier than the training. Now, I understood why the English captain refused to undertake the "horror swing!"

Outside the airfield, I took the number two spot for the second jump. On the plane, a young Englishman had asked if I would take his place in the number one position, for he feared that he would freeze when the light turned green. Given that I was already a veteran jumper (I'm kidding, of course; but, since I had been first in line before, I really did not object), I agreed. Just before we had reached the drop area, however, the sergeant interceded and told me to change positions. "Watch number one," he commanded, "and if he hesitates in any way, push him out of the door when the light turns green!"

That must have been a daunting prospect for number one; but, as luck would have it, he mustered up the courage, and jumped at the sight of the green light. As for me, my jump did not go so well. Unlike the first time, my parachute did not open, and I cascaded through the sky like a bullet. The sergeant had warned us that, if the parachute did not open immediately, the air pressure would cause it to remain closed. In that case, we would have to pull the opposite straps apart, allowing air to enter the parachute. In that crucial moment, I wasted no time in adhering to those vital tips. The feeling was indescribable—almost as if the straps would pull my body apart from the armpits; but, to my enormous relief, the parachute opened immediately. Later, a sergeant at the drop-off area who had been watching us jump told me that he feared my parachute would not open in time, and thought that I would become another fatality at the training camp. "It was a good thing that you pulled the straps apart. I've seen others die the same way, mate," he said, as he winked and patted me on the back.

In our last few days of training, seven-hundred-foot and five-hundred-foot drops were scheduled. Drops from these heights did not afford us the opportunity to look around; and, if the chute did not open, death would be a certainty.

"My God!" I exclaimed. "A five-hundred-foot jump? Why do we need to drop from such a low height? The airplane will be over the treetops just before we jump out."

"Since you are with the OSS, you must be prepared for a drop from any altitude. If you drop from two thousand feet and you take a couple of minutes to fall, Jerry could be watching and come quickly to capture you.[6] However, if you jump from five hundred feet (especially in an area where there are big trees), you may stand a chance at survival if you drop between them and hide. You should pray *first* that the chute opens this time and, *then*, that Jerry doesn't spot you!" one of the sergeants said, chuckling nervously at the thought of my closed parachute on my second jump.

---

[6]   "Jerry," of course, was a name the Allies used when referring to the Germans during World War II.

For me, jumping from an airplane was the most exhilarating experience—particularly on a dark, moonless night. There, with nothing but the vast expanse of blackness, I jumped out, saw nothing and heard nothing but the roar of the airplane above me. I prayed that the chute would open and, then, took a leap of faith, falling through the night sky, without seeing the ground. Without the ability to prepare to roll, I simply trusted in gravity, and hit the ground hard.

On one ill-fated night drop, I fell into an area with bushes and thorns, and the pin-like bristles stuck all over me. Trying to free the parachute (which was entangled in the thorn bushes) was a very difficult task. Because I had been delayed in appearing at the pickup location, I heard the sergeant on the loudspeaker call out, "Okay, number eight! Where are you?" Finally, the sergeant came looking for me with a big searchlight and gave me an assist. Always in a teasing mood, he commented, "You couldn't have found a better place to fall, eh, Yank?"

"Parachute jumping was a delightful experience with you. You were a very good group," the sergeant commended us at the end of our training. "If you have to undertake a jump, you should not be afraid now. I'm so used to parachute jumping, myself, since I have done so—more than eight hundred times— with each group that I have trained. On the descent, I unbuckle myself and hang onto the parachute with one hand before landing."

I remember that sergeant well, and it is very sad for me to think of him now. Just four months after his speech to all of us, whom he loved like sons, he died when his parachute failed to open on a five-hundred-foot drop. [7] Despite our grief, life had to move on for all of us, but not without looking over our shoulders and remembering, with love and reverence, the man who once warned us to expect the unexpected, to be alert to situations which he, himself, could not avoid, and to which he tragically succumbed. To the man who taught us to be fearless and to master the descent, we owe our heartfelt gratitude—more than he could ever know.

The Author, Second From Left, With British Soldiers (1943)

---

[7]   By that time, I had nearly completed my OSS spy training at the palace, and was about to embark on my behind-the-lines mission.

Chapter 13

An Interlude In Haifa

Our next mission at the English commando training camp involved introduction to all types of light firearms (e.g., pistols, machine guns, etc.) knives, and various types of training in combat-like environments. We also underwent grenade training, first with dummy and, then, live grenades. During training, we used both large artillery and small, .45-caliber guns, and were taught how to take out the enemy by cracking his skull using the gun as a club. The sound of firing the larger guns was so deafening, that I thought my eardrums would burst—even when cupping my ears with my hands, as per our instructions. As in basic training, we climbed ropes and ran over barricades and walls. Generally, the training was very enlightening for me, and I went through it with ease.

I was then assigned to survival training, which was but one of the many facets of commando training. Other, more sophisticated aspects of training included Special Operations ("SO") preparation for those who were bound for service behind enemy lines—with orders to enlist, organize, and embolden large groups of partisans for coordinated sabotages. By contrast, my training—for solitary agents in SI (Secret Intelligence)—was more defensive, aimed at hand-to-combat with and without a weapon. In the latter instance, we had to use our hands and feet to attack by hitting the enemy in the face or groin. I was also instructed on how to kill a person with a strong back-handed jab to the throat, the most vulnerable part of the body, and how to use an extremely heavy, sharp knife that could pierce the skin if held vertically on the palm. Through the course of my exposure to such gruesome methods of combat, I came to understand just how fragile life can be.

More refined, interesting ventures awaited me at the radio operator's training school just outside Haifa, Palestine. I was escorted to the most beautiful area of Haifa, where I gazed in amazement at the many luxurious homes on each side of a winding road that connected the harbor below to a hilltop, where the training school was located. Once inside the building, filled with many rooms, I was introduced to the English captain in charge, and prepared to train in wireless communication and Morse code. The twenty-student class had begun a week before I arrived; so, I had some catching up to do, and the captain was hesitant about accepting me. Finally, however, he agreed to place me in a separate room with a private instructor, and challenged me to absorb in two days what the others had learned in a week. If I proved myself, he said, I would be allowed to continue. Since I enjoyed the subject at hand, I learned quickly. On day one, I had the alphabet down pat and, on the second day, I was ready to accelerate.

The instructor thought that I was kidding. "Let me see your notes," he said.

"All right! Here they are!" I replied confidently.

The instructor looked at me with a surprised expression. "You're right. You can proceed more quickly, and you will have no problem joining the group."

So, on day three, I went into the larger class; and, from then on, not only did I keep up with the others, but I surpassed them in the speed necessary for sending and receiving Morse code. I even surprised myself.

During the evenings, I frequented the Haifa nightclubs with my fellow trainees. Since I was the only American in the group, everyone expected me to pay for drinks; but, given my monthly salaries as a corporal T5 ($105), and as a paratrooper ($55), I did not object at all. Those figures exceeded the wages of English captains, and far surpassed the $5 earnings of Greek or English soldiers! As a result of my earning capacity, I gained the reputation with the girls of being a big spender; and, each time I entered a club, they would flock to me. I learned (far too late, I'm afraid) that I was spending too much on those girls, only to receive a couple of kisses in return.

Lasting a couple of weeks, our memorable experiences in Haifa soon gave way to more spy training in Cairo. The demands of our schedules never allowed us to be in one place for too long, and goodbyes were commonplace. I shook hands with our English officer instructors and two Greek classmates (one of whom was a captain, the other a Cypriot), with whom I had become very close friends. Both were returning to Greece at the command of the English Intelligence Service. In taking our leave, none of us knew whether we would ever meet again— or, for that matter, if any of us would survive. Although I do not remember their names, the feeling of parting from them remains with me even now, and I wonder . . .

The following morning, we left for Cairo and, after a full day's travel, arrived once again at the spy training palace. Some things had changed during my month's absence. Most notably, some of my classmates were not there. Included in this number were the two Yugoslavians, who had been sent somewhere to the mountains of their homeland. My brother, George, as an SO agent, had amassed training in the use of explosives, as well as supervisory disciplines. Apparently, he was to assume a kind of leadership position involving sabotage. What I did not know then was that he would be sent to a place near the city of Volos, Greece, to organize six thousand five hundred partisans on Pelion Mountain. As an American OSS agent, using American supplies, my brother would utilize the partisan's force for sabotages with dynamite on the German supply depots and the rail system. He participated so honorably and successfully that, after the war, the United States Army decorated him with the Legion of Merit.

I always recognized George's enormous talents and potential, and I looked to him as a guide, mentor and friend, as well as a brother; but I also realized that I had to travel on the road of spy training alone, without knowing just what kind of mysteries lurked around every corner.

Chapter 14

Gentlemen Thieves

By now, I was used to embarking on new adventures. I proceeded to my next phase of training, therefore, as though I were walking from one room into another—and, in fact, that is just what I did: I entered a new classroom, where I encountered some familiar faces, along with new ones, and different instructors. One was a rather jovial lieutenant, who informed us that we were going to experience "serious" intelligence training.

"After your mission is over, you should try to forget your lessons in the art of stealing that you will experience here," he cautioned. "That is, if you want to lead normal lives, and you don't want to find yourselves in prison or rejected by society. In other words, the training that you will receive will transform you into thieves, cheaters and liars—for the sole purpose of accomplishing your goal as spies: to 'steal' information and documents in enemy territory, in order to thwart the Germans from carrying out their plans."

The lieutenant informed us that, most of the time, accessing the crucial information would be extremely difficult, given that it could be locked in an office. In that case, we would have to enter to confiscate what we required, and skillfully make our exit. The lieutenant provided further insight. "That's why we're going to teach you how to open locked doors, drawers and safes. In other words, we will make *gentlemen thieves* out of all of you. You will be invisible, mingling unnoticed with other civilians, but you will have the ability to steal the information that we need when you have the unique chance to get your hands on it. So let's start with outside door locks. We will give you a set of master keys." The lieutenant showed us a key chain with about two dozen sets of keys. As he explained, "Master keys are similar to these keys. For example, the cleaning woman in a big hotel has a master key that opens all of the hotel room doors, perhaps three hundred. With these master keys, you can open seventy percent of the door locks anywhere in the world. Each of you will receive such a set before you leave for your mission. So, now that you have the master keys, you must find the door to which each corresponds." The lieutenant paused to observe our attentiveness, then continued. "Imagine that you walk into an empty room and find a locked drawer which, you suspect, contains the vital information. Don't be discouraged if the documents are not right there on the table, before your eyes. Therefore, in order to open drawers and access their contents, you will use a tiny screwdriver, a thin wire, or a narrow metal plate, hidden in your jacket, wallet, or belt."

In demonstrating these techniques, the lieutenant led us to three desks in the room, all with locked drawers. Each lock was of a different type, depending on the mechanism—or tumbler. The lieutenant showed us a distinct method that was required in order to open each of those drawers. He had dissected the lock mechanism for each of the different types of locks, so as to easily unmask the concept involved. At first, none of us was successful; but after the lieutenant observed and corrected our hand movements, the task of opening all of the drawers proved to be very easy.

Upon seeing our smiles of satisfaction, the lieutenant looked very pleased, himself. He explained that under duress, however, the process would not be as simple. The elements of timing and the fear of being caught would add to the difficulties that we had initially experienced. Once we were in an actual, literally hands-on situation, we would have to open the drawers, take pictures of the information (we would be equipped with Nikon cameras for that purpose), and leave the scene as quickly as possible. "Know this," the lieutenant cautioned, "your hands will not be as steady as they are now, as you may tremble under pressure and fright. Your one or two attempts here, in practice, may take four or five in the field—or you may not succeed at all. However, if your hands are steady enough, you may be able to accomplish your goal." Looking somber, the lieutenant paused again, then resumed. "If you succeed in opening the drawer, and you leave it messy and in disarray, you must not exit the room; for if the Germans even *slightly* suspect that their troop deployments described in those confiscated documents have been photographed or copied, the documents will be altered and rendered obsolete. By the way, there will be a separate class on how to take pictures. The small, automatic Nikon camera that you will use, costing two thousand dollars, can take precise photographs even in poor lighting. Just point and shoot, and even in the worst conditions, we'll get what we're looking for. Also, it is very important that you place the documents in the drawer in the exact order in which you found them, and lock the drawer before leaving the room. Locking the drawer is a reverse process, which we will learn now, using the identical tools as before."

Closely following the lieutenant's hand movements, we observed how he opened and locked all three drawers. Together, we learned quickly and proved to the lieutenant—and to ourselves—that we were destined to be proficient "gentleman thieves."

By late afternoon, Major Vassos entered the classroom, and all of us stood at attention. Evidently, he had come to inquire about our progress and, observing the lieutenant's expressions of approval, we realized that he was satisfied. The smile on his face never dissipated as he told us that the following day's training would be even more challenging: opening safes. Once we learned that slight of hand, we would earn our diplomas as professional thieves. Although that title seemed like a dubious distinction, all of us were keenly aware of how essential it was.

The following day, we headed to our next class, where we saw one portable safe and three larger heavy combination-lock safes which, we assumed, would be our challenge for the day. The smiling lieutenant was poised and ready to commence the lesson.

"To open a safe," he began, "no instrument or tool is used; rather, you must utilize your ear and your sense of feeling and touch—on the dial. Turn the dial to the right, then left, and then right again. If you perform these movements in the correct order, and the plunger falls correctly into a certain slot (when you enter the right combination), you will open the safe. Otherwise, you will not succeed. When the correct combination is used, you must turn the dial slowly, stop when you reach the combination number, and feel or sense a very slight movement of the plunger. Then, you must change direction. You will now learn when and how to attain that sense or feel."

As with the door locks, the safes' mechanisms had been dissected open to visualize its moving parts and operation. I held the basic components of each safe in my hands, and was fascinated at the intricacy of its movement—especially when the plunger aligned with the correct combination number. "There are wheels inside the lock mechanism of every safe— which are attached to the dial by a shaft. The number of wheels is determined by how many numbers are in the combination— usually three," he said. "It's very simple."

After watching the lieutenant open all of the safes, we tried our hand at the task. When we first began, we could not sense the slight plunger movement. I didn't feel a thing. Then, the lieutenant told us the combination of one of the safes, and instructed us not to reach the combination number and not change direction—yet. "Wait and feel the slight movement," he repeated. I found the process to be very intense and exciting. Each one of us took a combination for another safe and slowly tried to achieve that "sense," first memorizing the combination and, then, proceeding blindly, without knowing what the combination was. I thought that, perhaps, the lieutenant was a locksmith or lock expert, and even others joked that he might have been a former criminal.

It took a while but, eventually, we really *did* sense something, even as we put our ears to the safe's wall. At the end of the second day, every one of us had opened all of the safes— even after the combinations were changed. The lieutenant was extremely happy with our accomplishments, and he called in Major Vassos, who again congratulated our swift learning abilities. Apparently, in two days, we had accomplished what the other classes took four days to complete. All of us agreed that we had earned our diplomas in thievery, and we celebrated by taking a break and passing cigarettes around.

After opening the safes, the lieutenant informed us of the importance of leaving the documents—and the room in which we found them—unaltered. If we moved around any pieces of furniture while getting to the safes, we had to replace them precisely as they had been situated before we entered. Certainly, we did not want to go through all of that trouble and risk our lives, only to have the enemy destroy our plans.

"A spy is a gentleman—a thief who does not take anything," the lieutenant explained again. "He only reads, photographs, or copies the information that he believes to be important, and ensures that nothing is disturbed after he is finished. A spy thief should actually be a 'phantom thief,' in order to be effective and useful to the organization."

Having made his message very clear to all of us upon completion of the course, the lieutenant concluded with one final point. "Aside from being a gentleman thief, a good spy should also be adept at cheating and lying." In order to avail ourselves of instructions in the art of lying, we had to move on to another classroom, equipped with movie projectors and various other equipment, and another instructor would present us with the next phase of our training.

When class ended on Friday afternoon, we were told that during the weekend, we could visit the yacht, docked only a short distance from the palatial OSS school. The yacht's rear deck was converted into small cabins, in which we could stay and be at our leisure. We were also provided with a private bus, which would take us to Cairo, where we could frequent The Grand Hotel. We were told to return to school solely via the private bus. If, for any reason, we missed it, we could telephone the school, and a special car would bring us back. Only later did I discover that the high level of security in place was due to the presence of a German spy ring in Cairo, gathering information and photos of OSS agents—particularly of the soldiers staying at the palace-school. At all times, we paid heed to every warning. Our very lives depended on that.

Chapter 15

Secrets, Lies, and Camouflage

Renewed and refreshed after a weekend in Cairo and visiting the yacht, we returned to the classroom to meet our new instructor (also a lieutenant), who managed to memorize our first names quite easily. For security reasons, we were never addressed by our last names, which were only known to OSS headquarters in Cairo. Thus, I was known only as "Helias."

In our first lesson, the instructor pointed out that, as secret agents, we would have to stay in various cities, integrating among people and communities, and we would have to provide mock proof of identity—a temporary form of identification, to be used en route to our final destination—in case we were subjected to a random Gestapo (German police) inspection. Therefore, we had to choose a last name, preferably something common and easy to remember, which would be placed on our pseudo-identification cards. Our first names would not change. The instructor gave us some time to think. While the others had difficulty in choosing a surname, one instantly came to mind. When the instructor asked us whether we had chosen, I wasted no time.

"I would like my last name to be Nikolaou," I said with conviction.

"OK, then. Your fake identification card will read "Helias Nikolaou," the instructor replied, as he wrote down the name.

"Now, the fake address at which you are supposed to be living will be chosen from the telephone book of the town or city to which you will be sent," the lieutenant said, looking around the room to observe our level of attentiveness. Then, he continued. "Once you have established a residence, you must find a way to get a permanent address. If, when you have reached your final destination, you find a place to stay, carefully examine the address on your temporary identification card. If that is a residential address, you should not replace the card; but if the address happens to belong to a store, hotel, museum, or other public establishment, it is vitally important that you replace the card as soon as possible. The replacement is not so much a means of avoiding scrutiny by the Gestapo (who will not easily be able to recognize whether or not the address is *legitimate*); rather, you must avoid investigation by the Greek police, who will immediately recognize whether or not the ID is *residential*." These types of subtle hints were essential to our very lives. We could only hope that, once at our destination, we could establish a temporary residence through someone whom we happened to meet, until we could find a permanent location.

Once we established a residence, we had to find a site in which to install the wireless and fifty-foot-long antenna, which would have to face south, toward Cairo. One caveat was that we could not live in the same place where we used the device. The secret location had to be well-guarded and frequented by only a few individuals with whom we would interact as though we were running a business—a cover which would justify our presence in a particular location and the nature of our association with specific individuals. The instructor suggested that we rent a storefront or warehouse, in order to meld into the community. The best decoy, the lieutenant told us, was to pose as merchants and pretend to sell items at wholesale prices (e.g., family heirlooms, which could be sold for food, clothing, wood, or oil). The main objective, of course, would be to sell these items at higher prices, in order to discourage returning customers. This would be an extremely unorthodox business tactic, but nothing that we spies did or endeavored to do was commonplace. We simply had to devise ways of deceiving and thwarting the enemy's objectives.

The primary reason for the dual locations was to ensure that we would have a place to stay in the event the wireless location was discovered and we had to avert capture. Conversely, if the Gestapo somehow found out where we resided, but remained oblivious to the wireless location, we would have to devise a way to communicate with our organization. A third scenario could also occur: "If the Gestapo knows both addresses—that is, where you live and the place where you operate your wireless—you need a third address, 'a safe house,'" the lieutenant warned us. His calm manner enabled us to process his instructions easily. "If you're chased by the Gestapo," he continued, still maintaining strict composure, "you cannot stay in hotels or run and hide on the streets. The most secure place will be in the safe house until you resume contact with us. Then, we will attempt to evacuate you from that city. Therefore, you should establish three essential addresses: one where you live; a second for operating the wireless; and a third for evading capture and reconnecting with OSS members, on whom you will rely for a rescue."

The instructor then elaborated on the fact that, in the event of a Gestapo raid, the location would operate as an escape route to the neighborhood's most remote sections. We would have to jump from one home's rooftop to an adjoining one or from one yard to another, rather than out in plain view on the streets, where the Gestapo could readily find us. In order to access a rooftop or yard, the Gestapo would have to gain access to a resident's home—a process which would buy us time for our great escape.

The learned lieutenant then proceeded to describe how to operate the wireless. "The radio and antenna have to be cleverly hidden from view, concealed on a table or desk behind office paraphernalia, so as not to reveal its existence to unanticipated visitors." Nonetheless, it had to be accessible to us at all times. When we would send a message, we had to be aware that we were exposed to every radio receiver in Greece, including the Gestapo's triangulation instruments. "So you must send your message and get off the air as quickly as you can," the lieutenant cautioned us. "Receiving a message is not a problem, but if, while you are sending a message, a triangulation receiver or a Gestapo agent with radio interceptor equipment hears you, the direction of your signal will be located immediately," he advised. Apparently, once the Gestapo ascertained the direction, they would place other triangulation instruments nearby, and pinpoint our signals' location. The strength of the signal would indicate our proximity to them. In other words, a very strong signal would mean that we were nearby. Knowing how many of their radios were in a given area enabled the Gestapo to restrict the activity of their devices in order to concentrate on our signals. Therefore, the lieutenant warned us that we could send only one or two short messages, at the most, containing not more than twenty-five words per message. We could only remain on the air for a maximum of five minutes, and if we needed to send another message, it had to be urgent in nature. "Remember to change frequency, and tell us which you want to switch to. You will require a unique code, which we will provide to you. The general rule is that you are allowed one frequency per message. You can send a second message and request a second frequency change and, then, a third, but not more."

At least two people had to guard us while we sent messages (telegrams). The first had to scour the area while the wireless was in operation, ever alert and committed to the operators' safety, and prepared to notify us of an impending Gestapo raid—even if that meant putting himself at risk of being caught. The second guard would be stationed in or outside of the building where we were working, scrutinizing everyone who entered the premises. He had to be willing to risk his life for ours and be ready to kill anyone who might attempt to enter the room where we were operating the wireless. If a stranger observed us at work with our headphones on or operating a wireless key, everyone in that vicinity had to evacuate the building immediately and go to predetermined locations. At every moment, we had to expect the worst, for that stranger would, undoubtedly, report the activity to others. Such were the lieutenant's admonitions, strict, precise, and to the point. He left no stone unturned.

As I listened to our instructor, I could almost read his mind. I instinctively knew that, at the moment I pressed and released the wireless key, I would be facing the most dangerous time in my young life. The lieutenant continued to appear stoic and focused when addressing the intensely serious subject at hand. Finally, he explained that, after all was said and done, the worst nightmare could occur, and we had to be on our toes at all times. The Germans could, potentially, randomly catch and interrogate us about our presence in the area. Because of our youth, we could convincingly state that we were students. Therefore, it was important for us to register at universities or trade schools in the regions in which we resided. Student identification would be plausible proof and justification of our presence in a given place. However, if the enemy suspected us to be spies, we had to learn the art of fabrication. In so doing, we had to maintain a calm exterior. As long as we were not caught with our wireless headset on, we could deny everything. Any display of fear would give rise to suspicion. The Germans were trained to investigate and analyze, and they could smell fear—quite literally. Therefore, the *way* in which we said things, the lieutenant pointed out, would often carry more weight than the story itself. Thinking quickly on our feet was the key to our success, saving our lives, and those of others. The swiftness with which we thought and acted would indicate that deliberation was not necessary (and, hence, that we were innocent). Therefore, saying the first thing that came to our minds was key. If we wished to succeed in the art of lying—and to live—this type of conduct had to become second nature to us. "In business, dreams are often built on lies," the lieutenant declared with conviction, holding forth on the topic for what seemed like hours.

At that moment, I could not have expected how much those vital instructions would come in handy and how, by employing wise methodology, I would save my life and be able to record these memories.

Chapter 16

True Actors of the War

Not only did we have to learn the art of secrecy and undercover activities but, also, how to escape quickly from dangerous situations and encounters. This was a much more involved skill than blending seamlessly into the Greek communities. For example, if we were in restricted areas, tallying airplanes in a German airfield, we had to be aware of the potential approach of German patrol units. We had to learn to make excuses, such as being uncertain of our whereabouts or losing our way. We could readily convince the enemy that such was the case, given our youthful, innocent appearances. Also, if we were not carrying weapons or items that would raise suspicion, we had a good chance of being released after a search. That is why we had to rely on our memories and refrain from note-taking at all times. If we had to recall the number of airplanes in an airfield before a scheduled sabotage (e.g., twelve small airplanes in field A, eight big-troop transport planes in field B, and approximately two hundred barrels of gasoline in field C), and we wrote these figures down on paper, there would be virtually no chance to prove our innocence. We would be presumed guilty, right then and there.

"That is why you must learn to memorize the information. Avoid making notes, even if there are many things to remember," the lieutenant said. He began by asking us how we might call to mind something from memory. "Use your ABC's as a way to help you remember: A for airplane, B for barrels [of gas], and so on. Take notice of soldiers' uniforms and patches using the same method: recall the unit number with a number you are familiar with. Let's say the unit number is '7.' Identify that number with something that occurred when you were "seven" years old, or a family you might know with "seven" children. If there is a flame, or lightning bolt on the patch, recall some event that occurred with a fire or lightning."

Like notes, tiny cameras were strictly prohibited in restricted areas. If we were caught carrying them, we would be detained until the film was developed; then, we would be tortured, and most certainly, face death. Our minds, therefore, were our ultimate sources of stored information.

In the event that we were approached by a single German guard who forced us to submit to his questioning and will, there would be no recourse but to kill him in order to avoid interrogation, an inevitable finding of guilt, and imminent death. Annihilating the guard would be our only chance. We could accomplish this, the instructor said, with a pen gun which would be provided to us before departure on our mission. We would keep this dangerous instrument (which looked like an ordinary pen) in our pockets. A single-shot gun, the weapon could be extremely effective in cases of imminent interrogation in isolated areas (particularly in encounters with a single German guard, when others were not nearby) or if the guard forced us to go with him to his station, where he would conduct a thorough examination. In that case, we had to take the pen gun from our pockets, point it straight at the guard's heart, and press the back, so as to fire a single small bullet. This act would either kill, stun, or wound the guard, and give us the opportunity to flee.

If we were alone with the guard in a room (which was not a prison cell), we could kick down the door, using methods that we had yet to learn. Another means of escape would be to jump from a window, or dress as someone else and walk right out of the room. If a guard was assigned to watch our activities, we had to use the pen gun (if we were dealing with only one guard).

However, if we were assigned to a house guard and threatened with interrogation, wishing that we had a gun on us, we could use another killing instrument: a newspaper. Understandably, one may wonder how a newspaper could be turned into a lethal instrument. In dire circumstances, we were taught, we could pick a point in the middle and left side of a multi-paged newspaper, and begin to fold the paper around that point. Doing so would make the newspaper hard and rigid. At just the right moment, we could swiftly jab the guard in the throat, crush his larynx (i.e., his voice box) and stop him from breathing. We had yet to learn and master these concepts, which were vital to our survival. All we knew was that we had to escape at all costs. "Escaping is a critical issue. There is no other choice," the instructor warned us.

To illustrate the above methods, the lieutenant showed us about a half-dozen four-page full-colored books (similar to those of early school-aged children), which depicted various fleeing tactics. In one example, a tree leaning against an outside wall, close to a window, was an ideal conduit for escaping through the window. In another picture, we saw a toolbox containing a variety of tools with which to unlock a door. In a third graphic, we observed a German soldier's overcoat and hat, which we spies were expected to snatch, put on, jump out of the window, and walk right past the German guards at the front gate.

As we carefully looked at each book, the instructor focused his attention on every one of us individually, made notes, and graded us on our responses to his questions, which he either approved or rejected. If he was unsatisfied with our answers, we had to go over that particular sticking point again. We listened to the lieutenant's praise and constructive criticism, while some of us invented new, logically thought-out methods of escape. Although we laughed at some of the outlandish ideas that some of us put forth, we were mindful of the seriousness of the moment.

After we had clearly defined the escape routes in each book, the instructor jotted down notes in his grading notebook. We wondered why we were being graded on our responses and performance time. Did this mean that we had to achieve a certain grade in order to be considered "spy material" and, ultimately, graduate? What if one of us failed and would be denied an assignment? It was obvious that, if the instructor would choose to fail any one of us, he would do so because he did not want to risk our lives, the lives of others, or place the OSS in jeopardy. By no means could he sacrifice crucial information or entrust someone incapable of following proper instructions with a spy mission. Where the greater good and the lives of countless people were at stake, one individual's failure meant very little.

As we discussed and thought about these matters, we became increasingly anxious, and drove ourselves even harder. We began to be in competition with one another, and to pay closer attention in class, viewing every situation as an actual, real-time event, as though our lives depended on how we reacted. We explored every option and tried to resolve each and every conflict that we encountered. In the following weeks, we came to realize that our suspicions were correct: our grades determined the nature of our assignments. The students with the highest marks were chosen for the most difficult missions.

The risk of being caught was very overwhelming, and made us think seriously about the types and degrees of torture that the Gestapo employed. The lieutenant did not elaborate on that topic very much, especially since most of us either had heard or knew of the methods used—the crushing or cutting off of fingers, electrical shock on various parts of the body, and other similar cruelties. Most certainly, we would be questioned as to our origins, our associations, our jobs, and our missions. If we were proven to be enemy agents, we would rather die by way of ingesting the so-called "Q pill" that we carried with us (a small glass vial containing cyanide for a "quick" death), rather than by torture. If we encountered a single German, we had to fight him, seize his gun and swiftly kill him. "If you die in the attempt, that would be preferable to dying by torture. At least, you will have died fighting heroically," the instructor stated somberly. As he neared the end of his instruction, the lieutenant looked around and saw our bewildered, fearful expressions. "The life of a spy is the most fascinating," he said, trying to encourage us. "It is the kind of experience that you will brag about to your family and friends, if you survive. You will be the true actors of the war." He paused and reflected. "You know," he continued, "my dream was to be sent to Greece as a spy, but my American accent did not permit me to go. I envy all of you for your opportunity to become spies in the SI, in a foreign city, as a stranger among strangers—civilians and Germans. That would have been a once-in-a-lifetime experience for me. I may be sent on a mission in another capacity—perhaps, as a saboteur as a Special Operations member (in the "SO") or as an Operational Group member (in the "OG"), working with partisans—both of which can be dangerous assignments; but an SI agent is someone special and unique."

Before concluding his lecture, the instructor mentioned a few things for us to keep in mind. He told us that living among civilians could also mean residing with those in collaboration with the Gestapo. Therefore, we always had to be on our guard and behave as appropriately as possible in various circumstances. The instructor warned us, for example, not to ask questions with answers that were of common knowledge, so as not to reveal our non-local status. At mealtimes, we had to use both hands when observing others doing the same, so as not to raise any suspicions. As consumers, we had to know the price of items and/or services. In our communities, we had to familiarize ourselves with the customary modes of transportation, the location of restaurants, post offices, banks, and other public establishments. As to our personal relationships, the instructor cautioned us, "Don't have a steady girlfriend or take your date to expensive restaurants. A jealous former boyfriend can be more dangerous than the Gestapo." He also warned us against spending money excessively in countries where the population was impoverished and starving. Doing so would bring attention to ourselves. "Most important, you will go on your mission with great spirit, energy, and faith, with the intention of doing the job that you are required to perform, and you will come back and talk about it. Good luck and a safe return!" he declared.

Emboldened by my instructor's words, I went on to engage in a few more sessions devoted to Morse code and learning to use the wireless device. A test revealed that I was able to receive at least twenty words per minute, each word consisting of five letters each. Evidently, my extensive training in Cairo and Palestine proved to be sufficient. I just had to learn how to cipher or code the message prior to sending it. To do so, I had to memorize a phrase, upon which the entire coding process depended. Then, by substituting the letters from that phrase, the telegram would be coded. The coding and decoding technique took a few hours of practice. Once we had committed the phrase to memory, such that it would not be lost in the following weeks and months, we had to burn the piece of paper on which it was written. An uncoded message could not be sent, and if we forgot the phrase, our entire mission would be worthless. Memorization, therefore, was essential. However, the more I tried to mentally retain the phrase, the more I realized that I was missing a letter or a word. So, I either sang it or related it to a story; and, at the end of the day, I was convinced, at last, that it was permanently etched in my brain. Then, I burned the paper on which the phrase was written, and swore to myself that I would never, *ever* forget it.

We also took lessons in how to use a specific type of wireless, how to attach the battery, make simple repairs and, generally, handle the mechanism. Most of us would infiltrate an occupied country via parachute, and the wireless would be dropped with us. Therefore, after hitting the ground, we would have to pick up the radio and make a few small connections, as we had been trained to do.

As the defensive training intensified, we learned how to disarm and kill a single opponent or two, while still focusing intently on our forthcoming mission. All the while, I constantly thought of the coding phrase, which I had set to music in my head, so as not to forget it. I also reflected on what our lieutenant told us about being a "stranger among strangers." Our mentor was right: life as an OSS spy was fascinating and frightening at the same time. As soon as the training sessions came to an end, all of us had to brace ourselves, knowing that our abilities and resolve were about to be tested in unimaginable ways.

Chapter 17

A Perilous Assignment

After completing my course of instruction, the chief, Major Vassos, called me into his office. I wondered what the nature of his communication would be—whether he had good news for me and whether I had proven myself enough to undertake a dangerous assignment. I approached the office slowly and tentatively, all the while expecting the worst. Soon, however, all of my fears were allayed when I saw Major Vassos, with his arms wide open and a smile on his face. "Bravo, Helias!" he exclaimed, embracing and congratulating me. "You are ready. Along with a couple of others, you finished at the top of the class, and your marks were quite high!" Although I was very relieved, another more worrisome thought quickly came to mind—*the higher the mark, the more dangerous the mission. Good grades could be my worst nightmare.*

As I sat down, eager to hear the news, Major Vassos revealed that there were two very interesting missions in store, and gave me a choice between them. One was to go with Captain James Kellis (the officer who had brought us to the OSS) as his radio operator. This would involve many parachute drops through a few mountainous partisans' concentrations to assess their need for ammunitions and report back to headquarters. On another assignment, I would be dropped via parachute outside of Salonica (or Thessaloniki), the second largest city in Greece, and form an underground organization with a team member, a Greek naval officer, who was very familiar with the city. Apparently, the team member and I would have to remain there until the end of the war.

Major Vassos emphasized that the Salonica mission, though more attractive, would be more risky. Due to its importance as the German troop distribution center for various fronts, the city had become intensely fortified and, therefore, more dangerous. Despite the obvious risks, I told him that I preferred the Salonica mission. "To tell you the truth," Major Vassos observed, "I believe that you're better suited for that mission. You're young and talented, and you speak without an accent. Captain Kellis had hoped to get you as his wireless operator, but Salonica will be your destination. I want to warn you of the dangers involved, however. Be careful when you are on the air, and don't stay on too long. The Gestapo will be listening. Remember what you were taught."

With that warning, I was told that I had to leave as quickly as possible. Major Vassos informed me that the sergeant in the next office would provide me with a nylon belt with one hundred fifty English sovereigns, plus extra money to purchase civilian clothes, underwear, and shoes. He also admonished me to remove all of the tailor's labels that disclosed where the garments were bought or made. "Also, you must not tell *anyone* where you are going," he added. After a salute and a handshake, I took my leave and went next door.

After another customary salute from the sergeant, I was given a belt surrounded by many small pockets, with a larger one on the right-hand side. The sergeant indicated that I could place a Colt .32-caliber gun in that pocket, if I so chose; but

**The Night Before Leaving For An OSS Airstrip Outside Cairo,
March 20, 1944**

I pointed out that the sovereigns would be hidden effectively beneath my clothes. The gun, on the other hand, could protrude through my pocket and be detected or palpated during a search at a possibly unexpected Gestapo checkpoint.

"I can't force you to take the pistol," the sergeant said. "But why not take it as far as you can, and before you pass through those checkpoints, throw it out beforehand, if you have to? Suppose you are approached and searched by a couple of soldiers who find your belt containing the gold. Wouldn't you rather be armed with the gun and ready to escape? Anyway, you're not guilty enough with the one hundred fifty gold sovereigns, are you?"

After listening to that amusing speech, I agreed and took the .32-caliber pistol, along with the pen gun. The following day, I went shopping with the Egyptian currency that I had on hand. Since all of the suits crafted in Cairo were made to order (it was impossible to buy off-the-rack suits), tailors' labels were prominently displayed everywhere on the garment. Fortunately, I was able to convince one tailor (without offending him, of course) to remove all of his labels. I had to pay a little extra, but it was money well spent. When I mentioned that I wanted to pick up the suit in two days, the tailor exclaimed, "What's the big hurry?" Predictably, a little more money was all it took to accomplish my objective of having the suit on time.

In a couple of days, I prepared to go to the OSS airstrip outside Cairo, where I would receive instructions about my drop and the wireless radio. To my surprise, a distressing message had come in from Macedonia, confirming heavy enemy troop concentrations near the area of my parachute drop. Although the region was some distance from Salonica, there was a high probability that I would be seen and captured. I was informed that an undetected parachute drop would be a miracle; and since I most certainly *would* be caught, the message suggested that I be sent by a different route, to a place far away from the city. Even though I loved parachuting out of airplanes, I was all too aware of the dangers of being spotted, possibly breaking my leg on the jump and, subsequently, being captured, injured *and* tortured.

I didn't know what to think or expect; but, given the obvious risks involved, I felt better about traveling in another direction. Instead of going to the OSS airstrip, I would be taken by car to Alexandria. From there, I would take a boat to Cyprus and travel north, very close to the neutral Turkish coast to reach Izmir, a large port city in western Turkey. From there, we would take the same boat to the southern shore of Salonica, where it would be up to my friends and me to find our way.

In the Alexandria harbor, I encountered a fairly conventional-looking boat that, originally, had been a Greek fishing boat, or *caique*, over forty-five feet long. The boat was typical of those navigating along the Mediterranean Sea. The conspicuous difference was that the OSS hired that particular boat and its crew in Turkey, and installed two tank engines, making the vessel very fast—and anything but "conventional."

Inside, I met a Greek officer named Spyros whom the OSS had recruited, wearing the same nylon belt as I and who, like me, was going to a city in northern Greece. His destination was Edessa, a city close to Salonica. I also met an American soldier (whose name eludes me now), going to the OSS station in Izmir, Turkey.

After the boat departed from Alexandria, the Greek captain told us that, in order to travel to Turkey, we would have to go by way of Cyprus. Along with the captain, two Greek sailors were on board. The captain recounted the story of how the OSS had recruited the three of them. After the Germans had taken over the boat in Greece and forced them into service, providing only food in return, the men attacked and killed their captors with only knives and escaped in the boat to Turkey, where the OSS recruited them.

Just after the captain related their adventures, one of the Greek sailors looked at the other, and said, "The Americans must have lots of money, and if we killed them, we would be rich." Upon hearing such a sinister threat, the captain told the sailor to shut his mouth. "I'm afraid that you don't know who the real enemy is!" he declared. "If I hear you say such stupid things again, I'll throw you into the sea!"

The captain's observation seemed very appropriate. We did *not* know who the enemy was and, therefore, I felt compelled to quietly warn my friend Spyros and the other OSS member not to stray from our group. Sticking together was essential for our survival.

Chapter 18

Rough Waters

Having reached Cyprus the following morning, we left for Turkey, after receiving the necessary provisions. At that point, the sailor about whom I had warned the others had been replaced by a very polite Greek man who, as I later discovered, was a very good fisherman. Since we would travel only during the daytime and make port in Turkish coastal villages at night, the sailor taught me how to spear a fish by using a strong light and a fork attached to the end of a stick. I always welcomed the opportunity to learn new things, and the fishing lessons gave me a break from the rest of the group, which I greatly enjoyed.

As we sailed, we sometimes flew two flags, each one with its own purpose. We flew the Turkish flag when we saw a German patrol boat, and the Greek flag when we spotted a Turkish patrol boat. Passing through the narrows between the Greek island of Samos and the Turkish mainland (less than a mile's distance), the captain warned us of approaching danger. As the Germans scanned the Aegean Sea from a post on Samos, we would be directly in their sights. Since we would fly the Turkish flag, the Turks would conduct a search of our boat prior to collecting their toll and allowing us to pass through their waters. Obeying their checkpoint rules was crucial. "If we don't stop," the captain said, "they may shoot or chase us down. In that case, the Germans may become suspicious and join in with the Turks."

As per the captain's instructions, we smiled and waved at the Turks, pretending that we were slowing down, stopping, and mooring alongside them. As we passed near the station, the captain called out, "Fall down!" He put the tank engines into full throttle and took us away quickly. Fortunately, the Turks didn't feel like chasing a small Turkish fishing boat, and left us alone. Deeply relieved, the captain made us aware that close calls of that kind were commonplace. "We were just lucky that time!" he declared.

We then traveled to Izmir, Turkey (or Smyrna as the Greeks called it). There, German spies, aware that the Americans were sending agents to Greece from Turkey, posed as photographers and took photographs of newcomers. Therefore, we were initially told not to go ashore. When it was finally safe to disembark, I was led to the secluded OSS office, where I was given an envelope that contained thousands of dollars in drachma, the Greek currency. I was also given my Greek identification card and asked what surname I would like to use. "Any name," the sergeant said, "except your *real* last name." I told him that I had chosen the name "Nikolaou" while in training and that I would use that common Greek surname now. My picture was taken and, while the identification papers were being prepared, the sergeant handed me a can of oil and said, "Here is a present for you. Be careful with it. It's heavy, so try not to drop it. Your radio is hidden at the bottom of the container, below another compartment that is filled with olive oil, extending to the top of the can. While you await the preparation of your identification papers, I want to introduce you to the person with whom you will be working."

When the sergeant escorted me into the next room, I met a Greek Naval Intelligence officer named Cosmas Yiapitzoglou, a man of about forty, who embraced me and spoke in a welcoming style. "I've been so eager to meet you and I'm so proud that the OSS has entrusted me with an American soldier who will serve as a wireless operator. I've lived in Salonica for many years, and I know hundreds of friends from all walks of life who will provide crucial information to the Americans."

Yiapitzoglou paused to look at the can. "What is *this*?" he asked, perplexed.

"It's a can of olive oil—a gift for us," I replied.

"What?" he said. "We don't need olive oil! We'll probably be eating in the finest restaurants in Salonica. Come now with me, and leave the can here. We have other more important items to carry," he said decisively.

At the bottom of this can is my wireless radio," I answered, smiling.

"Really?" he exclaimed. "A very smart idea. Who would ever think that there's a radio hidden in that container?"

Just then, Spyros walked in, holding the same oil can. When Yiapitzoglou saw him, he said, "Is this also a gift, or is he going to prepare us some food?"

I laughed and said, "Yes, as a matter of fact, he and his 'gift' will be with us for the next couple of days. The boat will drop him off at the same spot in Greece."

Finally, with my identification card in hand, I boarded, at the captain's instruction. We were heading to another American base in Turkey, near the Greek island of Lesbos; and, before arriving there, we would stop overnight in a small harbor situated between two hills. The captain, who knew that spot well, informed us that the calm sea would offer us an anchor for the night. The rough waters on the trip from Izmir to the harbor, however, provided anything but peace, and we waited patiently to reach that destination. The captain mentioned that, two years prior, the Greek cruiser, *Adrias*, exploded and sank after hitting a German mine in that same harbor. Tragically, twenty-one Greek sailors lost their lives. At the mercy of the elements, all that we could do was hope for safe passage.

Fortunately, we arrived intact and safely disembarked. After walking for a while, we reached the end of the harbor and turned back toward our boat. There, we saw a fishing boat (the size of ours), filled to capacity with women, children, and old men standing upright, without an inch of room to sit down, all of them weeping. When we asked the captain who they were, he informed us that they had escaped from the Greek island of Rhodes, hoping that the Turks would take them in. However, without the necessary food supplies for the thousands of starving people fleeing occupied Greece, the Turks had denied them asylum. Without further recourse, the captain of their boat tried to swamp the vessel, so as to force the Turks to save them from drowning and, thereby, offer them refuge. Their strategy, however, was all too obvious to the Turks, who had witnessed it before. They stood guard, therefore, displaying their weapons in the boat's direction, warning the captain and refugees not to carry out the plan.

Not having eaten for days, the refugees were in desperate circumstances, many of them begging for mercy. I will never forget the sight of one woman whose infant, less than a year old, apparently had died in his mother's arms. As she held the child close to her chest, the suffering woman wailed and screamed. Upon seeing what had happened, the refugee boat captain pushed past the others and ran toward the woman, grabbed the baby, and holding him by the feet, dipped him in and out of the cold sea water. Miraculously, the child survived. As we later learned, his mother had not eaten anything in two days and, therefore, could not produce milk to feed him. In order to satisfy the baby's hunger and stop his cries, she had given him some dried figs that she carried in her pocket. As a result, the baby choked, and needed immediate relief. Fortunately, the captain's intervention saved the child's life, but his piercing cries continued.

The sight of the refugees was insufferable, and I could not simply stand by and do nothing; so, I approached the captain of our boat and asked if I could take over a box of milk and other food. At first, the captain resisted, saying that we didn't have time; but, then, he finally gave in. "Since I'm working for the Americans, and you want to help, why not?" he declared. Eager to lend a hand, I hurriedly filled up a box with some milk and cookies and brought the small provisions to the beleaguered refugees. When they saw me handing the woman with the baby some canned milk, all of them stretched out their hands to receive something—*anything*. First, I gave the woman two cans of milk for the infant and food for herself. I then went back and brought another box-load of food. Everyone expressed their gratitude. One elderly woman said, "Thank you, my boy. God bless you and may He protect you wherever you go" (a common Greek saying bestowed upon Good Samaritans). "I will also pray for God's help for all of you to find safety," I replied. As

I turned to leave, I looked back at the baby, who, by then, had finished the last drop of canned milk and calmed down considerably. A sense of peace came over me, as I realized that I had done all that I could under the circumstances.

The following afternoon, we reached the American base in Turkey, where we spotted the Greek island of Lesbos just offshore. This was our last stop before leaving for Greece. The base was in a remote area where only Turkish guards patrolled. I recall that it was the Holy Thursday before Greek Easter, March 31, 1944. The captain told us that we should load the boat with supplies and, then, rest up before leaving for Greece. At that moment, we heard people coming out from the woods, and I saw three young Turks pulling a small wild pig that they had killed. According to their Muslim faith, the Turks were not allowed to eat pork, and they wanted to sell us the pig (assuming, of course, that we were Greek Christians who did not have that dietary restriction). *Not a bad idea*, I thought to myself. *This young pig would make for some delicious chops, but who will skin it and chop it up for us?* The boys agreed on $10 for the pig and another $10 to skin and prepare it for roasting. After I paid them, they hung the pig on a nearby tree to skin it. Yiapitzoglou and Spyros said they were very glad to hear of my intended feast that evening and the following day, prior to leaving for Greece. No doubt, we would have plenty of leftovers.

The next day, we noticed that the weather had turned ugly, and the sea became choppy with white caps. The captain became concerned about leaving, but said that he had seen worse weather. Nonetheless, he appeared anxious as he assured us that he would have no problem keeping the boat on course.

As we were thinking about the unfavorable weather, I heard a lot of squealing again, and saw four different boys pulling a large wild boar that they had slaughtered. Word had probably gone around of our previous purchase of a wild pig the day before. Therefore, these four boys caught a boar, which was four times larger than his predecessor. We told the boys that we were ready to leave and still had leftovers, but they begged us to buy the animal. One said that the creature charged after him after its initial wounding, and would have killed him, had it not been for the other three, who finished the boar off with their knives. I felt sorry for them, too, and told them that I would give them $10 for the boar and another $10 to dig a hole and bury it. They agreed and began to excavate a grave away from the base.

Before dark, the captain determined that despite the inclement weather, we could depart, and instructed us to stow our belongings in the stern of the boat. The two sailors loaded the boat with many supplies—bags of rice, canned food, guns, and ammunition. Once inside the boat, I observed that these food items were loaded in huge canvas bags and boxes, which occupied the entire stern. Rather than remain there, I looked for another less congested area to rest during the long boat ride to Greece. As I went up to the bow, I saw a porthole with an open hatch, above which the ropes were stored. I sat outside on deck, hanging my feet inside the porthole. At the start of our journey, the waves were not that big; but when the boat traveled farther away from the harbor, they began to crash against the hull and over the bow, and sea water came inside the porthole, and onto my head. Unable to navigate my way to where the others were and afraid of falling overboard, I kneeled inside the porthole, reached up, and pulled down the hatch, which did not have a watertight seal.

By the time the hatch came down, the waves grew larger, one right after the other. The compartment had already filled halfway with water and, as I kneeled inside, holding the cover as tightly as I could, a wave swept over the entire boat. I thought that we would capsize, for sure. The waves were so huge that, sometimes, I thought the boat would ascend straight up to heaven; then, a couple of seconds later, it was plummeting down to hell. Although I seldom suffered from seasickness, I could not help myself in that instance. I felt as though I were on a wild rollercoaster ride, unable to control myself, and I regurgitated.

In my state of distress, my mind wandered. I thought of my mother, who was probably in church at that moment, participating in the Good Friday Easter liturgy, singing sad Byzantine hymns about the death of Christ. No doubt, if she knew of my awful predicament and risk of drowning, she would have called on the priest to pray for me. Fortunately, she was spared immense suffering and worry.

For more than two hours, I ascended and descended with the waves, tossing about at their will. *I should have risked the parachute drop—even if that method of arriving in Salonica was more dangerous. At least, people would have known about my fate. Now, I'm facing an obscure death—in peril of vanishing to the bottom of the Aegean Sea*, I said to myself. Kneeling, I became dizzy and watched as the contents of my stomach floated around me, and I surrendered to what seemed to be my inevitable death. *To think that, just yesterday, I witnessed the refugees' immense suffering, and very unexpectedly, in the course of twenty-four hours, I find myself in an even more dire situation!* I said to myself. I remembered the elderly woman's prayer to God to watch over and protect me wherever I went, and I fervently hoped that He would listen. All of a sudden, the up-and-down motion ceased. A chill came over my cheeks, and I spoke to myself again. *We are sinking.* Instantly, I pulled the hatch tighter to prevent more water from flooding the compartment. Maybe, I thought, we had already sunk, and the boat had not yet reached the bottom of the sea. *Suppose the Aegean is a thousand feet deep! If I plan to get out, I should try to open the hatch and see if water comes in,* I thought.

To my surprise, as I opened the cover, no water entered. I stuck my head through the porthole and looked for the others. I tried to climb up but, having kneeled for five hours, I had difficulty doing so. When I finally crawled out, the others saw me, and I heard someone call out, "Look, there's Helias! He's alive! He was not thrown into the sea and swept away by the storm. It's a miracle!" I walked toward the group, and everyone stared at me—as if I had come back from the dead— from the depths of the inferno. Some laughed at my dirty, wet appearance. I looked at them angrily and asked why nobody came to look for me. Didn't anyone care? They said that they had seen me earlier, standing in the porthole; but, afterward, when I covered myself with the hatch, the wave that swept over the topside was so huge, that everyone thought the worst— the wave had swept me overboard; and, since everyone was hanging on for dear life, as well, they didn't have the chance to find out where I was or if I had survived.

As it turned out, Yiapitzoglou ordered the captain to turn back. He couldn't risk the chance of being detained during the day by a German patrol boat, and he didn't know what he would do in Salonica without a radio operator. Believing that I had drowned, he had already planned to request another agent. When he heard the news of my survival, however, he approached me warmly and said, "I am very glad that you are alive. I like you, and I believe that we will make a very good team. I think you're lucky, and we need luck."

"Thank you," I replied half-heartedly, in a much calmer state.

"Go and change your clothes before you get sick and we hit more bad weather," Yiapitzoglou advised me.

It was Holy Saturday, the day before Easter, and the captain instructed us to rest that day and the next. "Tomorrow afternoon, after we enjoy our Easter meal, we will leave for Greece, so pray for calm seas." Then, lowering his voice, the captain confided in me. "To tell you the truth, I was never more scared than last night. I did not want to say anything to frighten the others, but I thought I would not be able to control the boat, and we would capsize. We must have had over ten Beauforts of rough weather."[8]

The following morning, Easter, April 3, 1944, the sun shone brightly and the sea was much calmer, befitting the occasion. Turkish soldiers came to greet us as we were at breakfast; and knowing that we were celebrating Greek Orthodox Easter, they offered to bring us goat's meat in exchange for aspirin and

---

[8]   A Beaufort is a measure of rough seas and wind, where the number three signifies a light breeze (good sailing weather), and twelve indicates hurricane force winds.

canned food. We agreed, and with the meat that they offered, we cooked many chops—a fine way to celebrate the holiday. We ate and expressed gratitude to God for His son and for the miracle of surviving the previous night.

In the late morning or early afternoon, the captain told us to board and jokingly said that he did not wish to see me in the bow porthole again. Since many sacks of rice had gotten wet and were thrown overboard, there would be plenty of room in the stern for everyone. The captain informed us that we would arrive at the tip of the Halkidiki Peninsula in Greece around four o'clock in the morning, just before daybreak. Thankfully, the weather held out.

About an hour after leaving Turkey, we passed close to a small Greek island, where we spotted a tall lighthouse operated by a family placed there by German authorities. Once a week, the Germans brought food to the husband, wife, and their two little children. As soon as they saw us, they waved and told us to stop and provide updates on the war. We did so willingly, as the family didn't have access to radios, newspapers or any other forms of communication. They just whiled away the hours by fishing. Without revealing crucial information, we offered rice and cookies to the children, and took our leave. We had not another moment to spare, as new adventures and responsibilities awaited us.

Chapter 19

Unlikely Traveling Companions

Upon our arrival in German-occupied Greece, we were aware that, at any time, we might see a German patrol boat darting out from any one of the islands. In that case, a Turkish flag would not be of any use. After three hours of uneasy travel, the captain installed mufflers on the exhaust pipes of the boat's engines. He instructed us not to speak aloud, since sound travels far on open water, especially in calm seas. The sea had, finally, become more tranquil—so much so, that it appeared to be a lake. Perhaps, our prayers had been answered—or, maybe, the storm had simply ceased. The only sound that I heard was a mild *puff-puff* as the boat slowed to reduce the engine noise. As we approached Kassandra, the tip of the western peninsula of Halkidiki, it was close to 4:00 a.m., and we saw lights on the shore. Within them, we observed a blinking signal, beckoning the captain to set course in that direction. Slowly and carefully, we approached, assisting the captain in keeping a lookout for German patrol boats or other potential traps.

Since the captain perceived the area to be safe, we tried to dock along a small pier; but there weren't any open berths. We had to leave before the first light of daybreak, so as to remain unobserved, and the captain instructed us to begin unloading our supplies. Soon, he spotted a small run-down cargo boat, and told us to jump into it, and then, make our way toward the pier, where we would get out and walk.

Suddenly, a man ran out from a nearby house to greet us and shake our hands. As we soon discovered, he was our contact man, a member of the OSS in northern Greece, sending the signal lights out to us before we docked. Stepping up to introduce himself, Cosmas Yiapitzoglou then turned to me and said, "This is Helias Nikolaou, who will be our group's radio operator in Salonica." Lowering his voice, the captain reminded us not to dawdle or engage in pleasantries for too long. "Where did you dock? There are no open berths," the contact man observed. I told him about the captains' dilemma, and our plan to head for the pier. The man stared at me in disbelief and quietly exclaimed, "What? There are four German soldiers sleeping on that boat! It's a miracle they didn't wake up!"

When the time came to take my leave of the captain and the two sailors, I quietly thanked them for our safe return to Greece, and wished them well in their travels. I then proceeded to enter our contact man's house, where we partook of some much-needed coffee. While we relaxed and conversed, we asked the contact man whether he knew of the least dangerous route to Salonica.

"There are three ways—either by horse, car, or boat. Cars don't generally travel to Salonica anymore, since the partisans control many of the outlying roads. A couple of weeks ago, a taxi cab was stopped, men were taken hostage and forced to join "ELAS" [the communist partisans]. For this reason, traveling on horseback is also very dangerous, especially through the mountain passes. Boats are the safest mode of travel—*if* you find a boat, that is. The Germans have confiscated all of them for their own use." The contact man paused for a moment and said, "Wait! You're lucky today. I know of a German boat that arrived on Sunday, loaded with barrels of *retsina* [the Greek word for resinated wine] and resin bound for Salonica! Most of the time, there are only three Germans and three Greek sailors in that boat, so go and ask them if they can take you at least part of the way. The Germans know how difficult it is to travel through the mountains and, sometimes, they are kind enough to take civilians with them on board."

When Yiapitzoglou heard that we had an option to travel via a German vessel, he immediately refused. "I would much prefer to walk, since I'm carrying gold and guns," he stated.

Since Spyros and I were responsible for our precious cargo—the oil cans containing our radios—I disagreed. "Spyros, let's go by boat," I said. "They will never suspect us." Without pondering even for a moment, Spyros got his oil can and followed me out the door. We thanked the contact man, wished him well, and shook hands with Yiapitzoglou (who would meet up with us later). Once again, they tried to persuade us to travel on foot. However, because of our heavy radios, we had no choice but to opt for the boat. Upon our arrival at the northern-most part of the Kassandra Peninsula, Yiapitzoglou agreed to meet us in a café in a town called "Portes," a stop the German boat was scheduled to make on its way to Salonica. Attempting to encourage and give us hope, he added, "Well, if you succeed in getting to your destination, then it shall be written in the history books that two OSS agents were sent on their missions with two wireless radios, taking a German cruise!"

Recognizing the humor in our situation, we laughed as we walked toward the harbor. Spyros turned to me and said,

"Helias, do you really want to risk getting on that German boat? Wouldn't we be in enormous danger?" Spyros looked somber.

I turned and said to him, "Do you have any other suggestions? Would you rather be taken prisoner by the partisans? Follow me! We'll be all right," I said reassuringly.

When we reached the harbor, we had no difficulty in spotting the German vessel. Just as Yiapitzoglou's contact man had mentioned, three Greek sailors were approaching the boat, rolling the small barrels of *retsina* that they had purchased from the locals. With Spyros following behind me, I walked toward one of three Germans, a young sergeant in his mid-twenties, who was standing outside of the boat, counting the barrels. Speaking in German, I said, "For the last two weeks, I have collected olive oil in this can. I'm afraid that the partisans will take it; therefore, would you be so kind as to take me wherever you're going?"

Empathizing with my dilemma, the sergeant replied, "Yes, you can come along and bring your oil can with you."

"Can I take my friend?" I asked.

The sergeant looked at Spyros, who was much older than I (about forty-five), and hesitated. Then, he finally relented. "OK, tell him to come, too," he said.

I beckoned to Spyros, who followed me up the plank, trembling inside. We found an empty spot on deck, placed the two oilcans next to the German flag, and sat down with our backs up against them.

Visibly afraid and drenched in perspiration, Spyros needed some cheering up. So, I turned to him and said, "Spyros, do you realize the irony of our situation? Here we are, two American OSS agents, carrying a small fortune in gold and two guns, transporting two wireless radios aboard a German boat, right under the German flag."

"Stop! Stop!" Spyros replied. "I still don't know if we did the right thing. Who knows what's going to happen when the Germans come on board!"

"Relax," I whispered to my friend under my breath, smiling. "Nothing's going to happen. Stop showing them your fear. You're trembling!"

"Okay, Helias," Spyros said, "maybe I am not fit to be doing these things, or maybe I am just too old," he replied.

As the boat prepared to leave and I looked outside, I spotted Yiapitzoglou secretly waving to us. He wanted to be sure that we got on board before he began his own perilous trip through the mountains.

The boat left the docks and moved very quickly in the calm sea, keeping close to the shore. One of the German crewmen approached me as we passed by a small village, and inquired about its name. Not wanting to appear unfamiliar with my surroundings, I quickly thought of something off the top of my head. "*Vromohori*" (meaning "dirty town"), I blurted out. "*Ja, Ja!*" the German answered, apparently satisfied with my creative response. As he walked away, Spyros laughed, but he warned me not to converse with the Germans, so as not to arose their suspicion.

Around noon, as the boat headed north, all of us began to prepare for lunch. The German sergeant brought out cans of food, which he offered to us, as well. Our contact man had also given us a loaf of bread and some cheese, with which we began to satisfy our hunger. While we were cutting the bread, I noticed that one of the Greek sailors turned in our direction while talking to the German sergeant. "What is happening?" I asked Spyros. "Why is he pointing to our oil cans while speaking with the sergeant?" Spyros began to tremble again, and immediately thought the worst. "I told you, Helias," he said nervously. "They will suspect something is hidden in the cans!"

"Stop," I whispered. "Our radios are not visible. Stay calm, while I find out what the Greek sailor is telling the German." When I approached, I observed that the Greek held out a plate of sliced tomatoes, and asked if we could exchange some of our olive oil for our free ride. The German sergeant looked at me and awaited my reply. As soon as I realized the harmless nature of the request, I inwardly breathed a sigh of relief. I unscrewed the top of one of the cans, and poured out enough oil for the salad. The Greek man thanked me, and I carefully returned the can to its place next to the German flag. When I returned, Spyros appeared even more afraid, perspiring and trembling. "Relax," I said. "They only wanted some olive oil for their salad. Calm down, nobody suspects anything, including the Germans. If the sergeant notices that you're scared, our circumstances will be much worse."

We proceeded on course, and in the early afternoon, the boat entered the seaside town of Portes, next to a large ancient canal, joining the sea on either side of the Kassandra Peninsula. We were about to disembark, when the Greek sailor who had asked for the olive oil volunteered to help me carry the oil can. I thanked him and politely said I didn't need any help. "It's only olive oil and not that heavy." Had he become suspicious, he would have alerted the German soldiers nearby. Hoping to gain favor with the Germans, many spiteful, envious Greeks seized the opportunity to collaborate with them. By that time, I had learned, through calculated discretion—and deception—to create a shield around myself and my friends.

Before we climbed down the plank with our precious cans of olive oil, safe and intact, we expressed gratitude to the Germans—particularly to the sergeant who had so kindly given a free ride to two desperate-looking peasants. After walking a short distance, we spotted a few cafes, and I reminded Spyros that we had scheduled a meeting in the area with Yiapitzoglou the following morning.

With food on our minds, we could not resist going into a restaurant. After our meal, the cashier asked us to pay "seven." I was perplexed. *Did he mean seven, seven hundred, or seven thousand?* I wondered to myself. In training, we were taught not to ask questions about things which should be familiar to us. As I looked around me, strategizing, I noticed that the next customer in line gave the waiter hundreds of drachmas. Therefore, I correctly assumed that our bill was seven hundred drachmas, and averted unnecessary communication and suspicion.

Spyros then suggested that we find lodgings for the night. When we inquired at the restaurant, we discovered the whereabouts of a small hotel. Our only dilemma was that we would have to display our identification cards to the German police. Not wanting to take that risk, we had to forego soft sheets and pillows for an aimless walk along the harbor's wharf, not knowing where to find rest.

All of a sudden, I happened to pass by a large open tugboat whose captain was outside, painting the deck. Since only a small part of the boat's stern was covered over with a canopy, I was able to spot a little mattress rolled into the corner. I looked at Spyros and said, "How would you like to sleep on this boat? Watch the oil cans, and I'll be right back." I jumped into the boat and spoke with the captain.

"Excuse me, sir," I began, as I approached the captain. "We are traveling with oil cans, and we don't have any money or a place to stay for the night. Would you mind very much if we stayed here—anywhere on the boat?"

Looking at the oil cans, the captain said, "Okay, you can sleep on the deck, but the mattress is for me. If you don't mind sleeping on bare wood, you and your friend can come aboard and sleep—but only for tonight."

"We don't mind. Thank you," I said. I then went to inform Spyros, who looked puzzled by the fact that I had found comfortable sleeping accommodations. We waited outside until about nine o'clock, when I saw the man preparing his mattress. "Okay! Get ready for a memorable, relaxing night's sleep!" I said to Spyros.

By the time we brought the oil cans inside the boat and put them in a corner, the tired captain was already reclining and, in a few minutes, began to snore. I turned to Spyros and told him to choose his bed, pointing to a large, recently stripped wooden area of the deck. No sooner had I spoken, than my friend was stretched out on his back. While he tried to make himself comfortable, his nylon belt containing the one hundred fifty coins continued to hit the wooden floor, clanging and pounding on the deck's surface with a loud thud.

"Stop that!" I called out. "If the captain hears you, he will awaken, and you'll be in big trouble if he finds out that you are not simply carrying olive oil."

"Thanks for reminding me!" Spyros answered sarcastically. "Wake me up if I make too much noise, and I'll do the same for you."

The clamor of people running up and down the harbor pierced the daybreak hours. To our surprise, we also saw Bulgarian soldiers carrying automatic weapons, encircling and pointing their automatic weapons at all of the boats in Portes harbor. Anxious that they might be looking for us, we inquired about what was happening from the tugboat's captain, who was lying nearby. In turn, he spoke with a neighboring boat's captain, who informed him that the soldiers were searching for a Greek who had stolen a large quantity of gasoline during the night. We also found out that the area was handed over to the Bulgarians, allies of the Axis Powers.

Knowing that the Bulgarians were seeking out the thief and the stolen petrol, I feared that they might examine our oil cans, believing that they contained gasoline. In that case, even if we were not under suspicion, they could accidently discover the wireless radios. *What am I to do?* I asked myself. Thinking swiftly on my feet, I remembered where the captain had placed the paint bucket and brushes which he used on the deck. While he was talking to the captain of the boat docked next to us, I quickly poured out some paint where the search team had to step in order to enter the boat, and I began to paint the wooden deck. When the Bulgarians approached and saw the pool of fresh paint, they realized that they could not enter. The entire vessel was open and empty, except for the stern where we had put the two oil cans. Observing that the boat did not contain any large gasoline containers, the search party left, and I breathed a deep sigh of relief.

When the captain saw that I had spilled a large amount of paint on the deck, he became extremely irate, and began yelling and cursing at me.

"I know how to paint, and I'll help you to clean up!" I tried to convince him; but he was beside himself with anger, and told us to leave immediately.

"You've caused enough damage already!" he shouted.

As I turned to leave, with the oil cans in hand, I thought to give the captain some money; but, just then, I paused and said to Spyros, "How can I offer him anything, when last night I told him that we didn't have any money for a hotel!" Spyros laughed. "Your OSS training cetainly taught you many methods of deception, Helias!" he noted.

We disembarked, walked toward the cafés, and sat outdoors in one which was centrally located, next to the boats. "We should have breakfast here and wait for Yiapitzoglou to arrive," I said. The oil cans, which had only a wire-like handle, had calloused our hands; but, as we were instructed, we tried to conceal the fact that we were lugging heavy weight.

As we were eating, we noticed that a German police boat had come and docked right in front of us. Wearing large metal police insignias that hung from their necks, three German police officers (called the *"Feldgendarmerie"* or Field Gendarmeries) jumped out and ran toward the hotel. For a moment, we thought that they were after us; but, fortunately, that was not the case. Our fear nearly caused us to get up and leave; but where would we go? As planned, we had to wait for Yiapitzoglou in a café, making ourselves visible to him. Then, we would continue our trip to Salonica together (at least eight to ten miles away).

As we anxiously looked for our friend, we sat down and ordered one coffee after another. Finally, sometime before noon, we spotted Yiapitzoglou walking toward us, accompanied by the contact man whom we met the day before. We waved and beckoned them to our table, and both of them sat down, appearing exhausted and thirsty. They said that they were not able to find a car or a horse, and were on the run most of the time in order to avoid the ELAS partisans and the Germans. Yiapitzoglou admitted that it was foolish not to have gone with the German boat. He congratulated us on our safe passage, and said that we would never have made it through the mountains with the two oil cans and the partisans and Germans in pursuit. Once again, through all of our trials, tribulations, and risk-taking, Lady Luck and Divine Providence never left our side.

Chapter 20

❧

Children of Destiny

As we sat in the café, eating lunch, we were very glad to have arrived at our destination in one piece, and we hoped that the rest of our journey to Salonica would prove to be uneventful. Always wanting to be prepared, I looked around and asked people about the best way to travel to Salonica. Nearby, a man with a two-wheeled, horse-drawn cart offered to take us part of the way, after which we would hail a taxi cab. Our contact man did not want to use that means of travel, and decided to return home. The three of us—Yiapitzoglou, Spyros, and I, eager to get to Salonica, were more than willing, however; so, we placed our olive oil cans in the cart, and left Portes.

Not long afterward, the driver informed us, "There is something very important that I forgot to mention. The road we will be traveling will take us close to Salonica's airfield. The entrance to the airport is a German checkpoint and inspection area, where they conduct very thorough searches. Sometimes they even order people to strip off their clothes. I hope you don't have any contraband here in the cart, do you?"

"Of course not," I said. "Who do you think we are? We only have two cans of olive oil." All the while, without speaking our thoughts aloud, of course, the three of us were thinking along the same lines. *Not only do we carry the olive oil cans; we also have four hundred fifty gold sovereigns, three guns and two radios!* I turned to Yiapitzoglou and whispered, "At least

169

we stand a better chance if we get rid of the guns now. We can hide the belts and the gold, but not the guns."

Yiapitzoglou thought a few seconds about throwing them out along the side of the road, but then told me that the driver might be exaggerating about the extent of their pat-down. "The Germans see drivers transporting people from various places to the post all day long, and they don't search them." . . . "Let's wait, and when we near the airport, we'll see how thoroughly the Germans search the others. If they are as strict as the driver says, we'll give him the guns or toss them out."

Yiapitzoglou had not even finished his sentence, when we entered an open courtyard, at the end of which the German guards stood, watching us carefully. Since there was nobody else in front of us, we were entirely alone.

"It's too late to do anything," I whispered to the others.

The driver continued up to the gate of the military post and pulled at the reigns right in front. Next to us, there was a guardhouse, from the inside of which came the sound of voices. Having no clue, as to how many guards there were, I remembered that the gun in my possession had only eight bullets. In front of that structure stood two German soldiers holding automatic weapons. After the inspection, the driver instructed us to go behind the guardhouse and hail a taxi. The driver got out and took the two cans of olive oil from the cart, placing them right in front of the German guards. One of them was in his forties, and the other could not have been more than twenty. As the older guard approached me, I explained the contents of the cans. To facilitate verification, I unscrewed the top of one of the cans, and the guard dipped his finger in. Then, he commanded me to remove my jacket. As I did so, he came closer and told me to raise both arms. At that moment, I thought that my heart was about to burst from my chest and I wondered whether all of our valiant escape efforts would be dashed in an instant. I thought of the gold coins in the nylon belt—covered only by my shirt—and the .32 caliber gun in my right pocket. *What if he found these items? What if I were discovered? What would become of us?* I pondered, as my life briefly flashed before my eyes. Suddenly, as the guard frisked me, he stopped short and stared at me, transfixed, as if he had recognized someone or *something*. Chills went through my entire body, as I asked myself, *Why is he staring at me?* To my surprise, he paused and asked, "How old are you?"

"Twenty," I replied, trying to remain calm.

"I have an eighteen-year-old son, serving in the German Army. I haven't heard from him in six months, and I assume that he has been sent to the Russian front. You look just like him—with the same hair, the same eyes, the same expression . . ."

The pensive guard then continued his search, while gazing at my hair. All at once, his left hand touched the gun in my right pocket. He may have thought that he hit my belt. I will never know. In that one encapsulated instant, both of us were not at war. We were, simply, two people: a young man and a father yearning for his son who, like me, wanted to make it out alive.

As the German guard continued to look at me, I noticed that his eyes welled with tears, and the younger guard's eyes also watered. At that moment, I became emboldened and touched the older German on the shoulder. "The war will end soon and your son will return safely," I said, trying to encourage him.

"Let us hope so," the guard replied, with an affectionate smile.

Then, he approached Spyros, who just stood there, like a statue, trembling. The guard searched him by patting him down on both sides, but did not go near his waist or belt. Then, turning to me, he asked whether Yiapitzoglou was with me.

"Yes," I replied.

"Go ahead," he responded.

We took our oilcans and walked away, without a word.

At about a hundred feet away, Yiapitzoglou turned to us and said, "It was a miracle that Helias looked like his son. That saved us!"

"Yes, it was a miracle!" Spyros agreed, adding, "But what would have happened if the guard had searched me first?"

As he spoke, Spyros began to walk like a robot, opening his legs sideways. "Fellas, you have to excuse me," he said. "I need to change. I have wet my underwear!"

We laughed, but tried not to make fun of our friend. Yet again, fortune had smiled on us children of destiny. Once more, we had been at great risk, but lived to tell the tale.

"By the way, Helias," Yiapitzoglou observed. "Where did you learn to speak German so well?"

"As a high school student, I was excused from German forced labor one week per month, because I was willing to learn German, instead. I took lessons for six months, and that is why I can speak a little," I explained.

"As far as we're concerned, you did extremely well." Yiapitzoglou remarked. "We are alive because of your knowledge of the language—and the fact that you look like the German soldier's son. Maybe God wanted things to turn out that way. It is truly a sign that your mission will succeed!"

We passed through the restricted area around the airport, where we found stores and restaurants. However, the taxi stands were empty. As we looked up ahead, we saw a lone taxi approaching, and Yiapitzoglou quickly went to hail it. Two merchants had requested the ride first, and Yiapitzoglou was visibly distressed that we had lost our only chance of traveling to Salonica.

"Do you want me to get that taxi?" I asked confidently. "Just watch." I walked up to the driver and said to him, "What did the merchants pay you?"

"Five thousand drachmas," the cab driver replied.

"Suppose I give you ten thousand drachmas, would you take us?"

"Yes," he said. "Tell your friends that by the time I've filled the tank with gas, they should jump in the car. I will take you instead of the others. After all, they haven't paid me yet."

So, Yiapitzoglou, Spyros, and I jumped in, and the taxi left, while the two merchants chased and cursed at us. During the trip to Salonica, we asked the driver if there were any other checkpoints. "Only one for collecting taxes on imports, he answered. "For the two oilcans, you may have to pay about a thousand drachmas."

"Can we avoid going through the checkpoint?" I asked. "Is there another way?"

"Yes, but I took that route some time ago, and almost broke the cab's axle," the driver replied.

"Well," I said, "suppose I give you another two thousand drachmas, would you bypass the checkpoint?"

Not surprisingly, the lure of money changed the driver's mind, and he rode through some very rough terrain. The ride was very uncomfortable, but the detour seemed worth the trouble. When we were departing from the checkpoint, however, the inspectors spotted us, ran after and caught up to us, dragged the driver out of the car, and began to beat him.

"Stop, stop," I yelled. "What's the trouble? How much can I give you to stop this fight?"

They looked at each other and, then, at the two oil cans. "One thousand drachmas!" they declared.

"Does it pay to cease fighting for one thousand drachmas?" I asked. "Take two thousand drachmas, and leave us alone to continue on our way."

Accepting the offer, the inspectors warned the taxi driver, "The next time you bypass us, we will destroy your car!"

"Didn't I tell you?" The driver looked at me with a stern expression. "I'm sorry that I listened to you."

"Don't worry," I replied. "Because of the aggravation that you suffered, I'll give you three thousand drachmas instead of the two thousand that I promised you."

Money healed all of the driver's wounds. At that point, Yiapitzoglou turned to me with a grin and whispered, "I see that you know how to resolve things with OSS money."

"Why not?" I said. "That's what it's for!"

Within a few minutes, we finally entered Salonica, and Yiapitzoglou told me that he would drop me off at a pastry shop[9] near the famous "Aspro Kastro" ("White Castle[10]"), where I should wait until he returned to pick me up. He also said that he would take my oil can with him. Within the next couple of minutes, the taxi stopped in front of the pastry shop. Yiapitzoglou and Spyros remained in the taxicab. "Get out here," Yiapitzoglou said. Without asking any questions, I dutifully followed his instructions.

There I was, in Salonica, at last—the most dangerous spot in Greece, according to the OSS. Suddenly, I realized I had not even said goodbye to Spyros or wished him good luck on his mission. Quickly, I turned around, but the taxi was already gone. For over a month, since we first met in Alexandria, we had diligently looked after one another and averted danger on many occasions. Then, in the haste of the moment, we did not even say goodbye. I never heard from my friend again.

---

9   The famous White Tower Café was demolished after the war

10 Known by many names, including *Lefkos Pyrgos*, the White Castle was notorious for its reputation as a place of execution, where many Greeks had been tortured and killed. Built by the Ottoman Turks to defend Salonica, with a commanding view of the harbor, it was once part of a larger fortification. Today, it is Salonica's landmark.

Helias In Front of the White Castle, Salonica (1944)

Chapter 21

All In the Game

I entered the pastry shop and without waiting to be seated, I decided to take an empty table on the sidewalk. The waiter spotted me, came over and, like a soldier, stood at attention. "Yes, sir, can I have your order please?"

"A slice of pasta (Greek cake)," I said.

While enjoying my delicious cake, I watched hundreds of Axis soldiers mingling in the streets. Right before my eyes, I saw more German soldiers than civilians. Major Vassos's decision to send me to Greece via boat, rather than by parachute, had been a very wise move, after all.

I had hardly finished eating, when the waiter reappeared and asked if I would like another slice. Just then, I realized that I was seated at the best table in the restaurant, and the waiter demanded that either I continue to order, sit inside, or leave. There were others waiting to be seated, including some German officers. Imagine eating six slices of cake while waiting more than three and a half hours for my contact! That is exactly what occurred, and I felt sick to my stomach.

While trying to get through my malaise, I heard someone at the next table say, "Helias, come over here." I turned my head in the direction of the voice, and saw a man wearing black sunglasses. I approached the stranger's table and sat down.

"I'm Nicos Oreopoulos, a friend of Yiapitzoglou. I apologize for being late. Prior to meeting you, I had to find a place to stay," he said. Then, as an afterthought, he remarked, "I hope you tried the pastas. Some say that they are the best in Salonica."

"Oh yes! They are very delicious. I've had a couple!" I replied, without mentioning my overindulgence."

"They were really that good?" Nicos asked.

I just laughed. Then, as we got up to leave, the waiter approached again, with yet another "pasta." I suggested that Nicos sit down and taste the savory cake. After taking just one bite, he concurred that it was, most definitely, the best in Salonica.

As we walked out, I whispered, "There are more German soldiers here than there are civilians."

"Don't be afraid of them, Helias," Nicos reassured me. What you should fear is the German police, the SS [the *Schutzstaffel*], and the Greek undercover police. "I was told that you are an American soldier—most likely the only American soldier in Salonica—and the German police would really be happy to get their hands on you; so, we must always be vigilant."

Nicos, a member of Yiapitzoglou's inner circle, had found me a temporary place to stay until he could find a more suitable permanent residence. The temporary residence, which overlooked Salonica, was a house with a magnificent view in an area called "Panorama," so named for its panoramic vistas but, as I later found out, there were many communists concentrated there, and the Germans used the area to round up hostages. For this reason, I could not stay there for a long period of time.

My wireless location had to be at least fifty feet long, so as to hide the wireless antenna and accommodate its length. Within a short time, Nicos searched and found the perfect site: a deserted textile factory in Agia Triada, an area on the east side of the city, near Larnakos Street, once owned by a prominent Greek Jew, who provided work for people during the war. With the German invasion and savage destruction of Greek-Jewish properties (including the factory), the owner and his family had fled into the mountains. Never could we have imagined that the ruthless destruction of one man's business would become our place of refuge.

It is deeply significant to note here that Greek Jewry had once flourished in Salonica and Greek Jews fought valiantly alongside their Christian brethren in the Greco-Italian campaign. When the Germans occupied Greece, however, the Jewish population suffered extreme marginalization, which could not be thwarted by partisan protests or clergy edicts. Forced to wear the Star of David on their clothes, the Jews succumbed to unspeakable genocidal atrocities and were forced into concentration camps at Auschwitz and throughout Europe. The Greek citizenry aided some Greek Jews in escaping and finding sanctuary. Some who managed to flee fought alongside the ELAS partisans, others with the Greek royalists. Only one thousand Greek-Jewish Salonicans of the original sixty thousand returned after the war. Tragically, Greek Jewry in Salonica was virtually annihilated, Jewish properties were confiscated, and the Jewish cemetery was destroyed.

Given such a history of suffering, it was fitting that we OSS members, fighting for the cause of liberation, would utilize the factory for the accomplishment of our mission—a building once owned by a man who had, undoubtedly, sacrificed everything—possibly even his life.

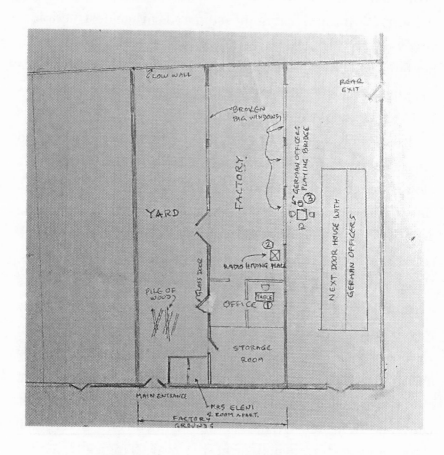

Author's Sketch of the Wireless' Location
From April to December 1944

Textile Factory's Yard With Odysseus (Yiapitzoglou's cousin), author, and Nicos Oreopoulos Sitting on Wood Pile, Nikitas in foreground (Mrs. Eleni's apartment in background with shuttered windows) 1944

Upon inspection, we discovered that the factory accommodated our precise specifications. The place was one hundred feet long and thirty feet wide, with the long axis of the building pointing south; therefore, the antenna would be well concealed. The factory's huge glass windows had been blown out, due to the Germans' detonation of bombs in that area. The factory occupied about seventy-five feet of space, at the end of which were two offices and a storage room, in which we kept the merchandise that we claimed to sell. The outside yard was about the length of the building. Facing the street was a huge gated door, next to which was a small two-room guardhouse with a kitchen and a toilet, which the city had given over to Kyria (Mrs.) Eleni, an elderly woman, who used it as her residence.

After we thoroughly examined the place, I said to Nicos, "Well done! This will be ideal. We can operate undercover as sellers of wood, coal, oil, and petroleum."

"Good idea," Nicos replied. "I will inquire downtown about renting this place; then, we will ask Yiapitzoglou for the money to buy supplies for our storefront."

As we left, Nicos said, "I forgot to tell you that I have also found a permanent place for you to stay. Why don't I take you there right now and show it to you? It's very close, and it would be very convenient for you to walk from there to the factory, if we decide to rent it." We walked for a few minutes to the address Serron 10, and entered a courtyard off a small street, where there were three separate apartments—one of which had three rooms, occupied by a fatherless family of four—a woman with three young children and her elderly mother. I learned that the woman's husband was a Greek officer, killed in Albania during the 1940 Greco-Italian campaign. The apartments also had been owned by a Greek-Jewish family who owned a huge lumber business. Before the German invasion, the patriarch of the household found a secure refuge for his family, and then joined the partisans in the nearby mountains that enveloped Salonica.

As we entered the apartment, Nicos introduced me to the young woman and her family. Tragically, the woman had been widowed at age twenty-eight, left to feed her family on no income during the German occupation. As a result, the woman agreed to take me in as a boarder and converted the living room into a bedroom for me. Instead of paying rent, I agreed to provide food money for the family (which I would leave on the kitchen table for them to retrieve), and I would dine with them at every meal, except lunch. The arrangement seemed very agreeable—particularly given the fact that the young woman was very attractive. By their exchange of glances, I observed that the woman and Nicos were close companions. This assumption was later confirmed by Nicos himself.

"Helias, you are a lucky man. What else shall I sacrifice for Greece?" Nicos winked at me as we left. At first, I didn't understand what he meant. Later on, however, I discovered that Yiapitzoglou had asked Nicos to relinquish his companionship with the young woman for "the safety of the organization." "Sultanitsa" (meaning "sultan's prize") would offer me her friendship and charms, so as to prevent distractions elsewhere. Whether "Sultanitsa" was her given name or a nickname was not clear to me; but, either way, it suited her perfectly, since her beauty was undeniable. Since I had to maintain a low profile, my search for female companionship outside of my home would, no doubt, draw attention to myself; therefore, the presence of Sultanitsa would provide the necessary diversion, while averting danger. *Now, that is a very desirable arrangement*, I thought. That notion was confirmed with each passing day and evening, when I came home and beheld Sultanitsa, who dressed quite beautifully—just for me.

Lady Luck herself was truly on our side. The Greek authorities agreed to rent the factory to us; and the three of us—Yiapitzoglou, Nicos, and I—met at a nearby café to discuss my ideas about converting it into a wholesale business venue, where we would sell coal, oil, firewood, and other products. My two colleagues agreed and complimented me on the plan, stating that it would be a very good undercover operation and would not arouse much suspicion. We determined that the necessary supplies would cost around ten thousand dollars.

Remembering my training, a light bulb switched on in my head. "In order to minimize the amount of customers, I suggest that we sell at a higher price than the black marketeers," I said.

Nicos, who was a merchant in Salonica, looked at me curiously. "This war is rewriting the rules of business! It's a system that I've never heard of—selling at the highest price to chase customers away!"

"It will suit our purposes well," I replied, laughing.

The following day, we paid the civil authorities, received the factory keys, and were open for business. Nicos and I visited the factory again, and examined its suitability for the wireless installment. That afternoon, the three of us met once more, and we told Yiapitzoglou that we had thoroughly inspected the factory and found it to be precisely what we needed. I mentioned to Yiapitzoglou that, at all times, we would need at least two guards who would masquerade as salesmen or workers. We planned to unload firewood just inside the front iron gate of the courtyard, which would serve to obscure the view of the factory and, also, to advertise our business as merchants. Yiapitzoglou said that during our operation of the wireless, one of the watchmen would stand inside the front gate near the woodpile and pretend to cut wood, serving as a lookout. The second watchman would be responsible for walking around the block while the wireless was in use and would be on the alert for strange movements, trucks, or cars. Two watchmen would be a good start, and if we required more security, that number would increase. Nicos purchased a one-hundred-fifty-foot-long antenna wire, which I planned to install with the help of one of the watchmen. It was very important that the installation be performed accurately, so as to conceal the wire. The factory had an A-frame metal roof and horizontal beams fifteen feet above its concrete floor. Each support frame was about three and a half feet away from the next one. As I looked around, I strategized our game plan. If we could climb the first horizontal beam and pull the antenna wire by jumping from one beam to the next, we could install the antenna from inside the building without any difficulty.

Intent on my purpose, I arrived at 1:00 p.m. and waited for the watchman to come and assist me, as Yiapitzoglou had promised. After an hour, when no help arrived, I became impatient, and decided to perform the installation alone. So, with the antenna wire wrapped around my shoulders and under my arms, I climbed to the first beam using some wooden boxes. Then, I jumped to the second beam, quickening my pace, so as not to be detected. With the windows blown out, it was inevitable that any passersby would see me and immediately suspect what I was up to, particularly with the wire wrapped around my shoulder. The Greek and German governments strictly banned all radios, and above all else, I did not want to get caught.

Helias With the Wireless and two Guards, Stavros (foreground) and Nikitas (unseen), 1944

While I was standing on the second beam, trying to hide the wire, I heard some people talking. Next to me, there was a very large window that had been shattered, through which I saw four German officers of various ranks, right below me, carrying a bridge table and four chairs. They situated themselves right under where I stood, and sat down to play cards in a nice shady area. I knew how to play bridge well, and from my vantage point right above them (the captain was sitting right below me), I amused myself by following their game, judging their correct and incorrect bids. In one case, when the captain bid 3 No Trump, I immediate said to myself, *He will never make it. He is missing two aces and one king.* The mechanics of the game, though serving as a diversion, were not in the fore of my thoughts. The main issue was, of course, that if, just by chance, one of the officers happened to look up, he would have spotted me. That would have been my ruination.

Aware of the dangers involved in my tasks, I tried to hide by moving behind a vertical column where there was only just enough room for one leg. I had to stand on one leg at a time, therefore, alternating between my right and my left leg. *How long would I be able to stand like this without being seen?* I asked myself. Even if I could remain hidden, there was so much dust floating around me, that I was in peril of sneezing or coughing. One such involuntary noise could be my undoing. *My God! Is this the way in which I will end my mission—by getting caught before I even had the chance to send a single message? What would Major Vassos and the other instructors say? I survived the escape from Crete, the boat voyage, the German inspection, and now that I'm ready to begin my mission, will I be caught like a mouse in a trap—all because four German officers decided to play bridge?*

As much as I possibly could, I resolved to take control of the situation. I was determined to stifle every inclination to cough or sneeze, and no matter what, I would stand on one leg, like an acrobat, for as long as I had to—regardless of how many hours the four officers decided to engage in their game. As I tried to ensconce myself behind the beam and the vertical column, I realized that I had inadvertently stuck my head into a spider's web, and a large spider (more than an inch long) was a breath away from my face. I tried silently to blow the creature away, but as an intruder, I knew that I would have a struggle on my hands. The creature did not seem to approve of my presence one bit, and I was all too aware that it might bite me; so, I moved my right hand slowly and tore down the web, throwing it and the spider away from my face. As I did so, the wind carried the web through the open window next to me, right on top of the table where the German officers were playing bridge! One officer grabbed the web and looked up to see where it came from. I held my breath, and in a few seconds—and some choice German obscenities later—the matter had summarily ended. The German officer tossed away the web, without spotting me. Unfortunately for the spider, its well-constructed web was destroyed. Ensnared once more in the web of life's unpredictability, I, however, had escaped certain peril, and I was thankful to be alive.

When the 5:00 p.m. dinner alarm rang for the German officers, they were still immersed in their game, laughing and talking. Then, a few minutes later, they finished their hand, collected their table and chairs, and went inside the neighbor's

188

house. Meanwhile, a feeling of immense gratitude came over me, coupled with the idea that I had been standing motionless on one leg for close to three and a half hours. I began to move and circulate my seemingly paralyzed limbs and, with great difficulty, I tried to walk. Given my discomfort, I decided not to continue with the wireless installation that evening. Instead, I would jump back to the first beam, and climb down some boxes that I had piled there. That was the plan—or so I thought. When I tried to leap from the second beam to the first, my legs felt powerless to sustain me. As a result, my body twisted, I fell, hit my head on the first beam, and tumbled face down, fifteen feet to the concrete floor below. I must have lost consciousness when I hit the floor, and when I regained my senses a few minutes later, I found myself covered in blood. It was then that I realized that my nose was broken.

In my state of distress, I made my way to Sultanitsa's home, where I was staying. When she saw me, she let out a high-pitched scream, and begged me to go to the hospital. I refused, telling her not to worry. "A piece of lumber fell on me and hit my nose. If you would bring me some ice, and just give me a kiss, I'll be all right in no time," I reassured her. Not only did she provide me with those remedies, but many others, which seemed to heal me almost instantly. Those tender, curative treatments were so effective, that I gladly would have repeated the entire episode, without a thought to what had occurred at the factory.

Yiapitzoglou, on the other hand, was not so easily placated. When he came to see me that night and I explained what had occurred, he stared at me in wide-eyed disbelief. "We achieved our goal of coming to Salonica and experienced so many dangerous situations, only to be caught because four Germans decided to play a game of bridge?" he asked. He could not believe that I was able to remain motionless for three and a half hours without coughing or sneezing. I laughed while he cursed the watchman who was supposed to come and help me install the antenna.

"Tomorrow, I will send both of those bastards with Nicos, and they will do all the work," he said decisively. "You will not go up there again, do you understand? You are too valuable. Besides, you will jeopardize all of us. I have to watch you more carefully—for your interests, as well as mine. Besides, what would we do without our lucky man who has miraculously avoided capture and death so many times in the past three weeks? Either you have been trained extremely well, God is on our side, or you're just plain lucky; but whatever the case may be, you have always survived." Yiapitzoglou squeezed my arm, adding, "We need you."

Soon, Nicos and the others managed to install the wireless. I suggested that we find a place to hide the wireless, the battery, and whatever else we would use in a safe, accessible place. Also, I had to have a .45-caliber gun on the table next to the wireless, the .32-caliber gun that I had brought from Cairo, and a couple of grenades, just in case we had to cause a diversion. Other than a pile of lint and pieces of material in a corner, the place was completely empty. The two rooms contained one table, on which we would put the radio and the guns, but we did not have any closets or shelves in which to store our other necessities. In my search for a place to hide the radio and the weapons, my shoe accidentally kicked a plywood board, hidden from view under the lint. Since the board was too heavy for one person to lift, I summoned Nicos for assistance, and to our surprise, we found a wonderful hiding place! "Helias, not only are you lucky, but you are always able to find a way where none exists," Nico remarked. After a brief pause, he continued. "Since the factory owners were Jews who were forced to leave," he thought, "maybe they hid gold or important things in the hole, as they could not take their valuables. Other Greeks [most likely factory workers who knew of the hiding place] or Germans must have searched and found their possessions. Most likely, they stole everything."

The hole in the floor seemed to be the perfect place of concealment. "If we keep everything the way it is—including the pile of lint—nobody would know what was under there, and those who might have inspected and ransacked it before will never suspect the presence of other items there now," I affirmed. Without another alternative, we proceeded with the plan, even though we had to work in a room with glass doors and windows through which anyone could see from the front gate and/or office entrance.

The next day, Nicos brought the wireless and the battery, the latter of which he put underneath the table in one of the two offices. I pulled the antenna wire down from its hiding place on the wall, behind the vertical column of the A-framed building. I strategically positioned the table on which the wireless sat a few feet away, so that the hidden end could be pulled and connected whenever necessary. I also made sure that I was able to look outside and observe the watchman. The only problem was that, since I was sitting at the table with my wireless in the front office, anyone walking in the courtyard could also peer into the entrance door's upper glass panel and blown-out windows on top, and see me with my headphones on. The entrance gate was also never locked, and no one ever compelled Stavros, the gate watchman, to ensure that no one came in. I considered using curtains, but I realized that, while they would prevent outsiders from looking in, my view would be obscured, as well. My situation, therefore, was quite unconventional. Usually, wireless radios were hidden in sub-basements; but there I was, out in the open and unprotected.

With little time to waste and intent upon finding solutions instead of obstacles, I focused on my escape plan. In the inner office, which was connected to the outer office by a glass door, a low glass window faced our neighbor's yard (i.e., the house where the German officers resided). Upon careful deliberation, I decided that my best means of escape was to jump through the small window into their yard and use their rear gate, which exited onto another street. To that end, I cut the putty out of the window frame with a knife, so that the glass was barely in place and could easily fall with the exertion of slight pressure. In an emergency, I thought, I might distract the Germans before my planned escape. For example, I could prevent them from rushing in by throwing a couple of grenades into the courtyard and, then, quickly exiting through the escape window. My mind never stopped strategizing.

Finally, with all of the preliminaries in place, the moment of truth arrived: our initial contact with Cairo. On that momentous occasion, I thought of everyone who had risked their lives for our mission's success. The two watchmen stood at their posts, the table was set up, and the wireless was prepared to receive and transmit. While in Cairo, we agreed that, every day at 3 p.m., a signal would be sent to me in order to initiate contact.

At 1 p.m., we became anxious about our communication. I saw Yiapitzoglou speaking to Nicos Oreopoulos, both displaying intense uneasiness. Only Stavros seemed calm and collected at his post in the courtyard, smoking a cigarette while cutting firewood, secretly scouring the passersby. Nikitas, the other watchman, began walking around the block, alert to what was happening. If he spotted German trucks or cars, he would quickly inform me to stop the transmission and, then, he and I would escape in separate predetermined directions.

As I thought of my first message, I remembered what Captain Kellis and Major Vassos had told me: the city of Salonica was even more important than Athens, known for its higher troop-concentration and as a deployment point for German soldiers. Therefore, the Gestapo would be focusing on the area. *What would happen as soon as I went on the air? Would the German triangulation instruments find my signal immediately? Would they capture and torture me?* My thoughts spiraled—justifiably so.

Thinking quickly, I moved the table to just the right spot, in order to view the courtyard as clearly as I could. I placed the two guns—the .45 and the .32—to the right of the wireless key, next to which I placed a small wooden box with the two grenades. Yiapitzoglou and Oreopoulos eyed my every move at all times. Looking up to observe their reactions, I noticed that they seemed withdrawn and frightened.

"Why do you look so gloomy?" I asked.

Yiapitzoglou replied, "If someone were to come in at this very moment and see what was on the table, we would be done for."

"I'm going out for a cigarette," I replied, unable to withstand the atmospheric tension.

I walked outside into the yard and told Nikitas to get ready. In fifteen minutes, he would begin his walk, continuously circling the block until Stavros informed him that the transmission had ended. I happened to see Kyria Eleni, the woman who lived in the next door apartment, and asked her if she wanted some oil or firewood. She shook her head. "I haven't seen any customers buying anything yet," the woman remarked.

"Oh, don't worry," I answered. "We're selling wholesale, and that is why you haven't seen anyone yet."

If only the woman knew that she was sitting atop a pile of dynamite! In the event of a German raid, hand guns would blaze and grenades would explode. I wish that I could have warned that good soul, but what she didn't know wouldn't harm her; and, as the perfect cover, she was doing us a service—however unknowingly.

At 2:55 p.m., everyone watched as I put my headphones on, listening for the signal. At exactly 3:00 p.m., I heard "Cando, Cando," my call name. I excitedly told Yiapitzoglou, "I hear them. They said 'Cando'!"

"What is Cando?" he asked. I put the headphones on his ears, and he heard, "-.-. .- -. -.. ---" which, in Morse code, is "Cando."

I explained that while in training, I was asked by what call name I should be identified. Since I hadn't given it much thought, the sergeant asked me to name the American city in which I was born. I replied, "Canton, Ohio." The sergeant replied, "We will call you 'Canto' or, better yet, 'Cando.' The Germans will never surmise what the name means."

"It is strange," I said to them, "but what you hear travelling in the air is my name. Even the Germans are listening to it right now, and they are probably asking, 'Who is Cando?'"

"My God!" Nicos exclaimed. "We've learned a lot of things during this war! To me, it is merely a sound, floating in the air. To you, it means that we have made contact with Cairo."

To myself, I silently said, *It's all in the game.*

Chapter 22

Mastering the Impossible

" **A** s you can see, we have established communication. We are in business," I said. Everyone smiled and breathed a collective sigh of relief.

I replied to Cairo and scheduled the next message for 10:00 a.m. the following morning. In the meantime, Yiapitzoglou asked that I send a small introductory message regarding his organization, which I did without incident or difficulty. We felt confident that, from that point on, everything would go smoothly. Wishful thinking often takes the sting out of reality's harshness.

As we busied ourselves, Yiapitzoglou established a network of collaborators (primarily friends) in different locations in and around Salonica, who would report the movement of German troops, the departure and arrival of cargo trains and/or ships, and the presence of weapons in a given area. Each site would be surveyed by a representative, who would gather information and report back to Yiapitzoglou (e.g., at the train stations, the airport, the harbor area, and even in German offices—including the bathrooms). These informants also monitored the numbers and whereabouts of British and American hostages. Yiapitzoglou would verify each piece of information, assess its level of importance, verify its accuracy with his sources and, then, prioritize it for transmission to Cairo. Then, I would divide the information into each message of at least twenty-five words without spaces, code and transmit the message to OSS headquarters in Cairo. In order to code a given message, I had to use a cryptographic technique, which involved a coded letter derived from a song known only to the OSS (now, nearly seven decades later, that vital piece of music eludes me but, as I mentioned earlier, I diligently had committed it to memory). I would write out the letters of that song under the text that I had to code, and repeat them until they matched the identical number of letters in the message, which would then be decoded in Cairo. As I already mentioned, I could only send one or two messages at a time (at most) within the space of five minutes. During that time, anything could happen. At any moment, the Gestapo could hear us and, with their triangulation equipment, determine our location. Sending two messages, therefore, posed the risk of "inviting the Gestapo for dinner," and as I had been warned many times, sending three was tantamount to "digging your own grave." If, however, I *had* to transmit three messages, I could change the frequency each time I sent a new one. While the Gestapo searched for that new frequency, I would have a brief window of time to send the third telegram.

It was not by chance that Yiapitzoglou had been chosen from the Greek Naval Intelligence, as he not only knew Salonica well but, also, had the necessary leadership qualities for our operation's success. Under his direction, many enemy ships descended to the bottom of the Mediterranean Sea. Once, a friend of a friend reported that certain ships were completely destroyed with troops and supplies on board. Everyone involved was literally fighting for life but, as young as I was, I did not comprehend the full extent of the danger. I was, simply, intent on carrying out my mission, hoping never to make a fatal error.

After a while, using the wireless became routine, and our fears dissipated. In fact, everyone in the neighborhood knew that we had rented the place, and we became instantly recognizable. For all anyone knew, we could have been running things on the black market. Our neighbors on the right (who housed the four German officers), those on the left and across the street would greet us every time we entered or exited our building. They were especially nice to me—the young man who ran a successful business and was considered to be a good catch for their daughters.

Not only had we become friendly with our neighbors but, also, with the German officers living next door. They played bridge two to three times a week in the shady spot between our factory and their home—the same area where I first encountered them. Soon, they realized that we were using the factory for business, and I wasn't afraid to approach or talk to them. From the small escape window near their bridge table, I often overheard them talking. One day, after sending two messages to Cairo and storing everything securely away, I opened the small window and said "hello" to the officers in German. "I see you play bridge. I do also," I said.

"If we ever need a fourth player, we will ask you to join us," they replied amicably.

I filled up a dish with almonds and walnuts and gave it to the four officers, who expressed their appreciation numerous times. That evening, when our group convened in a café bar, we laughed about my conversation with the officers. Yiapitzoglou remarked, "Now he is even going to play bridge with the Gestapo!"

Over time, information continued to pour in from all over the city—from the harbor area, the railroads, and the airport—so much so, that I had to make two daily contacts with Cairo, one at about 10:00 a.m., the other at 3:00 p.m. or 4:00 p.m., sending one or two telegrams each time; but without sensing the danger, my growing complacency placed me in situations that would put my training to the test.

As a form of diversion, our group would meet about two times a week near the waterfront taverns—just to relax and drink to our successful operations. According to those in charge, we deserved a few drinks now and then for all of our hard work. One night, we went out to a restaurant with Yiapitzoglou, Odysseus (his cousin) and Nicos, and ordered a huge meal, which included appetizers, shrimp, clams, fried potatoes, and other fish, along with a bottle of Greek ouzo. Our indulgence starkly contrasted with the economic climate surrounding us, with people literally starving to death, due to the scarcity of work and food.

While we were dining, a group of elderly people happened to be walking close to our table; and as soon as they saw our food, they looked at us with hostility, declaring out loud for all to hear, "The day will soon come when you traitors will pay with your lives. Eat now, you pigs. Soon, you will be hanging from the trees!"

So as not to incite the elders, all of us remained silent and continued to eat as though nothing had happened. They obviously thought that we were collaborating with the Germans. How ironic it was that we were endangering ourselves for the sake of peace! However, a retort would have been fruitless. "This was a bad idea," I whispered.

"We are successful businessmen. Maybe, they thought we were black marketeers."

"But even black marketeers need the approval of their German masters," I replied.

At that moment, emotion overtook me, as I reflected on the plight of our elderly detractors who may have lost their children, and my own parents, still living in Crete under the Germans' iron fist. I never ceased to worry about the Gestapo returning to my home and inquiring about our whereabouts again and again. With these thoughts in mind, I looked at Yiapitzoglou earnestly. "Next time, we shouldn't be so willing to eat out in Salonica's restaurants like Ali Pasha (the Ottoman ruler, notorious for his excessive eating and, most infamously, for his killing of many Greeks)!" I remarked.

Yiapitzoglou disagreed. "We are behaving as all Greeks do— even as accomplished businessmen; and, if we don't do things in excess, it's okay." My friend's way of thinking bolstered my confidence to such a degree, that I lost my fear; and, in so doing, I repeatedly exposed myself to danger.

In my oblivion to the perils surrounding me, I was able to do my job without reservation—and with time to spare. In my leisure hours, I took dance lessons three times a week and frequented the "Alexander the Great" swimming pool, one of my favorite spots. On one summer day, while sitting near the pool, I forgot to remove my wristwatch—an American-made, very costly military-style timepiece, given to me in Cairo. Nearby, two German officers sat tanning themselves in the hot sun. Turning to me, they asked whether they could have a look at the watch. *How am I going to get out of this?* I wondered. Clearly, I had made a mistake, but there was absolutely nothing I could do but remain calm and say the first thing that came to mind—just as I had been trained to do.

"I received this watch from a German soldier, in exchange for fresh eggs, nuts, and some money. Since the soldier had other watches in his possession—most likely confiscated from an American soldier or prisoner of war—he was eager to sell this one," I said, amazed at my impromptu fabrication.

The German soldiers looked at one another, then at me, and simply could not argue with my logic or my story, in general. Thus, they handed me my watch—and my freedom, along with the knowledge that my five months' training—and diligent obedience—had paid off.

Aside from my recreational antics, I enjoyed surprising Sultanitsa with groceries (since that was part of the arrangement). I had plenty of money and, often, I would bring the food home—to the neighbors' complete amazement. Across the street, a university professor resided with his wife and pretty eighteen-year-old daughter, Annoula. After observing Sultanitsa and her family's style of living and, most likely, hearing about me through his wife's conversations with Sultanitsa (who was always boasting about me), the professor persuaded his daughter to befriend me. Annoula would wait all day for me to return (usually after sending the 3:00 p.m. message) and serenade me with Greek songs under my window. Predictably, her gesture grated on the nerves of the lovely, but jealous, Sultanitsa. I, on the other hand, was thoroughly enchanted by the beautiful girl's melodious voice.

At first, I did my best to ignore Annoula and her friends; for, in truth, I enjoyed Sultanitsa's interest in me, and I did not want to aggravate her. All the while, as tensions mounted, she paid extra attention to me, and desperately tried to please me. As much as I took pleasure in Sultanitsa's company, however, she lacked Annoula's sultry nightingale tones. Regretting my initial rejection of Annoula, I finally opened the window one day, and saw her standing there with her friends, beaming from ear to ear. *What should Romeo do for the Juliets? Ah, I know! I'll play the musical accompaniment for their singing— if only I could find an instrument,* I thought.

One afternoon, while walking down "Tsimisky," a well-known market avenue, I happened to spot an accordion in a music store window. Since my early childhood, I had always dreamt of playing the accordion. I used to have a toy that showed the notes on a scale (as on a piano, for example), and I loved to play songs, which I managed to do with one tiny finger. However, since it was very expensive to purchase an accordion and take lessons in those days, the goal remained solely in the realm of my dreams.

As an OSS operative, however, with sufficient control over my own expenses, I hoped to fulfill my heart's desire. Without hesitation, therefore, I went back to the store via the same route (neglecting my usual detour, so as not to be observed or followed). As I suspected, the accordion was still there—as though it were waiting for me. I went inside and inquired about the price. The salesman looked at me, thinking I could not possibly have the money for it.

"The accordion is not for sale," he said definitively.

"Why not?" I answered. "I have money!"

To get rid of me, the salesman sent me to the manager, who also looked at me with a puzzled expression. "I admire your choice of instruments. When I was young, I also had a dream of playing the accordion, and began my musical career that way. Later, I sold musical instruments," he explained. Then, after a pause, he said, "This Hohner accordion that you see in the window, my boy, is the only one left in this store and in the entire city of Salonica. It is as precious as gold, and since it is the only one for sale, it costs a lot of money. I know you like it, but you cannot possibly buy it; so, go home." he commanded sternly.

"For how much gold would you sell it?" I asked.

"Really?" the salesman asked in disbelief; then, he added with a smile, "Twenty gold pieces for the accordion . . . and two gold pieces for the case!"

The manager assumed that I would be surprised by his answer, and fully expected me to turn around and leave. Instead, I stood my ground. "Okay, I'll bring you the twenty gold pieces tomorrow," I replied, as I turned to walk out.

The salesman and store manager stared at each other in shock, wondering if I was serious or playing a prank. As I left the store, I glanced at the accordion as if it were already mine.

Walking home through the theater district, I bumped into none other than my Juliet, Annoula and her parents. Annoula introduced me to her father and mother, the latter of whom observed, with a wink in her husband's direction, "This is the business-minded boy who lives across the street—the one about whom Annoula has spoken many times."

"Are you going to the theater this evening?" I asked politely.

"No, unfortunately, the performance has been sold out. We're so disappointed! This was the premiere."

"Just wait here. I will try to get those tickets for you," I said, as they looked at me with surprised expressions.

"No!" Annoula's father gestured for me to stay. "I have already inquired, and they are all sold out."

"Just wait here! I'll get them," I insisted.

The professor threw his hands in the air dismissively. "Go ahead, then!" he exclaimed, believing that I was delusional.

"I'll be right back," I replied, as I headed for the ticket office.

The price for theater tickets was five hundred drachmas, but in order to achieve my objective, I took out ten thousand drachmas, and placed the stack of bills on the ticket booth's window sill. "Please give me four tickets," I said, with conviction.

Gaping at the money, the manager immediately turned to the usher and said, "Give these four tickets to the gentleman, and place four chairs up front, in front of the first row."

I took the tickets, ran back and calmly displayed them to the professor, who could not believe his eyes.

"I know the manager, and that is how I was able to get the tickets," I explained.

We then went inside, sat down, and enjoyed the show. Since our four chairs were placed up front, everyone—including the actors—wondered who we were. Yet again, I had broken another rule of my training, and placed myself in plain view for everyone to see; but, as usual, I was unable to perceive the magnitude of the dangers lurking all around me, blinded as I was by the excitement of mastering the impossible.

Chapter 23

Departures

That night, I asked Yiapitzoglou to bring me twenty-five sovereigns in the morning (I had given him the gold for safekeeping).

"Twenty-five?" he asked, looking slightly suspicious. "What are you doing with the gold—selling it?"

"I'm buying an accordion," I replied without hesitation.

"What? Are you crazy?" Yiapitzoglou yelled at the top of his voice. "That gold is supposed to be used for paying off the Gestapo, informants, and other urgent matters. If someone sees you with that money, you might be reported to the Greek police or the Gestapo! The black marketeers will steal your gold—and kill us, for sure! And don't think that I haven't heard about the incident at the theater, and how everyone was looking at you, your neighbor's daughter and her parents."

I sat silent, as I allowed my friend to continue. "Did I hear correctly? You want to buy an accordion? The Gestapo is after us, willing to kill untold numbers of Greeks in order to find the only American soldier in Salonica, and instead of hiding, you're thinking of serenading the girls, showing off like a big spender! Obviously, you do not understand the extent of danger to which you're being exposed moment by moment—or maybe, you are just out of your mind! Just because you haven't been caught today doesn't mean that you won't be captured tomorrow. Do you know that, with twenty-five gold sovereigns, you can buy an apartment or even a house—a home like the ones from which the Jews fled for their lives! People are starving and dying, and you are buying an accordion!"

Clearly, my friend wanted me to retract my statement and admit my foolishness; but he did not realize how obsessed I was with the accordion. "I know what you're trying to say, Cosmas," I answered, attempting to calm my friend's wrath. "But I was initially given over one hundred fifty gold sovereigns, and you must be holding one hundred thirty five of them in your possession. Who knows? I may be killed tomorrow. What good would the gold be to me if I were dead? I want to enjoy the money now, while I'm alive. Besides, buying the accordion and playing it may help me to become friendlier with the neighbors, who might then cease asking, 'Who is that young merchant?'"

Cosmas Yiapitzoglou noted my determination and, recognizing my position—the fact that, at any time, I might be caught and my dream of having the accordion would never materialize, he finally gave in. "OK. I'll bring the gold pieces to you tomorrow; but promise me that you won't show the gold to anyone (except at the music store) and don't tell anyone what you paid for the accordion. In fact, don't let anyone even know that you just bought it. Let them think that you had it previously," he said.

So, the next day, after I sent two messages to Cairo, I went to the music store to purchase the musical instrument of my dreams. The store manager and the salesman watched in disbelief as I slowly counted out the twenty-two gold pieces and placed them on a table.

"My boy," the manager said, "I will not ask you how you came to have so many gold pieces, but since you brought me what I asked for, the accordion is yours."

The salesman placed the beautiful brand new Hohner accordion in its case and gave it to me.

"Enjoy it," the manager said. "But please don't tell anyone how much you paid for it." Obviously, he had overcharged me to such an extent, that he didn't want anyone else to hear about the sale.

"I also don't want to disclose anything," I responded.

Within minutes, the peasant boy from Archanes had realized his lifelong dream. Whether he would live to enjoy it was a matter of speculation, however. Therefore, the exorbitant price seemed irrelevant. I just wanted to savor life—at any cost. I took the accordion home to Sultanitsa's house, and tried to strap in on; but I could not do so alone. Yiapitzoglou kindly assisted me, and I roughly began to play the proper notes with my left hand only. I had no idea what the right hand was supposed to do; but, thanks to my childhood knowledge of scales, I roughly managed to tap out a couple of popular songs, and sing my heart out. Yiapitoglou and Sultanitsa sang along. I saw tears in my lady friend's eyes as she thought of her deceased husband. As we lost ourselves in reminiscences, we forgot about the Germans and, for a moment in time, the magnitude of my mission was not so overwhelming.

The hiatus, however, was short-lived. Soon, the entire neighborhood began to gossip about "the young successful businessman with the accordion." As word spread, Sultanitsa became more and more envious of the other girls—especially Annoula, who reveled in my daily concerts. Sultanitsa spoke with Nicos who, in turn, spoke to Cosmas Yiapitzoglou, and a meeting between all of us was arranged. Calmly, the older gentlemen attempted to explain the state of things. Some people enjoyed my singing, while others objected to it.

"Those who do not approve of your singing might complain to the Greek police, and who knows what will happen next?" By the second, Nicos and Yiapitzoglou's voices increased in volume. "Promise that you will end your concerts! If you like those girls, why not ask them to go out with you, instead of allowing them to stand outside the balcony window?"

I had no choice but to agree and put an end to my afternoon concerts. When those musical interludes ceased, so did the gathering of the neighborhood girls.

My Romeo persona became extremely nervous one day, when the Gestapo conducted a random inspection. Luckily, I was not approached and asked to show my I.D. card. Up until that point, I had neglected to check the address on my identification card, which I had been given in Izmir, Turkey. I was so busy having the time of my life, that these all-important details often escaped me. When I realized my negligence, I jumped onto a trolley and went to the address listed on my I.D. card. Was I stunned! My address was a waterfront hotel, where many Greeks and Germans were staying. I could not believe my eyes! When the sergeant presented me with the card, I was told that the address was taken from a telephone book, without knowing the precise location or type of address it was. He had instructed me, therefore, to find a place to stay and, then, change the I.D. as soon as possible. Since I failed to do so before, I had to seize the opportunity. I began to walk along the street and came upon a residential house number. That looked fine enough. The only problem was how to seamlessly insert the new address on the card. When I arrived home, I attempted to erase the old address and, in so doing, I made a small hole in the card. *Oh, God! Now, I'm worse off. I have to get a new card immediately,* I said to myself.

I was afraid that Yiapitzoglou would be furious and let me have it; but, thankfully, he simply suggested that I keep a very low profile until I could properly obtain another card. As it happened, one of Nicco's relatives worked in an office which issued I.D.'s, and we asked him to assist me. The issuance of such identifications was strictly prohibited and punishable by death, if the activity were discovered. Intellectually, I knew the dangers involved; but, in practice, I continued to behave with reckless abandon—despite Yiapitzoglou's warnings.

In the interim, as I was awaiting my new I.D., I hopped on a trolley. At the last stop, the conductor called out, "The Germans are looking for partisans, and every I.D. will be checked. Have your I.D.'s ready." Of course, the only card I had in my possession was flawed. *What now? They will see the hole!* I thought. *If only I had been more conscientious and spent less time playing the accordion, this wouldn't be happening,* I reprimanded myself; but without any more time to think, I looked up and saw the Germans weave through the streetcar's standing-room only section. When a German officer approached me, I took out my identification card, placed my thumb over the incriminating hole, and presented the card. The officer simply looked at me, saw the face of an innocent young man—so different from that of a partisan—and moved on to the next passenger. I had escaped certain peril—*yet again*!

The following week, Nicos informed me that his relative had agreed to issue the new card. "At exactly twelve noon, go to window number two, and say your name only. I gave our inside man your picture, your name, 'Helias Nikolaou,' and your address, Serron 10, Salonica."

At precisely the appointed hour, I went to window number two, where I encountered a man with a huge visor over his eyes. With his head lowered (so as not to see my face—or to be seen himself), he pushed a piece of paper in my direction for me to sign. I did so, and gave it back; then, the man stamped the paper and pushed it back to me. In the interest of the man's safety, neither one of us could see the other. The man's sole purpose was to legitimize my residency. Without a word, therefore, I gathered my materials and left as an ordinary, legal citizen of Salonica.

At home, Sultanitsa's attentiveness increased—particularly when the serenading ceased. She even offered to help out in the business. Given the dangers of her involvement, I discouraged her by saying that business was slow. She did not even know where the factory was located. Had she found out, that knowledge would have imperiled the entire neighborhood—not to mention our organization. Had the Gestapo inquired about my general whereabouts, Sultanitsa would have innocently directed them to me (perhaps, even while I was sending a message to Cairo). In that case, the German police would have dynamited the whole area—just to kill one American spy and topple our entire operation. For the time being, therefore, the neighbors knew me only as "a successful businessman." To Sultanitsa, I was, in her words, "a present from God."

Fortunately, Sultanitsa did not persist in her questioning, and I tried to avoid the subject at every turn. One morning, however, I noticed that she was ready to go out after breakfast. Suspecting that she wanted to follow me, I hid in an alley and, while she was walking along, I came up from behind her and grabbed her arm. "If you do this again, I will move out of your home," I warned her. She never followed me again.

Having been admonished again and again by Yiapitzoglou and Nicos about the momentous nature of my responsibilities, I began to realize that I was not on vacation. At first, I could not distinguish my clever, serendipitous antics and escapes from the seriousness of what I had to accomplish. Nicos always used to tell me, "Helias, for you, the war should never end." In truth, however, fortune had a way of playing games and reversing itself without warning. It just took me a while to acknowledge that fact.

"How will I ever know, at any moment, when the Germans are looking for me and awaiting me at Sultanitsa's house?" I remarked to Yiapitzoglou. Every night when I came home from work, I would stop at the corner and scout the neighborhood, to make sure that everything looked "normal" (i.e., that there were women chatting and gossiping outside their homes, and the streets were filled with people). If, on the other hand, no one was out and I suspected that something was awry, I would then have to go to the house at the top of the hill in "Panorama" (where I had originally lodged for a few days). From there, I would notify our organization's members that I required an exit strategy, in the event that the Gestapo raided the house. I even became more vigilant when entering the factory. After all, it was possible that the Gestapo would be there. As a result, I needed a decoy—and Kyria Eleni was the perfect person to unwittingly fulfill that role. Luckily for me—but, unfortunately, for her—she had made the mistake of accepting to live in that corner apartment. Her corner apartment had the best view of the courtyard, with two large windows facing the street, and the shutters prevented people from looking in.

Thinking that Kyria Eleni could be of help to us in scouting the area for any unauthorized person attempting to enter our yard or premises, I approached her one day.

"It's not easy to run a business in wartime," I said, "especially since jealous merchants would like to see us go bankrupt. Would you mind keeping an eye open for suspicious people or Germans who might force their way through our entrance gate and into our yard?"

"I would be happy to help out in any way," she replied.

"If you see anyone suspicious, just tell them that I will arrive shortly. Then, open the shutters on both windows facing the street to alert me of their presence."

"Very smart, Helias!" Kyria Eleni said. "If ever I see strangers or Germans looking for you, I will open both shutters immediately. After all, I'm thankful for everything that you have done for me."

"By the way, Kyria Eleni," I said, "would you like some olive oil or petrol for your lamp?"

"No, my boy," she said. "I haven't seen many customers in your store lately, and I feel sorry for you. You're wasting your father's money. I don't want anything; but if I see your business pick up, maybe then I'll ask you for some oil."

Poor Kyria Eleni, I said to myself. *She doesn't know that she is in harm's way—and that I put her there! If that terrible day ever comes, Kyria Eleni and her apartment might be the first casualties*; but I could not continue thinking along those lines. I was just grateful that she was such a good cover. She cared for me like her own son. Yet, by placing her in harm's way, the Gestapo would assume that she was an accomplice, for sure. And it would never have occurred to her that she was protecting an American spy—innocent to this fact—which weighed heavily on me.

With the Allied invasion of France, the war escalated, and the Germans began to leave Salonica, using the city to depart via airplanes and trains. Even donkeys and mules were used to transport heavy equipment and belongings. OSS Cairo wanted information regarding all of their movements, and I began to send two telegrams per day—one in the morning and one in the afternoon. Believing that the Germans were distracted with their departures, I underestimated their single-minded intent to find me. In the ensuing weeks, such a misguided notion almost cost me my life.

Since OSS Cairo was receiving my daily messages, the departures of a few German squadrons leaving by truck convoys or planes were too incidental. The big brass was not willing to sacrifice airplanes to annihilate a few hundred. So, they asked me to inform them of a brigade or division-strength departure—an event of much greater magnitude. As already mentioned, the German military order stated that any private home with two extra bedrooms and an extra bathroom was commanded to take in German officers, while lower-ranked (non-commissioned) soldiers were quartered in schools or factories. From our informants, we determined that the number of Germans in Salonica at the time exceeded fifty thousand. Many had arrived from other parts of Greece or from various fronts outside of the country.

The German officers' presence in civilian homes often led to close connections with the people with whom they lived—most often young ladies, who developed strong attachments to them. One such association was that of Katerina (a cousin of one of our organization's members named "Yianni") and a German officer who resided in her home. Each Saturday evening, the officer escorted her to the officers' entertainment events. Yianni warned her that her continued association would result in punishment and her hair would be cut by vengeful Greek partisans. Katerina, however, professed her love for the German lieutenant, and would not end the relationship. By all appearances, the German officer had fallen in love, as well. When the time came for him to leave, he would not allow Katerina to come with him to the train station. He stated that there would be thousands of fellow Germans there, departing on the 3:00 p.m. train on Thursday. Therefore, he would say his goodbyes the evening before, leaving her gifts and some of the belongings that he could not take along, and attempt to see her one last time on Thursday before his departure. Both of them parted tearfully.

That night, Yianni happened to go to his cousin's house. When the girl saw him, she said, "Now, you don't have to worry about me anymore. The German is leaving this Thursday."

Yianni quickly interrupted her and asked, "Is he the only one leaving?"

"No," Katerina replied, "his entire company is leaving, along with others. There will be thousands leaving from Salonica."

"Thousands? Where are they leaving from?" Yianni asked. "Are you going to say goodbye to him?"

"No, I can't. He is leaving by train at three o'clock on Thursday, and he told me not to even *try* to come. There will be police and so many soldiers at the train station. It will be impossible to go there. No one will be allowed near. Instead, we're meeting on Wednesday night. He is going to bring me some gifts. He said he will try to see me one last time on Thursday."

Acting on that innocent tip, Yianni called Yiapitzoglou who, in turn, notified me. I immediately prepared a message, which I sent on the following morning, a Sunday: "Thousands of Germans to leave Thursday at three o'clock in the afternoon at the main railroad station in Salonica." The OSS replied, requesting that Katerina verify that the departure would be on schedule. If she did so, they would send airplanes to bomb the railroad station on Thursday at 3:00 p.m. I responded: "I will definitely know on Wednesday night, when the girl will meet with the officer."

On Wednesday, at the appointed hour, the two paramours met and said their goodbyes, promising to reunite one last time behind the tavern at the railway station at 1:00 p.m., the following day (Thursday), if possible. Later that evening, Yianni pretended that he just happened to be passing by Katerina's house. During their conversation, he asked her if the soldiers were really departing the next day. "Yes . . . they are leaving," she innocently said as she cried, "Tomorrow . . . at three o'clock." Yianni left a short time later, and quickly called Yiapitzoglou, verifying what Katerina had said.

Yiapitzoglou immediately called me and I prepared a coded message that over three thousand Germans would depart from the train station on Thursday at 3 p.m. I suggested that the planes drop their bombs only on their target, avoiding the heavily populated civilian areas on either side of the railroad station. The OSS agreed to reply to me at 12:00 p.m. that day.

Yiapitzoglou was so excited to find out what would transpire, that he came to our factory to await the OSS' reply. He suggested that, just before 3:00 p.m. on Thursday, we should ascend to the rooftop to keep a lookout for the anticipated air attack and its aftermath, and report back to OSS Cairo. In all of Greece, only three people were aware of the impending bombing: Yiapitzoglou, Yianni, and I.

At precisely two hours before the scheduled attack, I received a message stating that American planes were scheduled to arrive at 3:00 p.m., and that we should avoid being in the vicinity of the railroad station. The message ended with the words, "Cando, most likely this time, you are going to hit the jackpot!"

I went home, feeling weak and sick to my stomach. Sultanitsa noticed that I looked pale, and asked if I was having difficulties in my business. "If I can help in any way, please let me know," she said, oblivious to my pain. If she only knew that, because of the telegram, coded by my hand, thousands of Germans in their twenties, the prime of youth, were going to be killed. "I'm just tired and need some rest," I assured her.

At 2:30 p.m., I went into the courtyard, searching for a way to climb to the rooftop of our house, as Yiapitzoglou had suggested. Suddenly, I spotted a tree leaning toward a wall. I had to climb up there before 3 p.m., but how was I going to do so without arousing Sultanitsa's suspicion? Suddenly, I had a thought. During one of her children's ball games, I took the ball and threw it up toward the one-story-high roof, and it got stuck near the chimney. *That's it!* I exclaimed to myself. *I will climb up on the pretext of retrieving the ball!* As

I began to ascend the tree, Sultanitsa spotted me, and called out. "Helias, Helias! What are you doing? You're going to fall and hurt yourself!" She grabbed my feet and started to pull me down, all the while screaming at the top of her lungs. I replied that I had inadvertently kicked the ball there, and that I was going to retrieve it.

"No, No!" Sultanitsa continued to chant, hysterically. Her cries alerted the two other tenants, who came out into the yard and joined in her pleas. "Stop, stop!"

"Leave me alone!" I beseeched my lady friend and the others. I looked at my watch. It was 2:50 p.m. I had to think quickly. I pretended to lose my footing, kicked Sultanitsa away, and continued the climb. All of a sudden, I heard *boom, boom*! The antiaircraft guns had already found the squadron and began to fire at the American planes.

Looking to the south, I saw a row of airplanes, one behind the other, heading toward Salonica's harbor. "What is happening?" asked everyone who saw me up on the roof. "I think airplanes are coming," I answered, unable to utter the terrible truth.

As the planes neared, I counted twelve, medium-sized bombers (most likely, B-25's, judging by their shape and size). To my surprise, the first airplane (which must have been the leader's plane) was directly hit. The plane's wing separated, and two parachutes descended. In a couple of seconds, the third airplane in line was hit and began to burn, while four parachutes fell from it. I noticed that the planes were traveling in a straight line, according to my recommendation; but the pilots obviously did not anticipate such fierce antiaircraft fire. After they witnessed their two lead aircraft being destroyed, they broke formation and spread out over the sky. Looming above me, each plane went in its own direction, dropping bombs on the railroad and its vicinity.

In less than a minute, all of the planes were gone. Tall plumes of smoke and flames encircled the railroad station. Quickly, I ran to the area. Passing by the harbor, I saw an open flatbed truck belonging to the Germans. Standing on top of the truck were five sad-faced American officers, still tied to their chute straps. Hundreds of people gaped at the American airmen who, in turn, remained silent and stared at the curious onlookers.

As I approached the truck, I yelled, "Hi! Hello there!" One of the airmen, a captain, turned briefly to glance at me silently, without uttering a word. How could he have known, in his wildest imagination, that it was I who had brought them to the spot where they had been captured?

What had happened was not merely conceptual, but profoundly real and tragic. I had to see for myself; so, I went to the railroad station. The Greek and German police would not allow me to come near, and I had to wait with hundreds of others, who looked on, wondering and waiting. An hour or so later, a Greek man who worked for the Germans came out and said that the trains had been completely destroyed. The search was limited only to survivors and wounded. The deceased bodies were so entangled, that it would take days to extricate them from the ruins.

"There must have been thousands killed," the man said.

"I heard that over one hundred homes were also destroyed or damaged and, under the wreckage, hundreds of civilians may have been trapped or killed. I saw a dead baby hanging from the telephone wires," another man said.

The fate of those thousands of German soldiers and captured American pilots still haunts me to this day. The thought that I had been the catalyst for so much death and devastation made me physically and emotional ill. Under the weight of a very heavy heart, I made my way home, with guilt pervading every fiber of my being. When I reached my block, I bumped into a neighbor with whom I frequently had discussed politics.

"Helias, do you see? The Americans did not forget us, after all," he said. Then, he silently looked around and added, "The Americans must have known about the German departures from the station. Don't you agree?" he asked, in a low whisper.

I paused. "Yes, they probably did know about it, but to tell you the truth, I wish that they didn't!"

"I don't understand. What do you mean?" the man asked.

Without replying, I simply hung my head and went inside. For the first time, I cursed my job. Until that moment, I considered my OSS duties to be a lark; but in the tragic aftermath of the bombings, I saw firsthand what a twenty-word telegram could do, and I felt as though I had dropped those bombs myself. Did I, a young boy, have the right to wield so much power as to send countless families into mourning, just because we were at war? What was the purpose of it all? As I tried to calm my mind, I realized that if the Germans had been allowed to enter France or Italy, thousands of American lives would have been lost—chaos and destruction, nonetheless. I asked myself why I had departed from my true nature—a loving, compassionate individual, who so enjoyed and valued life. The answer was that I had acted like a soldier—neutral and emotionless, carrying out my duties as I was told—as did countless others. I thought of Major Vassos, and my mission.

He had given me a choice: the more dangerous "Salonica mission," or the less dangerous "Captain Kellis mission"—and I chose Salonica. At such times, it was not for me to analyze the senselessness of humanity's inhumanity to itself; and all of my attempts at understanding were fruitless. As I have learned through the ages, things never change.

Somehow, the sun managed to rise the next day. The German-controlled newspapers wrote that "the barbaric Americans" bombed the city of Salonica, destroying eighty five homes and killing four hundred fifty civilians. The exact number of Germans killed remained undisclosed, but it was estimated that more than two thousand five hundred had lost their lives in the bombing, just as the train was about to depart from the station.

I notified Cairo that we had witnessed two planes shot down, and a third seemed to be smoking as they returned southward. Six pilots had been captured, one with a captain's rank. When I went to the factory to send that message, everyone there was happy and congratulated one another. As I walked in, however, everyone observed my dour expression and questioned why.

"Don't you know why?" I replied. "If estimates were correct, my message cost at least three thousand people—soldiers and civilians—their lives! How can I be proud of that?"

"It was your duty to send the message, and for this very reason, you were sent to Salonica, Helias. Don't be foolish. If those two thousand five hundred Germans were sent to the front, they might have killed who knows how many numbers of Americans. So, don't feel sorry. Have a glass of ouzo and be proud!" Yiapitzoglou tried to encourage me.

And so, I drank the ouzo, while Katerina (who innocently told her cousin, Yianni, about the German departure) patiently awaited a call from the German lieutenant.

"Now, you don't have to worry about me anymore, Yianni. The lieutenant and all of his friends must be dead," Katerina tearfully said a few days after the bombardment. "By the way," she added. "Do you still think that the Greeks will cut my hair after the war?"

"What? Cut your hair?" Yianni exclaimed. "Most likely, they will erect a statue of you, in your honor, Katerina!"

"What are you talking about? Why would they do that?" she asked.

"Do you know that the information you gave me about the Germans' departure is what brought the American planes here?" Yianni replied.

"What?" Katerina sat still, as though she were encased in stone. "Do you mean it? I killed them? I caused that misery? Did you know that my German lieutenant was an ancient Greek scholar and knew more about Greece than both of us? He told me that, after the war, he would return and marry me. He loved me and he loved Greece. He even wanted to live in Greece. I loved him, too. He read the Greek tragedies to me and now, I *became* his tragedy!" she cried.

"Please don't feel bad, Katerina. "You didn't know . . ." Yianni tried to comfort his cousin, who sobbed uncontrollably. Regretting that he had caused her so much pain, he continued, "It was *I* who did it!"

"What? Don't feel bad, don't feel sad? You tricked me!" Katerina wailed, furiously jumping on Yianni, hitting and kicking him, then finally collapsing to the floor in tears.

In the days that followed, Katerina suffered a nervous breakdown. Throughout her ordeal and her recovery, she continued to hope for and dream of the telephone call that would never come . . . .

Chapter 24

The Limits of Fortune

In the aftermath of the railroad bombing, Yiapitzoglou informed us that the Germans must have suspected the Americans' knowledge of the German soldiers' departure and our involvement in the sabotage. As a result, he instructed us to send only one message per day to Cairo and station a third watchman outside the factory.

"The Gestapo has many tricks up their sleeves, and will not stop in their search for us! From now on, be very careful!" he warned.

On one afternoon, German soldiers began installing telephone lines outside the factory. Noticing the available space inside, a supervising sergeant asked whether they could store equipment inside, so as avoid hauling it back and forth every day. Since no one was there to speak with the sergeant, he spoke with Kyria Eleni, who did not understand a word of his request. When the Germans brought their tools into our courtyard, Kyria Eleni opened the shutters to warn me, just as we had discussed. When I returned from my duties elsewhere, I noticed the clue, and was immediately alerted. Assuming that the Germans were inside the factory, I slowly turned, walked in the opposite direction, and awaited the rest of the work crew. I had half an hour until my next transmission.

Just as I spotted the Germans approaching, I signaled to Nikitas not to enter the factory.

"I'll get close to see whether or not the shutters are still open," Nikitas replied.

As he approached, Nikitas observed a German wearing a tool belt and Kyria Eleni, who began to close the shutters.

"Judging by his tool belt and general demeanor, I don't think that he's from the Gestapo," he said.

Both of us began to walk slowly toward the gate, believing (due to the closed shutters) that the Germans were not inside the factory. When we entered, Kyria Eleni greeted us and said, "The German left his tools in the courtyard, and that is why I opened the shutters."

"Thank you! Please continue to follow protocol whenever you suspect an intruder," I answered.

The following day, the German came to retrieve his equipment. "I'll be working in the area for the next ten days," he informed me. "Is it possible for us to continue to store tools in your courtyard?"

I could not deny his request. "Of course. I don't object at all."

Over the course of time, we became good friends. As it turned out, the sergeant was Austrian and very much against the war. At 4:00 p.m. quitting time, he would put the tools aside and sit and talk with us every day for about half an hour. An extremely friendly man, the sergeant enjoyed engaging me in conversation (in German) on such subjects as Greek mythology, history, and archaeology (in all of which he was very well versed).

I recall one particular exchange in which the sergeant spoke extensively about his friends and family at home. He was so immersed in thought, that he did not want to leave. The problem was that I had a 4:30 p.m. appointment with Cairo that day, and I did not know how I was going to get away. Nicos tapped his watch to remind me that it was time to assemble the wireless.

Finally, I interjected, "I have an important appointment, and I must end for today," I said, adding, "I'm so thirsty. Can I get you some water, as well?"

"No, thank you," the sergeant politely responded. "I've had a long day, and I'll just get a beer elsewhere."

Both of us rose. The sergeant went toward the gate, while I headed for the outer office. Unbeknownst to me, the sergeant began to collect his tools and, then, returned for a drink, after all. Without my knowledge, he approached the outer door and tried to open it—just as I had begun to assemble the wireless. I had my headphones on, and was preparing to send my message. As the sergeant opened the outer office door, Stavros jumped on him from behind, knocked him to the ground, and fell on top of him. Upon hearing the calamitous noise, I quickly took my headphones off, jumped out of my chair, and hurried into the outer office, closing the inner office door behind me.

"What is happening here, Stavros?" I asked, trying to remain calm.

"I changed my mind and came back for some water," the confused sergeant answered breathlessly.

"I am so sorry!" Stavros continuously repeated. Then, turning to me, he said in Greek, "I must have tripped and fell on him! If he wanted water, he should have told me. I would have brought it to him."

After a series of apologies on all sides, the Austrian took a drink of water and left. By sheer luck, two weeks prior to the incident, we had moved the wireless' table from the outer office into the inner room. Although the two rooms were separated by a glass door, the table with the wireless on top of it was, somehow, hidden from view. Had we left the wireless in its original location, the Austrian sergeant most certainly would have seen me with my headphones on; but, as things stood, we were almost sure that he did not. Chance was at work again and, miraculously, I had escaped what could have been a fatal mistake.

Later, when Yiapitzoglou returned that evening and heard what happened, his face turned red with anger. Being older and, consequently, more mature, he recognized the gravity of what had occurred. "What? I cannot believe what I'm hearing! You started to assemble the wireless while the Austrian was still on the premises? Never do that again!" he warned, pointing his finger at me. "Use your head and miss your scheduled transmission, instead of being caught! When there is a German, Austrian, or *anyone* else on the premises, don't dare to bring the wireless out again! If we were to be caught by the Gestapo, that would be out of our control; but to be caught while the German was still in the factory would have been plain stupidity!" he railed. Then, looking at Nikitas and Stavros, he added, "Have we lost our minds? How can we forgive ourselves?"

All of us agreed that a careless error had been made and that, moving forward, we would always comply with Yiapitzoglou's orders. Using the wireless had become so routine, that I neglected to employ the safeguards that I had repeatedly learned in Cairo. Our main objective had been not to compromise the mission; but, as time passed, we forewent the basic rules. Even Nikitas and Stavros did so; but they were untrained civilians—not soldiers.

Yiapitzoglou's reprimand deeply impacted me, and I began to recognize my careless transgressions. To clear my mind, I went for a walk, passing the Church of Saint Demetrios, the largest church in Salonica, with its streets lined with beggars. Evidence of the ravages of war loomed everywhere, and virtually no one was spared. Families were torn apart and killed, soldiers were either killed or captured, the partisans, resistance fighters, and hostages were shot. As I looked around me, I beheld the sights of abject poverty and desolation—beggars in tattered clothes reaching out and hoping to receive morsels of food or money to quell their pangs of starvation. I reached into my pockets, and gave them whatever loose change that I had, silently hoping for better days.

As I was leaving the area, I spotted an elderly woman, who looked like an admixture of my blind grandmother and the Virgin Mary as she beheld her son on the cross. Although the woman wore clean clothes, her downcast expression revealed that she was a beggar. I wondered what had brought her to that point in her life. Reaching into my pocket, I pulled out a wad of bills and placed them in her hand. Without looking at them, the woman turned to me and said, "Bless you, my son. May God be with you and protect you wherever you are."

"Thank you, and may God bless and help you also," I replied, taking care to leave before the other nearby beggars saw my monetary offering.

As per my custom, I took a different route on the way home. I noticed that, even though it was early afternoon, the streets were empty. Suddenly, I heard a pistol shot and spotted a man in a nearby window, beckoning me to approach slowly. "The Germans are shooting at the ELAS partisans, and you are going to get caught in the crossfire," the man said.

"Where can I go?" I asked.

"The neighborhood is surrounded, and the janitor of my building locked the entrance door. So, go down the street a little way to the overnight drugstore. The door there is usually open."

As I looked ahead, I saw the drugstore; and as I attempted to cross the street, I hit into a garbage can, which rolled right into the middle of the crosswalk. Upon seeing the moving object, the Germans began to fire at it. Bullets ricocheted around me, as the garbage can jumped up and down, hitting the sidewalk on both sides and making a tremendous noise. Hearing the resonant sound, I ran across the street and opened the pharmacy's door. I realized that, seconds later, the Germans would enter the store looking for partisans, and would search me.

"Is there a rear exit?" I asked the drugstore owner.

"Yes, there is," he replied. "But why would you have to leave? The Germans are looking for partisans, and you don't have to worry if you have an I.D. card."

Although the pharmacy owner was right, I knew that I would still be interrogated. Without any time to waste, I rushed out of the rear door and went home. On my way, my thoughts wandered. How fortunate I was not to get caught in that crossfire! Had circumstances ended tragically, Yiapitzoglou and every one of my colleagues—including the OSS—would have thought that the Gestapo had killed me while I was trying to escape. What are the odds of being saved so many times, only to be shot just because I happened to be walking down the street?

"What happened?" Sultanitsa asked, as I walked in with a distressed expression on my face.

I recounted my story about being in the wrong place at the wrong time—in a crossfire between ELAS partisans and Germans, and about the elderly beggar woman that I had met while passing the Church of Saint Demetrios.

As she hung on my every word, Sultanitsa remarked, "That woman *must* have been the Virgin Mary, testing whether or not you are a good man. By her mercy, she gave you protection and spared you."

I sat silent, so wishing to believe in the miracle of divine intervention; and I began to wonder just how long my good fortune would last.

Chapter 25

The Moment of Truth

With the destruction of the railway station, OSS Cairo focused its attention on ships' departure, particularly that of an Italian minelaying ship that was docked in Salonica's harbor. With the intention of sinking the ship, OSS Cairo repeatedly requested that our informants working in the harbor area notify Yiapitzoglou as soon as the ship was ready to leave port.

Soon (on a Tuesday, as I recall), we received word that the ship was loaded with provisions, and were assured that the vessel would leave within a few days—by the following Thursday, at the latest. When I notified Cairo, I received the reply, "Good news, Cando. Keep up the good work." That was the last sentence of OSS Cairo's message.

Meanwhile, in that month and year, September 1944, the Allies were resisting the Germans on all fronts. Almost all of the German troops had withdrawn from Greece, just before the Russians could cut off their retreat to Germany. The previous winter, hundreds of thousands of Germans died in Russia, and the Russians were pushing them to their country's borders. By that time, everyone knew that Hitler would be defeated.

The Austrian sergeant with whom I had become close friends was convinced that the Germans had lost the war, and dreaded returning to Austria and facing possible confrontation with the Russians. "When the war ends, I would like to go back to Austria; but if I happen to be taken prisoner, I would prefer to be in the hands of the Americans or the English—God forbid, not a Russian prisoner. They will kill me for sure, Helias. They will kill us all!" he said. "You know, we were forced to become German soldiers. We had no choice," he added.

In conversing with the Austrian sergeant—as on many occasions—I had time to pause and reflect on how many innocents were involved in the senseless engagement of war— no doubt, far more than my young mind could comprehend. Constantly poised between life and death, an unknown force was shielding me. Inexplicably, either by happenstance or divine intervention, I was being protected, and I just accepted that fact, without seeking answers—not then, anyway. Analysis had no place in the theater of war. Rather, my focus was on our informants working at strategic locations, reporting back to us at every turn. Spyros, for example, worked as a janitor in a secure area of Gestapo headquarters, supervised by a German guard.

Two days before the Italian minelayer was scheduled to leave the harbor (on Tuesday), Spyros went to work at 5 p.m., as usual, and began to clean the building. As he did so, he noticed that a lieutenant was still working in his office. Typically, the building was vacant at that hour—except, of course, for Spyros and the guards. Accompanied by the Gestapo guard, Spyros went into the main office and emptied the wastepaper baskets. When he entered the lieutenant's office, the latter said to the guard, "Leave, and I will watch him."

When the guard left, the lieutenant beckoned Spyros to sit down. As chills pervaded his body, Spyros obeyed.

"Listen carefully, Spyros. Don't be afraid," the lieutenant began in fairly decent Greek. "I want to speak with you candidly. Are you aware of any patriotic organization?"

Spyros felt his knees weaken. "No, sir. What do you mean?"

"I know that you are aware of *some* organization. Whichever one it is, is its purpose to discuss our prisoners' situation or other matters? Why do you meet someone in the park on Fridays? Is it the same organization, perhaps, which knew about a regiment departing from a train station? We have concluded that it must have been an American organization—the one that sent the information a few weeks ago which bombed our troop train filled with German soldiers . . . you know."

Spyros turned pale, stopped the lieutenant in his tracks, and managed to deny his connection to any patriotic organization. In truth, he never did belong to any such group. However, six months prior to Spyros' intimidating encounter with the lieutenant, his friend, Jim (who was also a friend of Yiapitzoglou), informed him that he was, in fact, a member of a patriotic group in Salonica; but he did not mention the organization's affiliation with either the Americans, British, or Greeks. Every Friday, the two men would meet at the park to discuss the presence of hostages or prisoners at Gestapo headquarters.

"I realize that you are involved somehow, Spyros. Don't worry. If you tell me, you will be safe," the lieutenant repeated.

Thinking that he was being tricked, Spyros insisted, "No, sir. I assure you that I don't know of any patriotic organization."

"Stop right there! Spyros, if you don't cooperate, I will show your file and the pictures that we have taken of you at the park to the Gestapo chief, and you know what that means," the lieutenant warned. "Even if you do belong to an organization, we have concluded that you are not a very important source. We made this determination when we intentionally left important documents around, and you did not even attempt to look at them. So, again, don't be afraid and listen to what I have to say."

"Please continue," Spyros replied, calming down a bit.

"The Germans have lost the war on all fronts," the lieutenant began, with a sad expression. "Soon, before the war ends, we will leave Greece, and most of us will be sent to the crucial eastern front, which requires immediate reinforcement. It is likely that I will be sent there to assist in stopping the Russians. If I end up as a prisoner in Russian hands, I will be killed. If not, I will be tortured for many years. Do you understand what I am saying to you?"

Pretending to be oblivious, Spyros simply replied, "Please continue, sir."

"Since we are close to capturing the American spies, I have a proposal for you," the lieutenant said. "The Americans have a radio, operating out of Agia Triada. If you help me, I will help them. Do what I tell you."

Spyros sat silent and listened, unsure of the lieutenant's every word and intention.

"On Thursday, all German radios will be silenced, as per the Gestapo chief's order, so as to easily locate the Americans' radio and position. We are *certain* that their radio will transmit messages on Thursday, and we will concentrate our search in Agia Triada. The capture there will be promising. So, for your own good and the good of the American spy, tell him to cease communications this Thursday and move far away from the area of Agia Triada." The lieutenant paused and looked at Spyros intently. "Now, Spyros, you may be asking yourself why I am telling you these secrets. Well, I will tell you." The lieutenant lowered his voice. "Besides speaking Greek, I also speak a little Russian. Therefore, I *will* be sent to the Russian front where I do not want to be—in the midst of a war that, sooner or later, we will ultimately lose. While I'm awaiting my orders to leave Greece, why would I care whether or not the American wireless is discovered this Thursday? I have thought this through, and I want to help you to escape capture on that day; but, in return, I hope to be taken prisoner by a member of your organization which is, hopefully, American.

Spyros could not believe his ears. He realized that during the war, people would do anything to save their lives and the lives of their families—no matter how impossible or incredible the measure would be. Quick-wittedness, spontaneity, and decision-making (either well-planned or miscalculated) were, ultimately, subject to the whims of fate, and outcomes were always unpredictable. With this in mind, Spyros continued to be silent.

"Finish up whatever cleaning you have to do in this room, and allow the guard to follow you through the rest of the building. Tell the organization what we have discussed, and inform me of their response within a few days," the lieutenant said, realizing from Spyros' non-responsiveness, that he feared for his life.

Spryos could not wait to leave, so that he could speak with Jim; but he was afraid that he might be followed. Spyros recalled every word of the conversation. Would anyone believe a word of what the lieutenant had said—especially about his intent to surrender and become a prisoner of war? As he got up to leave, Spyros could not conceal his trembling hands or the perspiration streaming down his face. With the guard at his side, he went on his way, continued to clean the offices, and quickly finished for the evening. Then, he went straight to Jim's house, not caring whether the Gestapo followed him, after all. The Germans already had Jim's picture and knew that the patriotic group to which he belonged was, most likely, American. *How could I have been so foolish? I'm going to kill that man*, Spyros thought to himself, writhing in anger.

Upon entering Jim's home, Spyros found his friend enjoying dinner with his wife, and the two asked him to join them for a drink.

"I think that you should pour yourself a large drink, Jim, especially after you hear what I'm about to tell you," he said, trying to remain calm.

After dinner, Spyros asked Jim to go outside for a walk through the back alleyways. They were not too far from the house, when Spyros turned to Jim and railed, "You son of a bitch! Why the hell didn't you tell me that you were working for the Americans? Why did I have to find out the hard way?"

"What's the difference? All of the organizations work for one common goal—to defeat the Germans. But let's get this straight. Who told you that the organization is American? For your information, they are right. It *is* American!" Jim exclaimed.

"Yes, and I received that information from the Germans— specifically from *a Gestapo officer!*" Spyros replied, still seething with anger.

Jim laughed. "Come on, now, Spyros! Tell me how you *really* found out."

"Look Jim, I had only one drink, and I am not drunk. I'm telling you the truth! This is not a joke, as you believe it to be. They have our photos."

Jim glanced around nervously, as Spyros recounted his entire discussion with the German officer, including his wish to become an American prisoner. Jim could not believe the truth of what he was hearing; but observing how much Spyros was trembling, he began to take him more seriously. That evening, Spyros called Yiapitzoglou, who was equally stunned, and immediately phoned Nicos the following morning (Wednesday).

That day, all of us met at the factory, where Yiapitzoglou reiterated Spyros' information. Up to that point, we surmised that the Gestapo knew more about our organization than we imagined; but, no matter how many informants we had, we could not prove our suspicion. Hearing Yiapitoglou speak of Spyros' conversation with the German officer sent us into a tailspin and, for the first time, we feared that our end was near. I thought the worst. If the Gestapo had photos of Spyros and Jim at the park, they would surely torture Jim until he divulged the names of everyone in our organization. *They will work tirelessly until they find me—the American*, I said to myself, shuddering at the thought.

Yiapitzoglou sensed our panic. "First of all, let's calm down. The Gestapo is aware that we are operating in Agia Triada. Since the Italian ship will, most likely leave port tomorrow (Thursday), they know that we will be on the air. However, no one knows anyone's name or address."

Everything that Cosmas Yiapitzoglou said resonated with truth and good sense. I did not know where anyone in our organization lived (though Nicos and Cosmas knew my address), and no one knew anyone else's code names.

"I understand why the Germans chose Thursday to cease operation of their radios: they want to locate me; but they don't know exactly who I am or where in Agia Triada I am located," I remarked, feeling somewhat more at ease.

Almost immediately, Yiapitzoglou interrupted. "Our first concern is to save ourselves. We must believe what the lieutenant says, and cease to operate the wireless tomorrow—even if he is lying. Do not go to the factory at all! Keep a lookout for radio trucks circulating around here from today, Wednesday afternoon, through this Sunday . . . the trucks should be all over Agia Triada tomorrow. Then, we will decide what to do later. Let's see if this German lieutenant is telling the truth." Yiapitzoglou ended with a look around the room, finally fixing his gaze upon me.

"Please listen carefully," I said. "Cairo has made numerous requests that we not forget to send the Italian ship's departure date," I ventured to remind Cosmas, who continued to stare at me.

"Helias, are you blind?" Cosmas nearly shouted. "The Germans are laying a trap for you, using the departure of the Italian ship as bait. Do you want to go on the air tomorrow and satisfy the Germans by slicing your own throat? If any of us come to the factory on Thursday, all of us will be shot! If you *must* send the information about the ship's departure, do so this afternoon, not tomorrow!" Yiapitzoglou sternly commanded me.

"But the ship hasn't left the harbor yet! And suppose it doesn't leave at all!" I quickly replied. "Do you want the Americans to send planes to sink a ship that hasn't left yet, and endanger the lives of more American airmen and Greek civilians for nothing? Remember the train station! We'll wait until tomorrow morning, and find out whether or not the ship will actually leave port. When your men notify us of the departure, I'll send a short message tomorrow morning—as quickly as possible," I insisted.

"I cannot stop you from doing your duty or order you to stay away from the factory. After all, you are an American soldier and must think like one, first and foremost; but I repeat: you are endangering yourself and others. All of us might be caught. Don't forget that a heroic decision can make you a dead hero," Yiapitzoglou warned.

All the while, Nicos remained silent, listening attentively. Then, privately, he told me, "If you go to the factory tomorrow, I will inform Nikitas and Stavros to be there also and warn them of impending dangers."

"I will be there at 8:30 a.m.," I replied, "and if the ship hasn't left the harbor, I won't send a message to Cairo at the previously designated hour, 9:15 a.m."

As we were leaving, Yiapitzoglou cautioned me, yet again. "Think twice before you decide to send that message, Helias! By all appearances, we have been set up—tricked to be on the air—and you have fallen for it. The Gestapo is like a fox. Just once, think of yourself, instead of your superiors. Don't think of me or anyone else. Even the German lieutenant—if he is telling the truth—is willing to become an American prisoner because that is his only recourse for saving his own life." My closest companion and team member, who had been at my side since Izmir, squeezed my shoulder.

When I went to the factory at 8:30 a.m. the following morning, I found Nicos there with the two lookouts, Nikitas and Stavros. "Two of Yiapitzoglou's informants called this morning to say that the ship is lifting its anchors. Even as we speak, the ship is most likely leaving the harbor," Nicos informed me.

"Thank you," I replied. "I'll have plenty of time to write and code the message to Cairo by 9:15 a.m. Since you are not needed here anymore, you can leave. At least, you don't have to be around in the forthcoming critical moments. The fact that you broke the news to me was enough. What you can do now is put Nikitas and Stavros on alert outside. If they notice anything strange or any type of radio equipment anywhere, tell them to warn me immediately. My life may depend entirely upon them."

Nikitas and Stavros assured me that they would never abandon their posts, and I trusted them. Both armed with pistols, as usual, they went on their way, one to cut wood in the front yard, the other, on a walk around the block.

I sat down and coded a message of twenty words, not more than five letters per word, *Italian ship has left port.* At 9:00 a.m., I set up the wireless, and I was ready at precisely 9:15 a.m., when I heard Cairo calling, "Cando, Cando." I answered back with a special signal code, indicating that I had an urgent message, warning Cairo not to interrupt.

I began to send the message, and had not advanced even three quarters through it, when I heard someone talking in the courtyard. The door flung open and Nikitas jumped into the room, throwing the gun on the table and screaming, "German trucks are surrounding the block! They will be here in two minutes! Get out of here! Save your life, and run to the exit!"

Standing near the gate, Stavros saw Nikitas running out. He came in, also dropped his gun on the table, and ran out, leaving me entirely alone with my headphones still on. Unaware of what was happening, Cairo signaled me to continue my message. I signaled back to headquarters to change frequency, and when I received a response, I finished the message. Looking back, I can hardly comprehend how I summoned the courage to continue that message. Even as I write, I can hear the closeness of those trucks so vividly—those sounds of seventy years ago that I detected even with headphones covering my ears.

Cairo tried to signal me again, but I refused to receive their repeated requests for me to accept their messages. Ignoring those communications, I removed my headphones; and for a moment, I stood motionless—as if frozen in my tracks, not knowing what to do. I looked at the wireless' table with the .45 caliber, Nikitas and Stavros' guns, and the box with two grenades. *Should I try to hide the wireless and the weapons? Why not just try to escape as fast as possible?* I thought.

Suspecting that I was surrounded and that, at any moment, the Germans would raid the factory, I determined to leave everything as it was—including the wireless. *Let them find the wireless. The most important thing now is to save myself,* I thought. Thus, leaving everything on the table, I put the .45 caliber gun in hand and the two grenades in my pocket, and walked to the front gate, toward the street. I figured that, in the event of a raid, I could throw the grenades at the Gestapo, escape through the window that led to my neighbors' yard, and exit from their gate into the street. If I were going to be captured or killed, I intended to die fighting—as any other devoted, well-trained soldier would do. I held my breath and just kept walking, certain of only one thing: this was the moment of truth.

Chapter 26

Another Waltz With Lady Luck

Peering through the wrought iron gate, I observed the absence of Germans and trucks surrounding the block. *Where could they be?* I wondered. I thought about going out and mingling with the people, laughing and walking casually in the street, as if nothing happened. Then, my mind focused on the guns and grenades in my possession. At that moment, I decided that it would be too dangerous to stay on the street with the weapons in my pocket; so, I decided to go back into the factory and drop them in the secret hole in the factory floor.

Once inside, I stared at the wireless and the battery (which was still connected), and determined that I should take precautions and toss it into the hole, as well. At that moment, I went into the street to join the others, thinking that, as before, nothing of consequence was happening.

Surprisingly, the casual scene that I had witnessed just minutes before was interrupted by loud shouts of *"Raus, raus!"* ("Out, out!") from German soldiers, dressed in black with high boots, commanding every civilian in sight. As I exited the gate, I turned quickly and heard the Germans approaching from about one hundred feet away. Thinking that they had spotted me and were coming for me, I ran inside the yard, and into the office. *My God! Now, I'm trapped in here without a weapon. My only chance is to escape via the rear window!* I hurried to my only outlet, the window facing the neighbor's yard.

Through the window, I saw two German officers chasing a man in our backyard, and a pistol shot rang out as he ran toward our rear wall. Behind the wall was another neighbor's yard which the man tried to reach. As he jumped over it, a second shot rang out. Without a moment to waste, I could not stop to figure out whether he had been captured or killed.

While pondering my next step and keeping a watchful eye on the front gate through the glass door, I saw a German police officer, wearing a large metal plate on his chest, enter our gate, accompanied by another German soldier. Both of them held guns in their hands. *These men must come from the trucks that Nikitas observed surrounding the block*, I said to myself. *The Gestapo will enter the office and question me. I must avoid capture!* I thought, deciding to escape from the rear window by simply pushing it open gently and jumping out, so as not to make any noise and raise the Gestapo's suspicions.

In my haste to get out of the factory quickly, I acted carelessly. Since the window frame was so loosely held in the wall, it collapsed as soon as I touched it. In fact, the entire frame moved outwards and, without thinking, I followed it. The window, glass frame and I just tumbled out to the ground, five feet below into the neighbor's yard. The broken window frame, glass and my fall on top of everything made a huge noise. As I tried to pull myself out of the wreckage, I was afraid that I was injured. Fortunately, however, I discovered that my hands were not bloodied—and, even more significantly, the Germans were not chasing me. So, I quickly ran for the yard's exit, and began to mingle with the numerous pedestrians in the street. Fortunately, the landlord was not in the yard, and the German officers were not playing bridge at that moment.

I expected that, with all of the noise, the German officer who was in my yard probably ran to the window, discovered that it was broken, and realized that someone must have escaped. For all I knew, he was watching me in the yard at that very moment! With that terrifying thought in mind, I should have fled through the back roads. Instead of getting away, however, I decided to satisfy my curiosity and see what was happening on the corner of the block, near our entrance gate.

Hiding myself among pedestrians, I proceeded toward the corner and saw a large enclosed truck, with two German soldiers in front, operating two triangulation instruments with rotating circular antennas. Behind them was an empty seat, and in back of the truck were five German soldiers (two on one side, three on the other). I immediately recognized the absence of the police officer and the sixth soldier who had probably occupied the empty seat, and realized that they must have been the ones whom I had seen previously entering our yard. In all likelihood, they were speaking with the German who had been chasing our neighbor, no doubt saying that he was tracking down a wireless. *For all I know, the Gestapo is searching every square inch of the factory, never suspecting that, in a covered hole, under a piece of moveable plywood and a pile of lint that covered it, was all of our equipment: the wireless, the battery, three guns and two grenades. It will take another miracle for the Gestapo to miss our hiding place!* I told myself.

Looking ahead two hundred feet to our entrance gate, I decided to remain in the area and walk in the direction of a German car containing two passengers in front. Mingling with the crowd again, I walked closer and observed a neighbor sitting in the vehicle—the very man who had tried to jump over the low wall. As I passed by the car, I tried to immerse myself in the crowd behind other pedestrians, so that he would not see me. In all likelihood, he belonged to a resistance organization and, somehow, the Germans had discovered his name. I felt for him deeply. Just by a twist of fate, he was there, in that car, and I was a passerby. The situation could very well have been reversed.

As I reached the gate and peered inside, I saw no one in the yard. Immediately, I realized that the German officers must have noticed the broken window and concluded that the foreign wireless operator for whom they were looking had escaped. As a result, they would probably conduct a thorough search of the entire area and, most likely, find the concealed hole and everything in it.

I walked away from the entrance, intending to verify Nikitas' information about the three trucks surrounding the block. So, I proceeded to the next corner and, then, to a farther corner at the opposite end of the block. To my surprise, I saw a similar truck on both sides. One German officer stood outside of each truck, both biting their fingernails as they waited for their triangulation instruments to pick up my signal that did not seem to come. I was gratified to see their anxiety. In those tense moments, I recalled learning in spy school that once the Germans located the block on which a given wireless might be located, they would hide their instruments in houses around the block until they honed in on the exact location and could catch the wireless. In my case, they did not count on the fact that I had secured guards to keep an eye on me. If Nikitas had not come in time to warn me, and the German had not issued his warning about the Gestapo's readiness to capture me, I most definitely would have sent another message and, consequently, have fallen into enemy hands.

For three hours, I inconspicuously sat at a sidewalk cafe, watching them from a distance, and thanking God at every moment that I had escaped. All the while, I never ceased thinking about whether the Germans had discovered the wireless and the other items.

Three hours passed slowly. After circling all around the block one more time, the trucks left. At that moment, the thought occurred to me that if the German officer in my yard had discovered anything suspicious, he would have summoned the other two trucks, and all three would have been parked in front of our gate; but since I saw all three trucks leaving from their original triangulation site, I surmised that the hiding hole had not been discovered. Obviously, the German officer had left the dirt pile of lint undisturbed, so as not to soil or tarnish his shiny black boots. Perhaps, the German officer was blinded by the curse upon the building left by the Jewish factory owner, who had to abandon his lifetime investment and was forced to flee to save his and his family's life. Clearly, Lady Luck was on my side, yet again.

My thoughts wandered once more to the German lieutenant who had saved my life. Had it not been for his warning, I would, most certainly, have sent at least one more telegram regarding the ship's departure. In that case, I would have received at least one more return message which, in turn, would have kept me on the air for a longer period of time. *Yes, the German lieutenant was, in fact, telling the truth. We should tell Cairo about him and have him surrender to us at the proper time*, I thought to myself, sympathizing with the lieutenant's predicament. In fact, I wished that I could have gone to Gestapo headquarters, then and there, and expressed my indebtedness to the lieutenant; but, after all that Lady Luck had done on my behalf, it would neither have been fair nor prudent to leave her all alone on the dance floor.

That evening, our group met at a quiet table in the back of a restaurant. We embraced one another and were so grateful to be safe. Yiapitzoglou squeezed my shoulders. "I told you to listen to the German and not to go, but you put your duty first," he said proudly.

Then, Nikitas approached me. "Helias, forgive me for running out without even asking if you needed any help. I was so scared," he said, with a sullen expression.

"You did what you had to do, and you did your job well," I replied. "Besides, if the Germans had come in and you were there, you would, most likely, have been killed. They were after me, not you. Your warning saved me."

I then turned to Stavros, who was equally apologetic about leaving me to fend for myself; but I reassured him that he had no other responsibility than to provide the appropriate alerts. Sensing my earnestness, both men felt more at ease.

Finally, Nicos also expressed remorse. "Helias, I thought that if you were caught and tortured, you would have told them about me. Since everyone in Salonica knows my family, there would have been nowhere for us to hide, and I felt the urgent need to flee. I'm so sorry."

"I told you to leave, since you weren't needed. Anyway, you did your job. I realize that you are a well-known merchant in Salonica, and before the torturer's hand ever could have touched me, I would have died with the poison pill in my mouth. Your name never would have been revealed."

At that point, Yiapitzoglou interrupted me, shuddering at the mere thought of what I had said. He filled our wine glasses, and we toasted to one another's good health, longevity and prosperity. "Don't send any more messages until we're sure that the Gestapo has stopped looking for us," he suggested.

"Does any one of you think that the German lieutenant might be waiting to hear from us regarding his forewarning?" Shouldn't we show our appreciation for his advice?" I said, feeling intensely indebted to the source of my survival.

Everyone sat silent and just glanced at one another with angry expressions. I tried to break the ice by making my colleagues laugh. "I thought that, maybe, the proper thing would be for all of us to go to Gestapo headquarters and introduce ourselves. I would say, 'I am Helias Nikolaou, a corporal in the United States Army and a member of the OSS. This is Cosmas Yiapitzoglou, a Greek Naval Intelligence officer and a trusted OSS representative in Salonica; and these are our guards, Nicos, Nikitas, and Stavros. First of all, Lieutenant, we would like to thank you for notifying us about the Gestapo's plans to seize our wireless; and secondly, we want to inform you that we are at your service and will accept you as a prisoner, whenever you wish.'" Suddenly, the charged silence transformed into uproarious laughter.

"Since you are the only American soldier, it would only be fitting and proper for you to go alone to Gestapo headquarters and offer the lieutenant the terms of his capture." Yiapitzoglou suggested.

Laughter rang out again and, then, we quieted down.

Cosmas Yiapitzoglou (1944)

"To tell you the truth," I said, seriously, "we have to think about the lieutenant eventually. After all, he saved my life and here we are, happy and laughing, instead of preparing for a funeral. I don't think that we should make a decision tonight, but let's not exclude the possibility of helping him altogether. Months from now, if we hear that the Russians have killed all of their captured prisoners, wouldn't you feel gratified that at least one has been saved?"

At that point, Nicos raised his hand to silence me. "I think that you should forget about it," he said, as his face turned crimson with resurgent anger. "If he expects help from us, he is stupid! That is impossible! To think that we would endanger ourselves to help him become a prisoner of the Americans! He will not dupe us with clever Gestapo games. Don't forget that he is still SS, and they are fanatics. So, you can forget about talking to the lieutenant!"

With that, Nicos got up to leave, while Yiapitoglou grabbed my arm, saying, "Spyros has fled. He left his job, took his family, and on the same night, left Salonica for Yiannena (a city miles away). Jim has also fled, but I don't know where he has gone."

Spyros' disappearance must have enraged the lieutenant. Therefore, all of us agreed that we would wait for a couple of more weeks before even trying to send more messages. I told Yiapitzoglou that, from the tone of my last message, Cairo must think the worst—that the Gestapo had captured or killed me. However, Lady Luck had given me her dance card again, and I was very grateful to have become so unconsciously proficient at her waltz.

Helias In Salonica, Just Before the Germans Left (1944)

Chapter 27

The End of a Nightmare

After our celebratory dinner, my friends and I left the restaurant and went home. To my surprise, Annoula was waiting for me to come home, as I usually did in the early afternoon. *Oh, my God! I hope that she and her friends are not going to serenade me in my present state and, somehow, see the fear in my eyes of the Gestapo chasing me!* I thought. Even though it had literally been only a few hours since that narrow escape, I still could not believe that I had not been ensnared in their plans and tricks.

"You have been avoiding me, Helias," Annoula complained. "I'm very glad that we're friends, and I would like to go on another date with you, like the one we had weeks ago, when we ate ice cream at the seashore café."

Annoula had barely finished speaking, when her parents came out, shook my hand, and invited me to dine with them. Although I had just eaten dinner with my fellow OSS team members, I felt compelled to accept the invitation. Apparently, Annoula's parents had already approved of me as their future son-in-law. If they only had known who I was and the nature of my business in Salonica, they would have kept their daughter far away from the American spy, the only American soldier in that city—a Gestapo target, for whom they would not mind killing hundreds just to catch! In any case, I was glad to sit and socialize with Annoula's parents and take my mind off my recent escape and all that I had been through.

"I still can't forget how you managed to get those theater tickets for us, even though the seats were all sold out. You got us the best ones in the house! Everyone—even the actors—stared at us, as though we were dignitaries," the professor remarked.

"Well, I have friends in high places," I said glibly, remembering how I procured those tickets with a handful of cash and cleverly averted suspicion.

Everyone laughed, and for the rest of the evening, I managed to dodge questions about myself—where I came from, and how I came to be successful at such a young age. Telling harmless falsehoods was my only escape, and I thought that I had managed to make the professor accept my stories, when all the while, he was just being polite by not asking too many questions. Before the night ended, I found a chance to be alone with Annoula, whose warm kiss vanquished the terror that had gripped me over the previous few days.

Time passed, and an increasing number of Germans were leaving Salonica with their possessions on their backs, walking to bus terminals and train depots, with their heads down, most likely contemplating the hard days ahead, many on the Russian front. From what I understood, the Germans feared the Russians most of all.

All of us were still avoiding the area of the factory after our close encounter with the Germans, seizing every opportunity to take time for ourselves. On one warm summer day in 1944, I decided to enter a bar to get a refreshing cold beer. As I turned on the bar stool to observe who was entering, I saw two

Germans carrying their belongings on their backs in huge duffel bags, one holding a wooden stick. The latter sat next to me, and spurred my memory. Something about that man and that stick looked oddly familiar. *Oh, my God!* I thought to myself. *It's Hans!* Suddenly, my boyhood encounter with Hans in Archanes flooded my mind. He was the officer who, in an effort to recruit me for forced labor, chased me on the terrace of my house and, later, hit me with that identical wooden stick! No wonder it looked familiar! Hans was probably bound for the Russian front where he, himself, would be forced into hard labor. The cliché is true: "Whatever goes around, comes around."

As soon as I recognized Hans, I turned the other way, thinking that he didn't recognize me; but, even if he did, he was no longer a threat. Since my first encounter with him, I had worked my way out of more serious and dangerous situations; and I was, therefore, armed with greater self-confidence. I had dined in the presence of other German officers before and I had gone to bars where German soldiers drank; so, it was a non-issue that I was sitting next to Hans at that moment. In one instant, I felt like turning to him and saying, "Hey, remember me, you bastard?" Then, I paused, kept my words in check, and left without speaking to him.

Within a couple of weeks, the streets were emptied of German soldiers, where there had once been eighty thousand (not including the Bulgarians). The Greek partisans were making their presence known, and because their supply lines were stretched, the Germans quickly realized that they would have to leave the area soon; otherwise, they would risk being cut off by the advancing Russians.

After a meeting with Yiapitzoglou, we decided to return to the factory and begin to communicate with Cairo again. We were sure that the triangulation units had given up and left, and that the remaining units would not care to conduct a search for and find us any longer, since almost all of the German troops had gone from the area, and the remaining few would soon be on their way out. Luckily, we found everything as we had left it, despite the absence of locks on the office and factory doors, and the hole in the corner of the factory's floor (which was fairly easy to detect). I went to the spot, brushed aside the lint, opened the cover of the hole, and found the wireless.

Wondering whether Cairo had given up on me, I connected the battery and the wireless, and sent my signal at the usual time, 10:00 a.m., "Cando, Cando." First slowly, then gradually faster, the signal came back. The increasing speed indicated how glad the operator was to hear me again. I had been absent for a month, and OSS headquarters must have thought that I had been captured. I sent a brief message, explaining why our communication had ceased and how close we had come to being caught. The operator responded again, expressing how happy everyone was to resume communication with me.

Thereafter, I kept busy, sending one or two telegrams daily regarding the schedules of departing ships, trains, or groups of trucks, all heading north. The final German evacuation was approaching. On one particular day, our contacts in the harbor notified Yiapitzoglou that the Germans were placing dynamite along the harbor's entire length, including the warehouses that contained thousands of tons of wheat and corn, where the Germans had stored the grain for their soldiers.

"We can't stop the Germans from lining the harbor with explosives, but it would be a pity if they destroyed those warehouses filled with so much food. The people are starving!" I noted.

Yiapitzoglou agreed, and sent someone to notify the archbishop to speak with the German high command in Salonica to request a cessation of their final act of savagery. So many people were starving, and the destruction of the warehouses would not have any effect on their withdrawal. Sadly, the German generals were impervious to reason.

The following day, dynamite exploded along the harbor and destroyed the warehouses, throwing hundreds of tons of precious grain into the air. Thousands of hungry birds filled the sky to feast, while thousands of starving Greeks in Salonica dreamt of bread that would never grace their tables.

Since the public was warned to remain at a distance, hordes of people poured into the streets to await the panoramic event, blaspheming the conquerors who, even at the last moment, showed no mercy for the people of Salonica. It was a hot autumn day, at the end of October, 1944, when we witnessed the last of the German infantry depart from the city in long columns, most of them advancing on foot, with their belongings on their backs, their heavy guns loaded on mules and donkeys.

"Leave, you animals! Russia is waiting for you!" the Greeks called out with raised fists, as they watched Hitler's once mighty army leave Salonica with their heads lowered in shame. As soon as the last soldier departed, all of the church bells began to ring, and everyone ran into the streets, disbelieving that their woes had come to an end.

"We are free! God has saved us!" Young and old cried, some dancing and singing patriotic songs, others destroying anything that called forth the memory of the German invasion. After three long years, the nightmare had ended, just as on the day of Greece's liberation from the Turks. Although most of the people appeared to be thin and pale from hunger, the Germans' departure resurrected their smiles.

As for me, I experienced a huge relief that I did not have to worry any more about the Gestapo or SS and, even more significantly, none of us had been captured or killed. It would take months, at least, for me to feel free and able to walk down a street without having to look over my shoulder, take an alternative route home, and wonder whether anyone was following me. However, just knowing that I had survived and accomplished my mission well filled me with pride. I thanked God, who had saved me countless times in perilous circumstances—too many to recall all at once. Years would pass before the memories would flood my mind again.

Chapter 28

❦

Farewell Salonica

After the Germans left, the ELAS partisans quickly followed close behind, as they shouted to the crowds that they had liberated Greece from the Germans. Since they were inspired by communistic ideas, Cairo suggested that I not reveal my identity as an American soldier to anyone— at least, not until the situation settled down. The fear that had once terrorized Salonica resurfaced—and escalated—as informants and pro-Nazi sympathizers were rounded up. What those unfortunate Greeks didn't realize at the time (though others had warned them) was that they had signed their own death warrants. Thirsting for blood, the partisans hunted down the traitors, as well as those who lined their pockets after four years of German rule. Some escaped and went into hiding, while others who were not so lucky begged for mercy. The partisans killed anyone who collaborated with the Germans, and I saw many injustices committed—and many dead people in the streets. While we waited to see what would happen next, I sent my daily telegrams to OSS-Cairo regarding my observations. Finally, the English and Americans arrived in Greece.

At home in Sultanitsa's house, I found my companion with a hammer in her hand, trying to tear down the walls in her kitchen and washroom.

"What in the world are you doing?" I yelled.

She began to recount the fate of the family which had once owned the houses where we lived—a story that I had heard all too often. The three houses in this complex belonged to a Greek Jew, who had a thriving lumber business before the war. He and his family were forced to flee when the Germans arrived, and could not take their gold or possessions with them. "So, they buried everything inside their home," Sultanitsa said. "A man living in the house told me so. I believe that some of their possessions may be hidden in the kitchen walls or beneath the toilet. Please, Helias! Help me to open the wall and find the gold. The owner may never return. For all we know, he may be dead. In that case, it's better that I find it, instead of someone else," she pleaded.

In order to satisfy Sultanitsa's curiosity, I reluctantly tore down one portion of the wall. Not finding anything, I tried to placate her. "You were misinformed," I said. "We are tearing down walls for nothing. After all, you are still living in this house, which does not even belong to you." Sultanitsa finally agreed, and eventually the walls were repaired.

A month after the Germans departed from Salonica, the political climate became more unsettled. Of course, people were ecstatic to see the Germans retreat, and were glad to witness the English army parading down the streets of Salonica. They were pleased, as well, with King George of Greece, who had escaped to Egypt; however, those who sided with the communists were not so content.

While I waited for my orders, I received word that an American colonel was coming to Salonica and wanted to know how he could contact and meet with Yiapitzoglou and me. I sent a coded message with my address, still unsure whether that was the right thing to do; but feeling more at liberty, I sent the telegram (minus Yiapitzoglou's address, which I never knew). That was my last message to Cairo.

Two days passed; and while I was having breakfast with Sultanitsa, the bell rang and she went to open the door. Running back inside to find me, she exclaimed, "A car with an American flag is parked outside. Can you go and see what this is about?"

Immediately, I declared, "They're coming for me!" I could not hide my huge smile.

"For you?" Sultanitsa asked with a puzzled expression. "Why?"

"I'll tell you in a moment," I said, as I rushed outside. In the American jeep, a uniformed American colonel sat in the backseat; in front were two Greek-American soldiers, both of them carrying automatic weapons.

When I reached the car, the colonel came out and shook my hand. Squeezing both of my shoulders, he said, "I am very glad to know you, Corporal Doundoulakis. I have heard you've done a wonderful job. Congratulations! I could have sent the two soldiers to pick you up, but I wanted to personally come along and see the place in which you had been working for myself. Please get your belongings and come with us. The OSS has rented a small hotel on the waterfront, where you will stay until you leave Salonica."

"It will take me some time to get my things in order, Colonel. Also, with your permission, I must inform my friends and acquaintances of my real identity. After all, I have kept that secret since I've been here."

"Don't worry, Corporal, I understand. You have my permission. Take all the time you need. We will wait for you," the colonel replied.

By that time, all traffic had stopped in front of my house. Hundreds of people who had never seen an American soldier in Salonica before asked one another what was going on. Everyone on the block came out of their homes, curious about what the Americans wanted from me—by all accounts and appearances a successful merchant doing business on their block. Across the street, my girlfriend, Annoula, was outside with her mother, making inquiries.

Before I went inside to collect my things, I seized the moment to reveal my true identity to Sultanitsa and explain the reason for the Americans' presence. As one might imagine, it was far from easy to divulge the fact that she had been sheltering an American spy.

"What?" she screamed. "You're an American soldier?" In disbelief, she looked at me from head to toe. Minutes passed as she stood frozen, like a statue, trying to absorb my words.

"Well," I said, "it makes no difference who I am or where I'm from. I was sending messages from the factory, where you thought we were doing business. Now you see why I didn't want you to know where I was going every day. I wanted to shield you from harm."

Sultanitsa collapsed on the floor and began to cry. Extending my hand to help her up, I felt a pang of guilt for having broken the news to her so suddenly; but, under the circumstances, I did not have any other choice. "Sultanitsa, I have to leave. The American colonel and soldiers are waiting for me," I said gently.

"Children, Helias has to leave," Sultanitsa sorrowfully told her three little ones, with whom I had bonded like a father. The boy and two girls (the latter of whom were three and five years old at the time), truly looked to me as a paternal figure, always sitting on my lap and delighting in the stories that I told them. The three-year-old girl was especially attached and considered me to be her father, since her own biological father had been killed in Albania, fighting the Italians.

After getting my belongings, I stopped to say my last goodbye to Sultanitsa. I gave her six gold sovereigns—one gold piece for each of her three children, one for her mother, and two for herself. "I will write to the American and Greek governments, explaining that you sheltered me, an American soldier, for nine months, with your entire family at great risk, and that you should be given special favor in any American organization."

Sultanitsa expressed her gratitude with a final kiss. As I was leaving, I turned to see her in tears near the door, telling her neighbors aloud, so that everyone could hear, "My Helias is an American soldier, and I knew it, I knew it all the time!"

Upon hearing these words, everyone expressed great admiration for Sultanitsa, whom they recognized as the widow of a fallen Greek soldier. As for me, I praised her, as well, and would forever be thankful for all that she brought to my life— her love, her attention, and her willingness to give me a home in my greatest hour of need.

Realizing that I had far too many belongings, I gave most of them to Sultanitsa, taking with me only the necessities, such as clothes and my cherished accordion, which I took care to conceal from the colonel. If he knew that I had been serenading the girls with afternoon concerts and had become the talk of the town, what would he possibly say?

Before I left, I turned around one last time to see all of the neighbors staring at me, especially Annoula and her friends across the street, who gazed at me with sad expressions. Filled with emotion, I asked the colonel whether I could have a little more time to say farewell. He understood perfectly and reassured me once more, "Please, take all the time you want!"

All of the girls—especially Annoula—wept at my departure. Annoula remarked, "Are you really an American soldier? Will I ever see you again? Will we ever sing together again?"

"Yes," I said. "One day, I'll come back, and as soon as I settle down, I will send you a letter." Annoula then smiled a little, and gave me a farewell kiss.

More kisses were exchanged with the neighbors. One gentleman with whom I had many political discussions over time, approached and shook my hand. "From what you said about the railroad bombing, I surmised that you were affiliated with some organization," he remarked. "But I would never have suspected you to be an American soldier, never! We had an American soldier right under our noses!" he exclaimed, looking at me intently, with a friendly smile. "Don't forget to come and visit us after the war is over."

"I will do that," I promised.

As I was waving goodbye to everybody and preparing to get into the jeep, I observed yet another neighbor standing on his balcony, staring at me with a sad face. That man never spoke to anyone, and all of the neighbors suspected that he was a German informant. I don't know whether that supposition was ever validated, but if it *was* true, he must have thought to himself, "How could I have missed an American soldier living right in my own neighborhood?"

"I'm sorry for having taken so long," I said to the colonel.

"Since you were living in this neighborhood for nine months, it is only natural that you made a lot of friends, and you had an obligation to say goodbye to them. So, don't worry about having said long farewells. I don't mind. After all, I came to Salonica just for you. There are no other American soldiers here. In fact, the news will go down in the record books that an undercover American spy remained in Salonica for nearly a year behind enemy lines. He sent four hundred messages and received two hundred, without ever being caught."

Clearly, the colonel understood the magnitude of the attachments that I had formed, and the emotions that accompanied my farewell. Even he waved to the crowd. With the gaping eyes of hundreds of people crowding the streets and peering into the jeep, we slowly drove away. A police officer who had been standing there and looking on, pushed back the throng.

After we had settled in, the colonel surprised me by asking whether he could see the factory where I had allegedly "worked"—the epicenter of our undercover activity. I agreed and, within minutes, we arrived there. I opened the gate and showed him the yard, the pile of wood that we pretended to sell, the place where the watchmen were stationed, and the office where I operated the wireless.

"Four German officers lived next door, and almost caught me while I was installing the antenna." I explained. Then, I took the colonel over to the table where I had placed the wireless.

Sultanitsa's Children (1944)

"You mean to tell me that you were sending messages from here—out in the open?" the colonel asked in disbelief. "Anybody could have walked right into the factory, the office, or the yard at any time! You had guts to operate here! That's all I can say."

Then, I showed the colonel the lint pile which conveniently hid the plywood cover and the hole in the floor. Amazingly, everything was still there.

"My God!" the colonel exclaimed. "There aren't any locks on the doors. The police could have come in at any time and found everything here!"

"Well, we had no other place to hide our equipment, and I thought that the least conspicuous place would be under that pile of lint," I replied, still astonished at my good fortune.

"Look, the Star of David!" the colonel observed. "The one exactly above the hole—the six-pointed star, painted in red. Before the war, this factory must have been owned by Jews."

"The owners must have buried their gold or money here," I said, echoing Oreopoulos' thought. "Maybe, they painted the star to indicate where it was hidden," the colonel replied.

"Who knows the real truth. I am just amazed that, for nine months, nobody discovered me or the wireless. The Star of David was enough to keep me safe from harm," I said.

After a long silence, the colonel spoke. "God looked after you, Corporal, and by the look of things, you have been blessed. I think you were very lucky not to have been discovered."

I went on to recount all of my near-misses and the fortuitous events that saved my life—especially about the German lieutenant, who told me not to operate the wireless on one memorable Thursday morning. If it were not for that tip, I most certainly would have been caught, and the course of our history would have been changed forever.

Still marveling at my good luck, the colonel ordered the two Greek-American soldiers to take the wireless, guns, grenades, and the pen gun to our hotel.

As we were leaving, Kyria Eleni saw me with the colonel and the two American soldiers, and figured that my association with them had to do with selling my 'unprofitable business.' "Are the Americans buying your business?

"Yes, Kyria Eleni, something like that."

"You are doing the right thing, my boy. I always had the impression that your business was not doing so well!"

"Goodbye, Kyria Eleni!" I said. Then, I bent down to whisper in her ear, "I would be very pleased if you would take anything that you may need for yourself, free of charge—olive oil, petroleum, charcoal, or firewood. Go, before I turn everything over to the soldiers."

"Well," she said, "This time . . . I will think about it!"

She never realized that she had been living in a hornet's nest. Unselfishly and unknowingly, she performed an immeasurable service on our behalf.

When the colonel overheard me and I explained the nature of our "business" in the factory, he commented again on our enormous luck, born of intelligent decision-making.

I agreed. "Because of that business," I said, "and with God and the Star of David watching over me, no one could ever have imagined that I was a spy, thank God."

"Yes, everything helped; but, most of all, either you played your cards right or you were just plain lucky! As of today, five of the students from the fifteen-man group with whom you trained in Cairo were captured and killed. The numbers may be even higher. I can't be sure, as I have not yet completed my tour of the remaining posts in Macedonia. As for Yiapitzoglou, I would like to meet him and receive a full, detailed report of his service. Since he is a Greek officer, he should report to his point of origin. I am only responsible for you. We should meet again tomorrow to prepare to travel to Athens."

With that, the colonel took his leave. What I did not know then (but later discovered) was that the colonel was a Jew, and felt deeply moved that our efforts to vanquish the enemy had been undertaken in a Jewish factory.

The following day, I met Yiapitzoglou at the hotel on the waterfront, at which time he informed me of a huge celebratory party that had been planned to rejoice in our survival and the success of our mission. The gathering (which included almost every person who had facilitated our objective), was to take place at one of the large downtown hotels. Of course, everyone was eager to attend; and, as it turned out, the celebration was a hit, replete with an orchestra playing Greek and American music, and plenty of libations. We all partook (I dare say, far too much Champagne) and had a wonderful time. Everybody wanted to meet me, the so-called "American phantom" (until then, my name and face had not been revealed). I must admit that such intrigue amused me—especially after the fact, among my peers.

The next morning, I found myself asleep on a bed in Nicos Oreopoulos' house, but to this day, I don't remember how I came to be there. When Nicos' sister woke me up, I was still filled with the excitement of being free (setting aside my tremendous headache). The colonel contacted me with the news that he was going north to other cities where wireless networks had been set up, and invited me to go along.

"If you agree, we will return to Salonica in two weeks. Then, I will take you to Athens."

"If you don't mind, I would rather go to Athens directly."

"Okay, I will arrange a flight for you."

"By the way," I said, "are you going to the Macedonian city called "Edessa" to find a Greek captain named Spyros? Both of us left together from Alexandria and experienced so many unforgettable moments, including a German search, in the course of which Spyros wet his pants from fear."

The colonel laughed. "Yes. "He is my first stop."

"When you see him, give him regards from Helias, and remind him about what I once told him: that he had nothing to fear, since *whatever we were doing was only a game!*"

"I don't know what you mean, Helias," the colonel replied. "But I'll give him your message."

The next day, the colonel told me that I would be on a flight leaving for Athens from Salonica's airport in two days, and I should report to the British office with all of my belongings by 10:00 a.m. "Our jeep will take you there," he assured me.

I called Yiapitzoglou and told him that I was leaving in two days, and wanted to say "farewell" to him and Nicos in person.

"I'll be there right away," he said.

Within an hour, Yiapitzoglou was at the hotel, carrying a bag. "Do you know what's in here?" he asked, smiling. "You forgot that I had your English sovereigns in my possession for safe keeping!"

Apparently, the colonel only asked for a return of the weapons, not the gold sovereigns. To my surprise, I later discovered that President Roosevelt had allotted an enormous, undetermined amount of money to the OSS, to be used by its agents behind enemy lines.

Yiapitzoglou pointed to the bag. "From the one hundred fifty gold sovereigns that you originally held in your nylon belt—after buying the accordion for twenty-five pieces, and after I gave you about five sovereigns a month—seventy-five gold sovereigns remain in the bag! Do you know what you can buy with that? A house or an apartment building—right now! What are you going to do with the sovereigns? Maybe, you should leave them with me, and after you're discharged from the army, I will return them to you when we meet again. Carrying so much money is not a good idea, as someone might steal it from you. Remember, these times are even more dangerous than when the Germans were here!"

"I know," I said. "The sovereigns would be safer with you, but I may need them before the war with Japan is over."

"Okay," he replied. "Be careful with them. They will be useful to you someday."

Before my departure, Yiapitzoglou met with the American colonel and gave him a full report, containing hundreds of pages of the organization's nine months' activities. He told the colonel that I had been very brave, endangering myself in order to carry out my responsibilities, and that I had done a wonderful job. He commended my devoted service, to which he attributed the organization's successful operation, and noted that, but for my knowledge of German and clever handling of dangerous situations, the entire group might have been caught or killed. Addressing Yiapitzoglou, the colonel emphasized that he expected nothing less, as I had been trained and chosen above others for this assignment. "His CO (Commanding Officer), Major Vassos, knew he struck gold when he assigned Helias to you," he affirmed.

We embraced each other, and each of us could not help but shed a tear when we said goodbye. We had spent many perilous moments together; and as we went in different directions, we felt like two brothers parting, promising to meet again in the future. In those nostalgic moments, neither of us could imagine what would happen before that hopeful eventuality.

Chapter 29

Sweet Victory

Paying heed to the colonel's instructions, I prepared to depart for the British military office at Salonica's Airport by 10:00 a.m. I looked around for the transport plane, but to my disappointment, I was told to load my belongings onto a British bomber, instead. I had no idea as to where I would fit, as there was no room with the pilots sitting up on top. When I questioned where I would go, I was told that I would have to sit in the gun turret bubble seat, located under the plane. It was a small compartment with a rounded glass, containing a double Browning machine gun, used to shoot down enemy planes during bombing missions. This meant that I could only look downward during the flight. While still wondering where I could put my suitcase and accordion (and recalling Yiapitzoglou's warning not to buy the musical instrument of my dreams), the pilot approached and suggested that my bags be placed in the cargo hold.

So, there I was, in the gun turret bubble, thinking that I was upside down, and if I stepped on the glass, it might break and I would fall out. Although the experience was frightening, the sight of the Greek islands in the ocean beneath my feet was indescribable.

As we landed with the bubble only two feet from the runway, I thought that we would, most certainly, crash; and I thought of the brave airmen who had risked their lives in those seats.

Arriving savely in Athens, I was surprised to find a jeep waiting to pick me up. Even more astonishingly, the driver called out my real name, "Corporal Doundoulakis!" Up until that time, I had been using the pseudonym, "Helias Nikolaou," at all times.

I climbed in and, in half an hour, we reached our destination, a five-story building, located at Phidias 3, in the center of Athens. Previously, it must have been an office building, which subsequently was rented to the OSS. I was assigned to a bed on the third floor, where there were big rooms, with six beds in each. I was given a spot in the corner, and told to store my suitcases under the bed.

Almost everyone there wore civilian clothes, and most everyone had heavy Greek accents, which clued me into the fact that they were, most likely, members of the "SO" and "OG's"—Special Operations, saboteurs, or Operational Groups, assigned with the partisans. They correctly discerned that I was a member of Secret Intelligence ("SI"), and asked how long I had been in Salonica. When I replied, "nine months," they didn't believe me. No doubt, each individual whom I encountered had their own stories to tell—probably of nighmarish proportions, worthy of their own narratives.

The building was without restaurant facilities, so we were provided with money to eat out. Since the lock on my suitcase was broken, I contemplated buying a new one. The seventy-five gold sovereigns were hidden with some dirty socks—a rather innovative method of concealment. I purchased some new ones, too; and in all, I had about twenty pairs of socks in which to store all the gold. Except for the coins and some clothes, my suitcase was practically empty. The rest of my belongings were in Sultanitsa's possession. Before I left for lunch, I tied the suitcase with a thick rope.

In the chaotic period of December, 1944 (the "Dekemvriana," or "troubled times of December"), Athens was in turmoil. A civil war erupted between the right-wing monarchists and the English, and the left-wing ELAS partisans in Athens. The English ordered the leftists to surrender their weapons, but they refused. I found myself in the middle of the street, looking around, and seeing thousands of people running about, communists and royalists, screaming at one another.

"King George is coming back," said one.

"The king is dead. The Russians are coming to save us! Fight with us!"

Fist-fights broke out here and there, with no peace in sight.

In the midst of the upheaval, I had forgotten to buy a suitcase. *It will be all right to buy one in the morning,* I thought to myself. I went back to Phidias 3 and, as I entered the building, I happened to meet a lieutenant, who was one of my self-defense and gymnastics instructors. He told me that he was going to Volos, a port city about two hundred miles north of Athens, and asked if I wanted to travel with him as his interpreter.

"You're going to see my brother?" I asked excitedly. "Is that where he is—in Volos?"

From the colonel who had taken me to Salonica's airport, I had learned that my brother had done a wonderful job in organizing thousands of partisans up in the mountains; but he did not tell me where George was stationed. Happy to learn that he was just a car ride away, I eagerly accepted the lieutenant's invitation.

George In Volos (1944)

Chapter 30

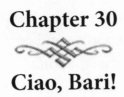

Ciao, Bari!

We met at 8:00 a.m. the following day in the lobby. "Don't take a lot with you," the lieutenant told me, "since we will be back in Athens in two days." When I went back to my room, I remembered that I forgot to buy the suitcase. *Suppose somebody opens that broken piece of luggage and steals the seventy-five gold pieces?* All night, I thought of those coins under my bed in a room where five other soldiers slept. Yiapitzoglou was right, yet again!

The next morning, I decided to take twenty coins with me, in case they opened it. *At least I would have twenty*, I thought. I found more rope, and I tied the suitcase some more. I wrote my name, rank, and serial number on two sheets of paper and stuck them, with glue, on the outside of both the accordion case and the suitcase with the other coins, and pushed both of them under my bed.

Since I thought I was returning to Athens, I didn't take much with me; but while deciding what to take, I found the cyanide capsules in my jacket. It seemed I had been carrying them around with me forever for luck; but I finally parted with them by flushing them down the toilet. That act was a literal and metaphoric affirmation of life. I met the lieutenant downstairs, still thinking of the fifty-five sovereigns, but feeling more secure.

When we arrived in Volos a few hours later, the lieutenant said to me, "Why don't you go and surprise your brother? He doesn't know you're here." I hadn't seen George in close to a year, and neither of us knew where the other had been sent; but we never forgot the day of our parting. With the prospect of being exposed to perilous missions, George deeply regretted involving me in the resistance movement in Crete. The last time we saw each other, he said, "Now that you are trained as a spy, you are not my little brother anymore. I hear you have made the top of the list, but I hope that they don't send you to the most dangerous place. Be careful. Don't take any unnecessary chances, and good luck on your mission. I am leaving soon. Let's hope that both of us come back alive!" We embraced, and parted—an event that I vividly recall to this day. I could not wait for the moment when we would see each other again.

Bringing myself into the present moment, I asked a man if he knew Sgt. George Doundoulakis. With a smile, he said, "Oh, so that's his real name, 'Doundoulakis'? We thought it was 'Papadakis.'" For a moment, I thought that I erred in revealing a secret; but then, I realized that the mission was over, and he didn't have to hide any more. As I saw him coming down the corridor, our eyes met, and he smiled as only a brother could, with intense understanding and pathos that only we understood. We had survived, and we could not believe that we were seeing each other again.

George told me how he had organized over six thousand five hundred partisans, both leftists and monarchists, into one group, who were fighting among themselves before he went to Volos. He supplied them with American weapons and shiploads of food, boots, and blankets through the American base in Turkey. By using explosives for sabotages in the airports or ships in Volos harbor, the supply of German troops was severely affected. He was well known as the "American in charge;" and at the Liberation Day parade in Volos, he represented the United States Army, laying a wreath at the Tomb of the Unknown Soldier.

The following day, the lieutenant received a telegram with orders not return to Athens, as the civil war between the royalists and leftists had escalated. The fistfights usually led to bloody street battles, and it would be unwise to go back. While anxiously following the civil war by radio, we received another telegram which confirmed the first warning not to return to Athens. Instead, we were ordered to leave Greece and travel to Italy with an English ship that was leaving from Volos' harbor, loaded with Italian prisoners.

When the lieutenant told me that I had to go with him and could not go back to Athens, I couldn't believe that I would not see that city again for a long time—and, of course, the fifty-five gold sovereigns and the accordion. I could only imagine Yiapitzoglou's face, and his warning about leaving the coins with him.

Soon, I received direct orders not to identify myself as an American soldier and to withhold wearing my uniform. I said goodbye to my brother again and went to the English ship in civilian clothes. The lieutenant, in constrast, wore his uniform. When we reached the ship, we couldn't believe our eyes. The decks were filled with over fifteen hundred Italian prisoners, most of them standing and shivering in the cool December air. Many were without shoes; some only had rags tied around their feet. All of them were unshaven and dirty, and many looked sick.

George and Helias Reunited (1945)

Our accommodations were much better. We were given a clean room containing two bunks. The lieutenant went to eat in the officers' quarters, while I went to the mess hall with the other soldiers. I noticed, though, that because I was wearing civilian clothes, the sergeant in charge refused to allow me to eat, assuming I was a Greek civilian. Since the Greek communists were now fighting against the English in the Greek Civil War, he must have been angry with the Greeks, especially after so many British, Australian, and New Zealand soldiers had given their lives defending Greece. I felt that this English behavior toward me was a personal affront, and I became so angry, that I left. I found the lieutenant in the officer's mess hall and explained to him what the English sergeant had told me. He advised me to wait while he went back to our room, and brought me his army jacket. I put it on and went back to the mess hall. That same sergeant saw me wearing the American army jacket and apologized; and, although there was a long line of English soldiers waiting to be served, he told everybody to let their guest, the American soldier, go ahead of the others. As I did so, I expressed my gratitude.

The following morning, I woke up early, and heard a lot of noise and singing. I put the lieutenant's army jacket on, and went up on deck. What I saw was truly unbelievable and difficult to describe: we were entering the harbor of Bari, Italy; and, as I found out, our ship was carrying the first group of prisoners returning to Italy. While less fortunate ships carrying thousands of Italian prisoners were sunk by German bombers in reprisal for deserting them, this ship was the first to survive any German retaliation!

All of Italy had been notified of the arrival of the first prisoner ship to make it without being sunk by the Germans. Wives, parents, and relatives of missing soldiers came out, hoping to see if their loved ones were coming home. As the ship maneuvered slowly inside the harbor, tens of thousands of civilians on the dockside and all the prisoners on deck began singing the Italian national anthem. The prisoners wept as they readied themselves to swim ashore. At this time, an English officer saw me up on deck. He approached and suggested that I return to my cabin, since he was afraid that, as soon as the ship docked, the prisoners might knock me down in their frenzy and crush me. However, as it turn out, everything remained orderly, and the lieutenant and I were the first ones to be called off when the ship docked. As a result, I didn't witness any happy reunions.

Our taxi driver reached our destination quickly, taking the address that the lieutenant had been given. As with the prior OSS stations, OSS-Bari was no different. It looked like a hotel or exclusive resort. The lieutenant turned to me and said, "Well, being an OSS member has its advantages." After registering, I was sent to a supply room where the sergeant in charge informed me to procure any clothes I wanted, including two more uniforms, cartons of cigarettes, boxes of candy, or chocolates.

I was assigned to a beautiful room on the second floor, with a wraparound balcony. I opened the balcony door, went out and saw, to my surprise, many people and children with their hands raised, begging for me to throw something down to them. Italy seemed worse off than Greece. Without hesitation, I went inside and brought out the boxes of cigarettes, chocolates, and candies I had just retrieved from the supply room and started tossing them to the crowd below. In no time, there were hundreds of people under my balcony, like birds feeding on bread crumbs. The soldiers in the adjoining rooms heard the shouting and also came out, joining my effort to throw down whatever they had. The men asked for cigarettes; the kids shouted for candies and chocolates. Even a policeman was begging me to throw him some cigarettes.

Later, I registered in the main office, where the sergeant warned me that if I needed to exchange American dollars or English sovereigns for Italian lire, I should do so only in his office, as exchanges out on the street were prohibited. I agreed, but I didn't understand the reason. Some time later, another soldier advised me not to be foolish and listen to what the sergeant had said. Outside on the black market, he said, I could get three to five times whatever they exchanged in the OSS office. I then understood that since Italy had been liberated only recently, the Italian lira was so devalued, that everybody wanted American dollars and gold. On the black market, you could get many times more than the official exchange rate. I was also informed that if I were transferred to another country, the lire would be converted into dollars again with the official exchange rate, and I would amass a lot of money.

With twenty-five gold sovereigns in my pockets, I went out in the street wearing my American uniform. I hadn't even gone a hundred feet when a well-dressed man approached me and asked if I had American dollars or gold sovereigns, offering me four or five times the official rate of exchange. Without even thinking of the sergeant's warning, I said, "Yes, I have gold sovereigns."

"Follow me, please," he said.

For ten minutes, I followed him first through the main streets, then smaller streets; and suddenly, we were in a dark alley. A sinking feeling gripped my stomach. *I have made a mistake,* I told myself. He said, "Do not be afraid; nothing is going to happen to you. Right now, know this: you are protected by the Mafia. Please come in." Although it was dark, I could make out a door to a small house, which he told me to enter. Years have passed since that incident, and still, I can't believe that I followed him. Upon entering, a woman approached, welcomed me, and told me to follow her.

"Go downstairs to the basement," the woman said.

"Nnn ... no ... I'm leaving," I stammered.

"You see, we're both members of the Mafia," the man informed me.

"The Mafia is making money through those money exchanges with you Americans. If anything happens to any American, the Mafia will kill my entire family. Since they have seen you coming in here with me, you are safer here than in your own home!"

When I heard that and saw the woman bringing me a glass of orange juice, I calmed down and trusted them. The man told me to sit down and to put the currency I wanted to exchange on the table. Since the rate of exchange was so high, I thought I would have difficulty exchanging the currency into dollars. Without blinking, I said, "Fifteen gold sovereigns." I took out fifteen from the twenty-five I had with me. The man agreed, and calculated how many lire he would give me. When he came out and placed a pile of money on the table, a-foot-and-a-half high of large denomination Italian lire, I thought, *What am I going to do with so much money? Where would I hide it? This time, I will have to buy a trunk!*

"Do you want to count it?" the man asked.

Wanting to leave that place as quickly as I had entered, I answered, "No. I trust you."

The woman brought me a cloth bag, where she placed all of the money.

"Someone is waiting outside, wielding a gun for your protection. He will take you to where you will be staying. We are responsible for your safety, until you return," the man said.

That night, since I had not bought a suitcase yet, I kept all the money under my pillow, afraid that it might be stolen. With the rate of exchange at the office, I calculated that by converting the lire to dollars, I should get a few thousand dollars.

The following morning, the captain called me into his office and told me that he heard about my excellent service in Secret Intelligence ("SI") and was very impressed by my accomplishments. "The OSS has commended you and will honor you with the Good Conduct and Excellent Performance medal," he said. "In the afternoon, in front of the other officers, you will be decorated, and you must not forget to come to my office at 3:00 p.m." At the appointed hour, I arrived at the captain's office where, in front of three other officers, he awarded me the aforementioned medal, of which I am still very proud.

It was Christmas in 1944, and I remember that the OSS-Bari office celebrated it with all the trimmings—Christmas trees, turkey dinners, and music with Italian bands and singers. The two opera houses in Bari, idle during the war, were now lively with performances almost every day, so I enjoyed frequenting them as often as I could.

I wasn't the only one who had a lot of money to spend. Most, if not all, of the other Americans were also financially fluid, and were exchanging their dollars on the black market, as well. All of them had plenty of spending money! Also, I realized that since the OSS had brought over a huge number of materials to Italy, the supply sergeants were selling various things to civilians on the side, and their pockets were filled with money. I observed that, almost every night, high-rolling dice games were taking place in the OSS building's basement. The games were getting so wild that I could hear the supply sergeants bid, "Shoot $200" or "Shoot $300," at those dice games. Once, I saw $5,000 in their hands; at other times, they were penniless.

I had stayed close to two months in that OSS station in Bari, Italy. One day, the captain called me in and told me that he was sending me back to Cairo to report to the academy where I trained. "They will tell you where you will go next." I was pleased to hear that I was finally going back to the palace and would see my old classmates and whomever was lucky enough to have survived their mission.

As I was walking away from the captain's office, I thought of the million Italian lire I had in my room, which had to be converted to dollars. So, without even thinking of the consequences, I took the pile of lire and placed them on top of the sergeant's desk. He checked my record book, and saw that I had not exchanged any money in his office, so he went inside and called the captain. The captain, of course, came out and asked me where I had come upon all that money. It became apparent to all that I had gone outside to the Mafia for the exchange, a forbidden act.

"You were warned not to convert any currency with the Mafia, didn't you know that?" the captain shouted at me. "For this, you will be punished."

Instantly, I thought, *I was trained to fabricate stories. I was taught to lie, and I have to find a quick response right away, even if it were to my OSS superiors!* After all, when my life depended on it, I always conjured up the proper retort, which even the Germans believed. *Why not find it now?* So, I replied, "Sir, have you ever gone down to the basement at night, where those big dice games are being played almost every evening? Obviously, Captain, you haven't. That's where I won all those lire. If you want, go tonight and see for yourself what I'm talking about. I played a few times and, surprisingly, luck was on my side!"

The captain, of course, was not blind, and could see through my story; but since he knew that I was an SI agent and had been trained to lie, he looked at me out of the corner of his eye, smiled, and with a softer voice said, "Yes, Corporal, you must be a very lucky man. Sergeant, give the corporal his money. Besides, Corporal, it was only last week that I decorated you with the Good Conduct medal!" With that, in the blink of an eye, all of the lire were converted into dollars—a few thousand, in fact.

Just as I was about to walk out, the sergeant then said, "You know, Corporal Doundoulakis, it would be wise to deposit the money in the army bank and withdraw it any time you want, or even when you're discharged. After all, you're still owed your salary while you were in Greece at $155 per month, and with this money, plus interest, it will be a substantial amount. What do you think about that?"

I agreed; and as I was leaving the office, I thought, *I can't believe it. I never expected that whatever I had been taught in the OSS would be so rewarding, particularly how to be a good liar!* The next day, I was notified that I had to go to the captain to get my air passage to Cairo. Even though the captain was disinclined to see me again, I had no other alternative. He said that he couldn't find air passage from Bari to Cairo. Instead, the plane would leave from Naples, so I would have to travel from Bari to Naples the following morning at seven o'clock.

The following day—a wintery day in February, 1945, I met the driver who would take me to Naples. His army truck, which was covered with canvas, was still very cold inside. Outside, the roads were covered with more than a foot of snow. The trip would last a couple of hours, and the five soldiers sitting in the back beside me were not at all happy about it. They complained about the transportation and hurled insults at the driver.

"Keep quiet, and bear up!" our beleaguered chauffeur called out.

For more than three hours, we waded through the snow-covered roads, without moving very far at all; and when the truck had to go uphill, the tires spun out and remained frozen. The driver said he had forgotten to get the chains for the wheels and, therefore, decided to go back! This was followed by expletive-inflected utterances from all of us. It took us another two hours to return, and the driver told me to go back to the captain and get air passage for the next day's flight, reminding me not to forget to be out at 7:00 a.m. again.

I ran to tell the captain; and as soon as he saw me, he said, "What the hell happened? The plane refused to take you?" I told him about the delay we had due to the icy roads. He gave me new air passage and told me that it was the last one; so, I couldn't miss the flight the following morning.

Once in my room, I set the alarm clock for 6:00 A.M. but, as luck would have it, I forgot to turn it on! When I woke up the following morning, it was eight o'clock. "*My God!*" I cried out. "*I overslept. Now what am I going to do? I can't go back to the captain again. He'll throw me out, and this time, he'd be right . . . . And that truck driver . . . . Why didn't he come and wake me up?*" For an hour, I was strategizing my next step. As a matter of fact, I was willing to even give up the gold I had if only I could find a different way—even public air transportation to Cairo—anything, rather than see the captain again!

After an hour of mental wrangling, I decided to go back. As soon as the captain saw me, he smiled a little bit, shook his head, and said, "I cannot get rid of you, Corporal, can I? I just don't want to hear your excuse again. I know you always have an excuse, *or can make one up*; but this time, you're lucky. I just got two tickets, which were returned to me. So, I guess you can have one." At a loss for words of gratitude, I simply accepted the ticket, and left.

The following night, I found two alarm clocks; I then located the driver and told him that I would give him $20 just to wake me up at 7:00 AM, in case I overslept! Since I froze the first time, I put on long johns, two jackets, double sweaters, and an overcoat. We arrived in Naples later that morning and boarded the airplane. I was still clad in all of those layers, when we reached Cairo a few hours later. The temperature was over ninety degrees, and I had difficulty breathing. The pilot told me that I should go outside and find the army car that was waiting to pick me up and take me to the OSS spy school. I found the car; but as soon as the driver saw me, he said, "Gosh, where did you come from, Alaska?"

We were four soldiers in all. The other three had orders to report somewhere outside of Cairo. The driver saw where I had to go, and told me that my destination was peculiar. "You must be of a higher rank, yes?"

"No," I said, "just a different job."

"I understand," the driver said. "Maybe I shouldn't ask too many questions!" Then, he asked me if I didn't mind taking the other three soldiers to their destination first, even though it was a little farther than mine.

I agreed and said to him, "Yes, go ahead." After all, if they saw me going into a king's palace, what would they think?

Chapter 31

Savoring the Present

I was filled with excitment about reaching the palace school; and when the driver pulled up in front, he turned to me and said, "I wonder what your qualifications have to be in order to stay in a place like this." I looked at him and answered with only one word: "Guts!"

It was so wonderful to be back that, when I reached the main gate, I went right past the guards who followed behind me, opened the door, and went straight into the main hall. Most of my instructors were there and knew I was coming. All of them were so glad to see me, and expressed their joy with handshakes and slaps on the back; but my sense of elation was marred with grief, when I heard that some of the original fifteen students, with whom I had begun my training, had been either caught or killed. Seven of them, as opposed to five (as the colonel told me in Salonica), had lost their lives. Two of the seven were the Yugoslavians, with whom I played ping-pong almost every day. I was devastated, and tried to distract my thoughts with the present realization that I, myself, was free, and I could, at the very least, live with the memory and pay tribute to those who were lost.

Being in the moment was all that I could do. I had no other option. All of the instructors debriefed me, and wanted to know where I went and if I had a rough time. They wondered if the Gestapo ever came close to catching me and, most important, whether my training had helped me in performing my job. They were very glad when I told them that without their instructions, I would have been caught on the first day!

When I went to my room, I found my old uniform, which I put on; but now I inserted my medals and ribbons, together with a star, indicating that I had taken part in frontline action. I looked in the mirror and said to myself, *I was never caught, and now I have returned—alive and well. I couldn't believe it.*

The next day, I went to Cairo to meet my relatives who lived there. They were relations of my grandfather's sister on my father's side, who had left during the Ottoman rule of Greece to become a maid in Cairo to wealthy Egyptians. When they saw me after more than a year's absence, they were so happy and anxious to hear what had happened while I was in Greece. They listened in awe, as I told them where I had gone. The younger cousin of four, named George, persisted in asking me to retell my perilous near-misses with the Gestapo.

I had a great time while on that visit. Cousin George and I went rowing, boating and walking along the waterfront. In addition, I offered to take my relatives to the "Bridge de Pyramid," the best nightclub in Cairo. To my surprise, fifteen of my relatives came; and since I had to pay for their admission and drinks, it cost me four or five months' wages; but what a night to remember it was!

By March 1945, my brother, George, came back from his Volos mission. I didn't forget to mention to him that, as a result of my surprise visit there in December of 1944, I left fifty-five gold sovereigns in an unlocked suitcase under my bed in Athens; and since I was unable to go back, I had lost them together with my accordion. He regretted that I had sacrificed these possessions just to see him; but "what is more precious than life?" he said. How true that statement was! The value of our lives immeasurably exceeded material possessions.

My pride in my brother cannot be adequately expressed (even to this day, words fail me). George was promoted to first sergeant and, at the time he was decorated with the exceptional Legion of Merit medal (which, customarily, was given to generals), six generals were decorated with that honor along with him. As mentioned earlier, George received that honor for organizing six thousand five hundred partisans, uniting them into a coordinated front to fight the Germans near the Volos mountains. After the war, in addition to receiving the Legion of Merit for his OSS mission, George was notified that he had to go to England to be decorated with the King's Medal for Courage, England's highest decoration awarded to civilians, for his role with the SOE as leader of a resistance group on Crete from 1941 to 1943.

In the beginning of April 1945, we were told that my brother and I would be sent back to the United States. Just as we began to prepare for our return, the supply sergeant approached me.

"Is your first name 'Helias?' . . . and how do you spell that?" he asked.

"Yes, my name is Helias. Why?" I replied quizzically.

"Well," he said, "a few days ago, two suitcases came through the Army Delivery Service from the OSS Bari station in Italy. I couldn't read the last name, as indicated on the tag, since it was torn out; and I wanted to find out whether the suitcases belong to you."

"What?" I said. "Two suitcases, you have two suitcases?"

"Yes," he said. "Please come on by and see if they belong to you. I don't know what to do with them."

Right away, I followed the supply sergeant, hoping that, perhaps, my possessions were recovered. There, in front of me, were my two suitcases, the accordion and the other suitcase— still tied and unlocked! I could not believe me eyes! Only the first name was readable, and the last name had only the first four letters, DOUN; but my serial number was still there (10675040, as I distinctly remember). Reading the papers stuck to the suitcases, I discerned that they had gone from Athens to Bari, Italy; and from Bari, they were sent to Cairo OSS headquarters, then to the palace spy school, travelling for a period of three months. I carried the suitcases to my room, cut the ropes, and took out the shirts on top. Beneath, I spotted twenty dirty socks with the fifty-five gold sovereigns still in them! *My God*, I thought, *an unlocked suitcase went around the Mediterranean, carrying a treasure in it, and nobody found it?*

When I told my brother that I found the fifty-five gold pieces, he suggested that I still keep them in that unlocked suitcase if I didn't want them to be stolen. I thought about the wireless in Salonica, unlocked and unprotected. My brother was a wise man, indeed, and I could not argue with his rationale.

Since I didn't dare play my accordion on the school premises, I took it to my relatives and played a few Greek songs for them. They enjoyed my playing so much, that I decided to leave that treasured instrument there, and play it for them until I was ready to leave for the United States.

The next time I visited, my cousin, Popi, began crying when I told her to bring me the accordion. Popi was married to a man who was much too fond of alcohol, and when he was home, spent most of his time in an inebriated state. Eyeing the accordion, he apparently saw an opportunity to purchase libations; so he secretly took it from Popi and sold it. When she found out what her husband had done, Popi was mortified. The two had a huge argument, and Popi offered to pay me; but of course, she didn't know that the accordion had cost me twenty-two gold sovereigns! Anyway, that was the end of my accordion, lost again–this time forever! Once again, I thought, *I should have listened to Yiapitzoglou.* What I could have done with those gold coins, and instead, I used them to buy an accordion!

Without the accordion for diversion, and with nothing to do before we received definitive word about leaving for the United States, I thought to divert myself with a sail on the Nile, which was a short walk from the palace school. With my OSS identification card, I could enter anytime I wished. The yacht had a restaurant, an entertainment room, and even an exercise room. I felt that, soon enough, I would leave the OSS' many luxuries, and life would never be the same; and, so, I seized the opportunity to indulge in that luxury. *So, why not? Would I have another chance to go sailing on the Nile?* As mentioned, before being sent to Salonica, I often went to the yacht and was offered a ride, which I declined. This was the time, the moment.

The following morning, I asked my brother if he wanted to accompany me. George, who was always reading, looked distracted and dismissively waved his hand at me.

"George, did you hear me? Would you like to go sailing on the Nile? It's our only chance."

"No!" George answered emphatically; then, he added, "I thought that all that spying around would have made you a more serious adult, but I see you are still just a boy."

"George," I said, "you were born serious, and in your seriousness, you will miss the joys of life. Sailing *is* done by adults, you know," I replied angrily, and went on my way.

**Helias with His Famed Accordion,
Serenading Cousins In Cairo (1945)**

Egyptian Relatives, Joanna and Popi, With Their Father In Cairo

The Brothers With Their Cousin in Cairo (1945)

Chapter 32

Revisiting the Good Life

Since George declined my invitation to go sailing, I decided to seize the opportunity to venture on my own. The yacht to which the sailboat was tied was only a short distance away, and I entered using my OSS I.D. The Arab gentleman in charge was all too glad about my eagerness for a sailing venture, given that I had previously rejected his offer.

As we broke into the open waters of the Nile River, slight anxiety overtook me. For a while, the wind picked up and the boat pitched at a forty-five-degree angle. "Don't worry! The boat may tilt, but it won't turn over. It's all in the joy of sailing!" my companion told me. I enjoyed myself; but, then, as my mind wandered back to my near-drowning on the journey from Turkey to Greece, I couldn't face the thought of that experience again. I got cold feet again, and told him to return. I was glad to have had the adventure, even if it was not the most memorable experience. Each endeavor held a memory for me. Soon it would be time to leave, and I soaked up every chance to take in my surroundings.

In April, 1945, George and I were told that we would depart for the United States, at last. To think that my brother and I had survived so many perils and seemingly insurmountable obstacles, and we would see our hometown of Canton, Ohio again, after more than twenty years! I was exhilarated, and my heart filled with anticipation. Many times, I truly felt that the moment would never come.

Rowing on the Nile (1945)

The Brothers, Prior to Leaving Spy School (1945)

The mere thought overwhelmed us. We only hoped that our dear parents were still alive in Greece. We truly had no way of knowing. George had tried to reach Patrick Leigh Fermor via SOE members in Cairo, in order to establish some communication; but these individuals only replied, "We're looking into it," and did not provide further information.

After organizing our itinerary, we learned that we were bound for Miami, Florida. Since we did not have a definitive home address in the States, location was irrelevant.

We said our farewells to all of the instructors at the school, including Colonel Vassos who, by that time, had been recently promoted. He shook our hands, and expressed pride in all of our achievements. We were living proof of the excellent training that we had received.

"Not only did you do a wonderful job," Colonel Vassos said, but you learned how to do your job right, and both of you came back alive. Most important, we taught you how to avoid being caught." Leaning forward, turning to another officer, and pointing to me, the Colonel continued, "I am even more gladdened by your second achievement. The German Gestapo gave up on him. He was too well-trained to be caught."

We shook hands again, I saluted Colonel Vassos, and we said 'goodbye.' That was the last time I saw him.

George and I had breakfast and, then, climbed into the jeep that was waiting to take us to the airport. Turning to look back, we absorbed one last impression of that magnificent building and all of the indelible memories that it had given us.

In a couple of hours, we arrived in Casablanca, and slept peacefully through the night. The following morning, we stopped off in the Canary Islands, where everyone ate "breakfast" again. I said to myself, *Breakfast again? Doesn't anyone eat lunch?* Then, I realized that we were traveling westward, catching up to breakfast time wherever we went.

When we finally had lunch, we were sitting on American soil. The pilot could not have given us a better sightseeing tour. Miami looked absolutely beautiful from the air. We were told that we would have to stay in Miami that day and, then, leave early the next morning for Washington, D.C. by train.

As we were walking around in the afternoon, we noticed buses heading for Miami Beach. Having heard of the famous Miami Beach resort city, we took a bus and got off at 14th Street. There, we sat on a park bench, admiring the luxurious hotels, gardens, flowers, and beautiful palm trees all around us.

In the late afternoon, a gentleman approached us and identified himself as a real estate agent from across the street. "Do you have funds to place a deposit on an inexpensive piece of waterfront land?" he asked affably. "I don't know if you realize that Miami is built up to 50th Street, at present. The farther north you go from 60th Street, the cheaper the land is. Please come to my office across the street, and I will show you wonderful inexpensive waterfront acres at around 70th and 80th streets."

Intrigued by what the agent said, we followed him to his office, where he showed us aerial photos of Miami Beach, which seemed to extend at least fifteen miles or more north of 50th Street. "Depending on what you want to purchase, I can find beautiful waterfront or interior land for you—as many acres as you want, at very cheap prices," he said.

At the time, I had seventy-five sovereigns in my pocket, $1,000 in cash, and an Army savings account passbook containing four-thousand dollars—enough for a down payment for many acres of land, if we wanted to buy. I was ready to sign, but George tempered my enthusiasm. "You will surely lose all of your money on that alligator-infested land," he said. "I'm going to invest in the cargo ship that Kastrinogiannis has spoken about—for practically nothing. He wishes to be partners." Kastrinogiannis had escaped with us from Crete and was a trusted friend. "What better cause is there than rebuilding Greece?" George declared emphatically. "We could make money, while unselfishly giving back to a country in desperate need of help."

"You're right, George," I replied. "We should forget the Miami Beach investment. I may also invest in the cargo ship that Kastrinogianis is talking about."

That settled it. We told the real estate agent that we were not interested in the Miami Beach properties, thanked him for his time, and left. In the months that followed, I proceeded, therefore, to invest almost all of my money into the cargo ship. As time passed, I witnessed how rapidly Miami Beach expanded, with large hotels building up in the North Beach area, as well, north of 60th Street. By all appearances, the seventy-five gold sovereigns would have become millions!

As it turned out, Kastrinogiannis' cargo ship met with disaster, he went bankrupt, and my investment evaporated. Tragically, he was later murdered, possibly by an irate, vengeful investor. I often thought of Yiapitzoglou's warnings about being frugal, but my youthful mind and heart just wouldn't listen. It took some serious mistakes for me to see his point.

The following day, we went to the train station, and were told that we had been assigned two berths in a Pullman. The trip to Washington was sixteen hours. Fatigued, but excited at the prospect of being there, I called OSS headquarters, and a jeep came to pick us up. As we drove through the streets, I noticed that barricades lined the sidewalks.

"Was there a parade here?" I asked.

"President Roosevelt's funeral procession just drove by. He will be buried tomorrow in New York," the driver informed me.

"What? George! How could we have missed that news?" I exclaimed.

My brother looked on in equal sadness and shock.

We remained at OSS headquarters for a brief time, after which we left Washington with our driver, and headed for Bethesda, about fifteen minutes away. When we arrived at our destination, I said, in amazement, "What's this? Another resort?"

"It's the Congressional Country Club for members of the House and Senate, where they relax and have weekend meetings. Now, it has been assigned to OSS members only. I don't know why I was told to bring you here," the soldier replied.

Approaching the reception desk, we saw a beautiful lady who directed us to our rooms.

"Will we be staying here?" I asked.

The lady looked at me with a puzzled expression. "Of course! The Congressional Country Club is the resting quarters for *chosen* OSS members only."

I couldn't believe it! The building was a beautiful structure, containing dance halls, exercise rooms, billiard rooms, and many living quarters. Outside, there was an artificial lake with fishing provisions, next to which was a tremendous golf course.

"I'm so tired of living in palaces and villas. Do we have to live in a country club now?" I quipped.

George laughed. "Let's enjoy the royal treatment while it's still offered to us, Helias. After we're discharged, we will only *dream* of these good times."

Yet again, as with most matters, my big brother was correct. We could not have spent time in a more enjoyable, exciting place. Four times a day, a bus left from the club for Washington, D.C., and George and I could go into the city at any time we wished. Every Friday night, USO girls put on shows, and kept us company while we danced the nights away.

"For the last two months, I relaxed at the palace in Cairo, visited relatives and friends, and sailed on the OSS yacht. "Now, maybe I can learn how to play golf or to fish," I remarked.

Two months passed, and I found myself becoming bored. I was a spoiled child, who didn't know what I had or what I was searching for. While visiting Greek-American OSS Special Operations (SO) members living in a nearby hotel, I was persuaded to come and work as a guard and receive accommodations at the hotel. "You'll have the time of your life," the SO members told me.

Before I approached the captain in charge at the Congressional Club about my change of venue, I thought to speak to George. When my brother heard my reasons for leaving such a glorious place, he repeated his harsh observation.

"Your training and work as a spy did not transform you into an adult yet. Do you know that millions of American soldiers all around the world cannot even dream of being in this place, and you say that you are 'tired of doing nothing'? I was just told that it may take up to a year for us to be discharged, and you want to leave this dream of a place for who knows where! Maybe, you'll be sent to a training camp and go through the Army's basic training program. You are dancing with girls every Friday night, fishing, playing ping-pong and billiards—all for free. We also have the privilege of registering for English classes a couple of days a week at George Washington University in D.C. If this type of life is boring to you and you want to abandon all of these comforts, you will find out the error of your thinking in years to come."

Without heeding George's wise admonitions, I went to see the captain the following morning. In no uncertain terms, I told him that I was bored, and would rather be a guard at OSS headquarters, along with my SO friends, in Washington. He listened with a little smile, called the sergeant in from the next room, and asked me to repeat what I had just said.

"Sergeant," the captain said, "please listen to the corporal. He says that he is bored and tired of doing nothing in the Congressional Country Club. He wants to be transferred to Washington!" The sergeant's smile also revealed his amusement.

"If that's what you want, Corporal," the captain said. "You can be transferred to Washington; but after you leave, you cannot come back."

"Yes, sir," I replied.

When the captain told the sergeant to make the necessary arrangements, I reported for duty at OSS headquarters in Washington, where I was to stand guard at the front desk of the main entrance, and not allow people in without verifying their OSS ID cards. I was told that if someone forcibly tried to enter, I should immediately press the alarm button, which was carefully hidden under the rim of the desk. This would signal for help from the heavily armed guards inside.

A week passed quickly, as I enjoyed my evenings in the hotel where my friends and I were staying. Just as I had been told, there were plenty of girls in my midst. *I made the right move,* I told myself. I had the time of my life.

During the second week, a two-star general arrived by car at the front entrance, and without showing me his I.D. card, proceeded to walk right by me. Without observing his rank and not knowing who he was, I stopped him and asked for his I.D. Naturally, he paused, put his hand into his right pocket, and produced the card. He then continued on his way. Not five minutes went by before a woman ran down the corridor, screaming bloody murder.

"What did you do? You stopped and asked a two-star general for his I.D.? He is one of the big chiefs here at OSS!"

"My instructions were to inspect *everyone's* identification card and that I should not allow *any* unidentified personnel through that door!" I said decisively.

"Yes," she said, "everyone, but him!"

"Suppose he was a spy?" I yelled back.

"If someone had the courage," she said, "to come inside this building pretending to be a general, then we all deserve to be shut down! In any case, you insulted the general and, therefore, you're fired! Go back to the Congressional Club!"

With my head down, I returned to the captain and told him what had just occurred. He responded that he could not take me back, but rather, would find some suitable job for me until I was discharged.

Washington, D.C. (1945)

"Oh!" he said, as he snapped his fingers. "I need someone to burn classified documents in the basement."

Needless to say, I was not intrigued; so, in three days, I found myself again in front of the captain's desk. "What's the complaint this time?" he asked with a mildly annoyed expression.

"Burning the documents will make me sick and burn my eyes."

"Report back in a couple of days, and wait until I decide what to do with you. You should never have left the Congressional Club, Corporal," the captain replied, looking at me out of the corner of his eye.

The next time I reported to the captain, he said that I never had basic training and thought about sending me to boot camp.

"Why can't I get discharged now?" I asked.

"Well, when the war is over, those with the most years in service have priority."

Finally, I discovered that I had to submit to basic training at Camp Crowder, Missouri. This event, I realized, was the result of my ungratefulness, pure and simple. The captain at the Congressional Club was not at fault. With such understanding, I readied myself for my next venture.

After a two-day train ride from Washington, I reached the camp and reported to the admissions office. The colonel in command looked at me with a puzzled expression. He observed the Good Conduct and Excellent Performance medal, the OSS pin, a star on top of the European ribbon, and my paratrooper wings. My records were handed to him by a sergeant, which he read very carefully. Then, he directed me into his office, along with the captain under him, and two lieutenants.

The colonel turned to the other officers and said, "You're going to witness a bad reassignment today. The corporal here has been a member of the OSS since he enlisted two years ago. He had five months of spy training, and performed a nine-month mission in Greece. As you can see, he was decorated for his excellent performance, and now, he was sent here to get basic training, since the captain didn't know what to do with him. My God, isn't that the craziest decision by an American officer?"

Then, he turned to me and said casually, "Did you really finish that strange spy training school?"

"Yes, sir," I said.

And your superiors in Washington," the colonel said, "knowing your record, sent you here for basic training?"

"Yes," I said. Fully aware that the colonel held the trump card, I continued. "It's my fault. I requested a transfer of duties to OSS headquarters; but if you don't mind my saying so, Colonel, even if that captain is in charge back in Washington, you are in charge now."

At that point, the colonel told the other officers to resume their duties. Then, he turned to me. "You have gone through enough, and you don't deserve more punishment. Why do you need this torture before your discharge?" Breathing a sigh of relief, I thanked the colonel for his kindness.

During my stay at Camp Crowder, I took English classes provided for foreign draftees. Another ten months would pass by and, in the spring of 1946, I would be notified of my discharge. With civilian life looming on my horizon, so much had changed—especially the boy from Archanes.

Camp Crowder (1946)

Chapter 33

Cloudy, With a Chance of Sunshine

With civilian life quickly approaching, my first inescapable thought was to find and visit my long-lost relatives in Canton, and explore my birthplace. George agreed, and with a week's leave, we boarded a bus to Canton.

I was only three and George was only five when we left our home in the United States for the island of Crete. One may imagine the surprise of our Uncle Manuel, therefore, when he first set eyes upon us after nearly two decades! He was so excited, in fact, that he threw us a huge party, to which he invited all of his friends. Although I was only three when I left, I could almost swear that I knew some of the people and even recalled some of their names.

The following day, Uncle Manuel took us to the house in which I was born, located on Cherry Street. I was so moved to see the place, and I had a strange, warm feeling of dejá vu. Then, before I knew it, I had to return to Camp Crowder for another ten months, from April, 1945 to January, 1946, where I engaged in the same "boring" activities to while away the time. Finally, in January, 1946, I was notified that I would be sent to Fort Dix Army Camp in New Jersey, and from there, I would be discharged. It was a surreal, almost unbelievable occurrence. I had gone into the Army as a boy, and I was emerging a man, with so much experience behind me, but with so many memories yet to create.

George With "Theo Manoli" (Uncle Manuel) and Colonel Betinakis' Niece and Nephew in Canton, Ohio (1946)

Once at Fort Dix, I was examined by a slew of doctors who, predictably, discovered the break in my nose, caused by my fall while installing the wireless antenna in Salonica. The doctors informed me that, later on, I would have to have surgery; but, for the moment, they labeled me as a disabled veteran with a thirty percent disability.

All went well, except for the the sergeant's question about my address, which I almost didn't know how to answer. "Well," I hesitated. "I don't have an address in the United States, since I've been away for almost twenty years. My parents are now in Crete," I explained, feeling pangs of longing for a place called "home."

"But you must provide us with a home address," the sergeant insisted, "in order to receive your mail and your checks!" All of a sudden, I recalled that my father had a cousin in Brooklyn, New York, named Zambia Doundoulakis; so, I scrambled for a Brooklyn telephone directory, hoping to find her name. At the time, George, a First Sergeant, was preparing to be discharged in another area of the camp. What I really hoped to accomplish was to utilize that address as my brother's and my home address until we could find an appartment.

As fate would have it, I found "Aunt Zambia" (as I called her) at 260 Pacific Street, Brooklyn. At first, I thought of surprising her; but, upon reflection, I realized that it might be prudent to call her first and identify myself, instead of shocking her with an impromptu visit. So, I quickly grabbed the telephone, and dialed. At first, I had difficulty in making Aunt Zambia understand who I was; but, then, all of a sudden, she let out a scream. To my surprise, she said, "Are you the little one who left America almost twenty years ago?"

"Yes!" I answered in disbelief.

Aunt Zambia was very pleased, and offered to provide room and board for my brother and me, until we were able to find our own apartment.

Realizing that I would be living in Brooklyn, New York, for a while, I provided Aunt Zambia's address as my home address. The discharge sergeant then handed me a ticket to Penn Station, New York. Since I had never been to Brooklyn and did not know that it was one of New York City's boroughs, I said, "Sergeant, this ticket says 'Penn Station, New York.' I want to go to Brooklyn!"

The sergeant lowered his voice and said, "Here is a guy who doesn't even know how to get home. My God! We sent people like this overseas, and we still won the war!"

Without a clue as to what he meant, I did not reply. One of the other hundreds of soldiers surrounding me slapped me on the back. "Don't worry! You have the right ticket," he said.

So with a duffel bag over my shoulder and a suitcase in my hand, I walked with the other soldiers to the train station, bound for New York City. Upon my arrival to Penn Station, I immediately looked skyward to witness the famous New York City skyscrapers. I was particularly excited to see the Empire State Building. Beholding that structure and its complex design, I thought about someday designing something grand. Twenty years had passed since my infant's eyes had taken in that scene. Little did I know then how much more unimaginable scenarios I would experience and witness elsewhere in the world!

"Excuse me," I said to a police officer passing by. "How do I get to 260 Pacific Street, Brooklyn?"

"Come with me," the officer replied, acknowledging that I was a newcomer, and directing me back to Penn Station,

318

so that I could board the proper train and get off at the right stop. Finally, Brooklyn—that mysterious place—was right before my eyes. Luckily, I got off at the appropriate stop. To my disappointment, however, Aunt Zambia's apartment was on the fifth floor, and there were no elevators. It was very difficult to climb five flights of stairs, while lifting a huge Army bag filled with clothes in one hand, and carrying a heavy suitcase in the other. Gone were the days of being driven around and helped by Army or OSS drivers.

Once I reached Aunt Zambia's fifth-floor apartment, she welcomed me with embraces and tears in her eyes, marveling at the fact that there, in front of her, stood a decorated Army man—not the three-year-old boy she remembered from twenty years before!

As promised, Aunt Zambia gave George and me an extra bedroom to use for as long as we needed to stay. Our search for an apartment together did not yield anything at first, except an attic apartment in a very old house. Ultimately, though, we ended up renting an upstairs apartment in the large private home of Bea Jackson, in Brooklyn. As it turned out, our landlady was a descendant of President Andrew Jackson. Bea was most kind to both of us, and even gave me a marble statue, passed down to her from President Jackson, himself. I still have that statue in my possession.

Soon, we reunited with our parents who, at the end of 1946, came to live with us, having traveled to the United States from Greece by boat. When I arrived in Cairo after I had completed my mission, I received word that both of my parents were doing well. However, we had to await their arrival in the states (specifically, Washington, D.C.), where mail could be freely sent and received. Since that time, we had been corresponding with them, anticipating the moment of our reunion. Never will I forget that day, that exhilarating, emotional moment.

"Do I really embrace both of my sons . . . and they are all right? Both of them survived? I have been dreaming of this moment for so long! Demetrios, it is really true?" My mother sobbed.

"Yes, Evanthia, it is really true." My father's eyes also welled with tears. "Your dream came true! Let us rejoice and thank God for this happy reunion."

All four of us lived in the same rented apartment. My parents stayed in a second-floor bedroom, while George and I occupied an attic room, where the temperature would often get close to one hundred degrees; but we made due with the small fan that Bea gave us. No doubt, George and I weren't living in luxury as we had been at the palace spy school or the Congressional Country Club, but I dare say that three years of opulent living was quite enough; and the joy of being together as a family again was priceless.

The reality of my new world—the universe according to a civilian boy in his twenties—lay before me. George and I were enrolled in college and, as a disabled veteran, I was able to receive one hundred fifty dollars per month, plus the cost of books and tuition. In addition, I had unlimited time to complete my education, and I could take any courses I wished. Having these benefits truly filled my heart with gratitude to George for enlisting us as soldiers, rather than as civilians. I had always begrudged those bridge-playing German officers for my fall and consequent injury; but I suppose that virtually every cloud has a silver lining.

Settling Into Brooklyn - The Author Near the Manhattan Bridge

College Days (1947)

At the City College of New York, I struggled for five years. Ultimately, however, I had the best time of my life. I vividly recall a conversation with my mathematics professor, whom I approached and asked what I could do to improve my overall grade. He said that he would think about the matter. Just then, he glanced down at my OSS pin, which I always wore on the lapel of my jacket. When I told him that I was in the OSS, he looked surprised and remarked, "I wish that the CIA (Central Intelligence Agency) were as efficient." He always seemed deeply sympathetic to veterans, and I was grateful for his display of approval. In the end, I got an 'A' in that class—possibly due to my veteran status, though I cannot be quite sure.

My primary goal was to become a civil engineer which, given my mediocre knowledge of English at the time, was not an easy task—particularly having to tackle exams. Notwithstanding these obstacles, I passed and began living the American Dream. All the while, life continued to unfold in magical ways. While earning a good salary, I had an opportunity to become acquainted with the Gianopoulos family and their beautiful daughter, Rita, whom I married in 1952. While still working full time, I received my Master's Degree in Civil Engineering, thanks in no small measure to the intervention of Rita, who typed my master's thesis.

By that time, George and I had purchased separate homes on Long Island, and my parents moved to their house in Tarpon Springs, Florida, from where they traveled to Greece every two or three years. Upon my father's death, my mother alternately stayed at my and George's homes on Long Island, gracing us with her presence until the age of ninety-three.

The Young Doundoulakis Family (1957)

Over the course of forty years, life continued to be filled with activity. I had a very exciting career as a civil engineer, working on such prestigious projects as the lead design for the foundations of the sixty-five story Pan American Building on Park Avenue (now the MetLife Building).

During the early 1960's, when the space program prepared to send men to the moon, I inquired about a job at Grumman Aerospace Corporation in Bethpage, Long Island. My background allowed me to slide easily into employment there. Since I had been hired early on, I took part in the actual design of the legs, the oxygen tanks, and various other parts of the Lunar Excursion Model or "LEM." For eleven years, I worked in the Apollo Space program, during some of those years as a group leader. My position gave me the privilege of shaking hands with many of the astronauts. The first two groups of astronauts from Apollo 11 and 12 left my signature, written on a plaque with others from Grumman Aerospace, on the moon's surface. The Apollo 13 astronauts, led by Jim Lowell, acknowledging my design of the oxygen tank which was used for the crew's return to earth, gave me a piece of netting torn from the LEM, which they had abandoned in space.

With all of the excitement and joy of the foregoing achievements, I consider the greatest accomplishment of my career to be my possession of the only existing patent for the design of the Arecibo Antenna, the largest radio telescope in the world. As my patent clearly shows, my brother and I hung the three-hundred ton antenna eye and revolving structure on cables, at a height of four hundred fifty feet above the one-thousand-foot antenna dish. Ultimately, the antenna was built on our design. The telescope was shown in the James Bond

Apollo 11 Astronauts

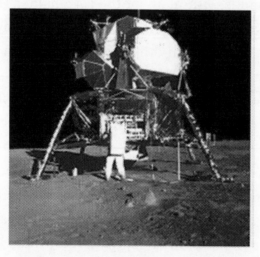

The Legs of the Lunar Module were Designed by the Author

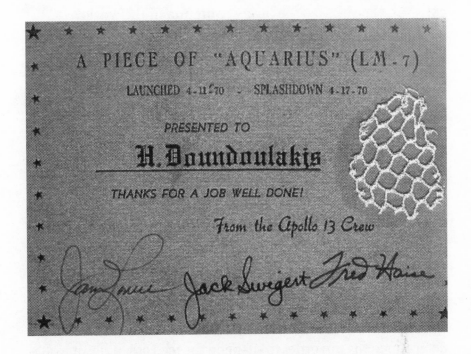

A Piece of "Aquarius" which never landed on the moon, but utilized the oxygen tank (designed by Helias Doundoulakis) to return to earth (1970). The three Apollo 13 astronauts presented Helias with the net that they brought back from the moon, thanking him for "a job well done."

movie, *GoldenEye*. In contrast to a conventional telescope, the Arecibo Antenna can receive signals from outer space up to ten billion light years away.

The question may validly be raised: how could I, an ordinary civil engineer, be given the opportunity to design something so colossal, classified as the largest antenna in the world?
As with all things, my dear brother, George, was always my right arm. He graduated from Brooklyn Polytechnic with a degree in electrical engineering, and was appointed Director of Research of General Bronze Corporation, an antenna design corporation. In 1959, George received an invitation from Cornell University to design a suspension system for what would be the largest telescope of its kind. He asked me if it would be possible to suspend the antenna's three-hundred-ton feed assembly above the reflector. Both of us studied the topographic maps of the proposed sites on which the antenna was supposed to be constructed. The reflector, a device resembling a huge bowl, was to be placed in a natural crater in the earth, or sinkhole, in Puerto Rico. After consulting with one another, George and I determined that, in order to suspend the feed assembly, it would be best supported by a cable system bolstered by steel towers, instead of a gigantic tripod, as Cornell University had suggested.

The antenna was finally built, as per our design specifications, at the National Astronomy and Ionosphere Center in Arecibo, Puerto Rico (now simply called "The Arecibo Observatory"). The suspension system was patented under my name, Helias Doundoulakis, on September 16, 1966. Assignees on the patent included my long-time friends William Casey (who was appointed CIA director under Ronald Reagan and also served in the OSS as Europe's SI chief), and Gus Michalos.

Twenty-five years after I left Crete, Yiapitzoglou visited the Greek Army Department's office in Athens, and requested special permission for me to return. As it happened, when the war was over, the Greek government discovered that George and I were registered in Crete as Greek citizens, and wanted us to serve in the Greek Army for a two-year period. Despite the fact that we wrote letters to the effect that we had served in the American Army for two and a half years, and were decorated by the American and Greek governments, the department did not accept the fact, and displayed our photos everywhere, intending to seize and imprison us if we ever returned to Greece. The general to whom Yiapitzoglou spoke said that he knew of two brothers, but was not apprised of the details of our circumstances. Finally, he signed a release letter, stating, "It's a shame to keep two brothers away from their second country."

After receiving the general's permission, I went back to Greece with my wife and three sons (the youngest, Thomas, was only seven at the time), and met with Yiapitzoglou, his wife and two young sons. It was exhilarating and deeply moving to see my friend again. We embraced, reminisced about the "what-if's" of our survival, and thanked God many times for the gift of being reunited and together again, this time in the presence of our families. Yiapitzoglou passed away about ten years later. Our connection lasted a lifetime, and our children still remain the very best of friends.

George later revisited Greece alone, leaving his wife and young family at home. After learning of his arrival, some of his friends threw a huge party for him though, sadly, he found out that some of his close friends had passed away.

329

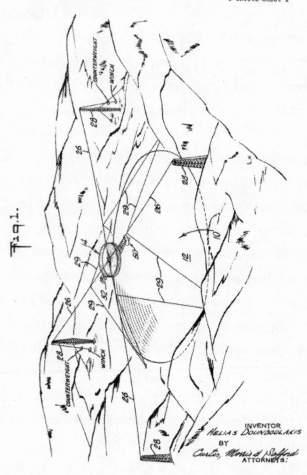

Sept. 13, 1966   H. DOUNDOULAKIS   3,273,156
RADIO TELESCOPE HAVING A SCANNING FEED SUPPORTED BY
A CABLE SUSPENSION OVER A STATIONARY REFLECTOR
Filed Sept. 11, 1961   6 Sheets-Sheet 1

**The Author's Patent for the World's Largest
Radio Telescope "Antenna" (1966)**

Aerial Photograph of the Arecibo Antenna

In 1999, after requests from many friends and patriotic organizations, George published his memoir, entitled *Shadows in the Night*. The book was presented at a public school in Archanes, our hometown, and two hundred fifty of the five hundred books printed were distributed to the people in attendance. The work describes George's participation in the SOE from 1941-1943, his association with Monty Woodhouse, Thomas Dunbabin, and Patrick Leigh Fermor. He also chronicles the sabotage of the Kastelli Airport and his OSS mission to the Pelion mountains.

Over sixty years after I left Salonica, I revisited the area again in 2004. Time and other thoughts had supplanted my memories of the place, at first; but, slowly, as I stood on the street and looked around, the Salonica of my youth materialized before me. It was all there—the waterfront, the statues, and the churches stood untouched, surrounded by modern buildings. Seron 10, the address at which I lived for nine months, was still there, too—replaced, of course, by modern apartments. The city was bustling all around me with a renewed heartbeat, but nothing disturbed my personal recollection of times long gone.

Suddenly, my eyes followed a familiar face. *Could it be?* I went over to a corner kiosk, asked for a phone book, and looked up the name of Sultanitsa's oldest child, Apostolis Asteriou, her little boy, whose name came to mind. I had long forgotten the names of his sisters. Two people were listed with that name; so, I called them, but neither one was the right "Apostolis." As I left the neighborhood, I hearkened back to the sound of Sultanitsa's voice, calling, "Apostolaki, Apostolaki, come for dinner!" I fantasized that he would hear his name and come running; but, sadly, just as so many of Salonica's people—Christians and Jews—Sultanitsa and her family had vanished.

Memories drift before me like clouds—whispers of the past—of those who shaped and literally *saved* my life, most especially, my brother, George, whose levelheadedness constantly kept me grounded and served as my compass. He passed away some years ago, but his legacy of brotherly love is indelible. There are no words that can ever express how much I love him—not only as a brother, but for helping me to evolve and for making me who I am.

John Androulakis, my high school friend, showed me the intrepidness and gentility of his heart, along with his fierce, unflinching resolve in the face of the enemy, and the definition of true heroism. Toward the end of the war, he was captured by the Gestapo near Chania, and was released only after the Cretan partisans paid for his ransom in gold. He eventually came to the United States and lived with us for a while in Brooklyn's Borough Park neighborhood while he studied naval engineering. He passed away after a long illness, but always remains in my heart.

Our hero, Patrick Leigh Fermor (a/k/a "Mihalis") became a travel writer, a veritable lyricist of the written word. After the war, he lived as an honorary Greek citizen in Kardamylli, Greece. He remained a true friend, and came to visit and stayed at my and George's homes on Long Island during the many tributes in honor of the Battle of Crete. In 2011, he passed away at the age of ninety-six.

And as for yours truly, I have been very happily married for sixty-one years (as of 2013) to my incomparable wife, Rita. We have four accomplished, extraordinary sons: James, a dentist,

John Androulakis (1960)

Stephen, a physician, Plato, an environmental engineer, and Thomas, who holds a Ph.D. in organic chemistry. We have ten grandchildren. Noelle, Elias, Tabitha, Justin, Sirena, Thalia, James Jr., Zoie, Brienne and Aurora. At the mere mention of their names, my heart bursts with pride.

As a ninety-year-old OSS veteran, my never-ending curiosity continues to get the best of me, and my world is still clouded by "what if's." What if that German guard outside Salonica did not have a son who resembled me? What if the bridge-playing Germans saw me? What if I were spotted with the wireless headset on while sending a message to Cairo? What if . . .

In response to requests for my own memoir from many of my friends in Greece, I wrote and published, in Greek, *Anamniseis apo tin antistasi kai diastimiki dimiourgia* (*Recollections of the Resistance*) in 2004, presented in the same auditorium where George spoke five years earlier. Of the one thousand books printed, I distributed five hundred gratis copies that night. The teachers explained the book's contents to a packed auditorium. One may imagine my surprise at seeing so many faces in the crowd, when I only anticipated relatively few. The choir's presentation of many patriotic songs brought me back to my fortuitous meeting with Sofia Vembo. She was right: we had prevailed, after all.

The evening was unforgettable, filled with memories and a renewed feeling of triumph and purpose. Afterward, at the reception, I enjoyed poignant discussions with the family members of those who participated in the resistance movement, some of whom lost their lives in the war. The audience's receptiveness truly touched my heart, and I gratefully received the praise that everyone bestowed on behalf of those fallen who could not be there with me. Subsequently, I published the book in English, and in 2008, *I Was Trained To Be A Spy* went to print, followed by *I Was Trained To Be A Spy, Book II*, in 2012. In that same year (2012), *My Unique Lifetime Association With Patrick Leigh Fermor* was released. Now, here I sit, expounding on my first memoir. There was so much to tell, after all!

Thus far, I have led a very full life, and I owe the Office of Strategic Services an enormous debt of gratitude. I also extend my unending appreciation to the United States Army, the men in the OSS who trained me, and the countless numbers of individuals who trusted me along the way. My life has been filled with plenty of excitement, joy, and rewards. As I reflect upon all that I have done, I realize that my life can be summarized in one sentence: My life was a game that had many interesting phases, played dangerously but, generally, properly—and, luckily enough, the winning way! At every step, good fortune and God continuously remained at my side, helping me to weather every storm. That is why *nothing*—not even the wrath of Mother Nature which has beset my hometown of Freeport, New York with many hurricanes, of late—can ever get me down. From experience, I realize in the depths of my heart that, no matter how gray the sky may appear, there is always a chance of sunshine, and I am forever looking up!

With Patrick Leigh Fermor (1981)

Cosmas Yiapitzoglou (1963)

With Cosmas In Athens (1971)

Visit to Salonica With Rita, In Front of the White Castle (2004)

A Christmas Family Reunion (2005)

**A Medal from the Greek Government was Presented to
Helias Doundoulakis by Col. Leontaris of Greece and Steve
Statharos of the OSS Society, Astoria, New York (2008)**

**With Archbishop Demetrios and Gus Vellios of the Greek OG's
at one of the OSS Society's ceremonies, Astoria, New York (2008)**

With Elizabeth Dole at the World War II Memorial, 2009

**Trip of Disabled Veterans to the World War
II Memorial Washington, D.C. (2009)**

Index

Arecibo, Puerto Rico, 328
Arecibo Antenna, 325, 328, 331
Arecibo Observatory, 328
Aspro Kastro, 175
Asteriou, Apostolis, 332
Astoria, New York, 341
Athens, 272, 338
  arriving in, 276
  Greek Army Departments
    office in, 329
  leaving for, 272
  orders not to return
    to, 281, 294
  preparing to travel to, 271
  turmoil in, 277
  university in, 57
Auschwitz, 179
Australian army, 25, 283
Austria, 233-34
Austrian sergeant, 228, 233-34
Axis, 46, 165, 177

B

Bandouvas, Manolis, 37
Bari, Italy, 283, 287-
  88, 290, 296
beaufort, 154
Bethpage, Long Island,
  14, 323, 325, 333
Betinakis, Antonios, 52-53
black market, 199, 285, 288
Bridge de Pyramid, 294
Brooklyn, New York, 265, 317-19

Brooklyn Polytechnic, 328
Bulgarians, 165, 257
Bulgarian soldiers, 165

C

caique, 143
Cairo, Egypt, 80, 101-2,
  240, 253, 288
  American soldiers in, 103
  arriving in, 292, 319
  contacts with, 192, 195,
    200, 208, 212, 225,
    227, 241-43, 258, 263
  Grand Hotel in, 102
  leaving for, 78-79,
    115, 122, 290
  meeting Ms. Vembo in, 88
  meeting relatives in, 294, 308
  OSS in, 15, 94, 142
  photographs in, 15, 75,
    89-90, 299-300
  sending wireless
    message to, 51
  spy training in, 115
  suburbs of, 83-84
  suits crafted in, 142
  time bombs from, 42
  transmission to, 197-98
Cairo OSS headquarters,
  94, 296
Camp Crowder, Missouri,
  312-13, 315
Canary Islands, 304

346

Printed in the United States
By Bookmasters